***

Matt Cunningham was born in London in 1969,
the youngest child of a large Anglo-Irish family.
He lives in Sussex with his wife and daughter.

***

MATT CUNNINGHAM

A Girl Named Dennis

Finding a way through losing a child: a father's story

ISBN-10: 1519507364
ISBN-13: 978-1519507365

For Ali and Molly May

Before

I thought it would go something like this:

One day, a year or so into our marriage, my wife Ali would tell me she was pregnant with our first child. She would be just shy of thirty years old. I would be knocking on forty. Yet even so – touch wood, it would have come easily to us. No excessive attention paid to fertile days, sperm counts and the like. Just love-making and what follows in its wake when all is well.

Initially I would be unnerved by the responsibilities heading my way. I might even imagine an overdue death knell sounding for a once-upon-a-time skirt chaser. But nothing that mattered. Nothing that wouldn't be outweighed by my sense of fortune and the frisson of satisfaction that at my grand age I had at last announced myself in the game: still young enough to kick a ball around the park when it came to it, without being too embarrassing or too knackered, even if it meant taking up jogging, upping the intake of blueberries and green tea.

After three months or thereabouts, when the pregnancy was safely established, we'd declare, and Ali and I would get to bask in the glow of approbation that always accompanies well-timed baby-making. Our families would rejoice at the prospect. Our friends would hug and kiss us, slap our backs. And the parents among them would shake their heads, draw air in through their teeth, tell us how exhausting our lives would be from now on. And then, with glassy eyes, how wonderful too.

Things would proceed then, without complication naturally, until full-term, give or take a day or two, when a beautiful baby girl (always a girl) would be born to us, healthy. We'd name her Molly. And within days our home would be deluged with pink:

pink flowers, pink balloons, pink baby clothes, pink everything. And there at the heart of it I'd be: a modern dad on paternity leave, carefully cradling his first-born, feeling like he was holding the beginning, middle and end of the world.

Later no doubt there would be horrors aplenty: schools that cost more than I had, boyfriends with leg tattoos, teenage rebellion. But all far, far into the future.

First there would be years of it being just us: Ali, Molly, me, maybe more.

First there would be games and songs and bedtime stories, piggy-back rides, dressing up, home-made fudge.

First there would be Mondays.

I don't work Mondays – and the way I saw it, that one day a week would be kept just for Molly and me. While Ali went out to work, my daughter and I would go in search of adventures, beside the sea, in the parks, on the Downs, at the supermarket, anywhere and everywhere. And one day I'd capture the wonder of it all in a book: a tender, light-hearted memoir of a dad out exploring the world with his little girl.

I even had the title: *Mondays With Molly*.

I thought it would go something like this – because I hadn't really thought at all.

Part One

Dennis

Padstow, Cornwall

When I think back to the beginning, exactly the way it was, the first thing I see is the thirty-nine-and-a-half-year-old me pacing up and down outside a Ladies toilet, working myself up into a mood. Every minute or so I come to a halt, theatrically (though I'm alone), to squint down through the twilight at the clock on my phone and mutter something ungracious about women, about the amount of time they spend in bathrooms while the rest of us die slowly outside.

I was hungry, you see.

I had a particular kind of pizza in mind, a bottle of Chianti. Ali and I had been on our way out to dinner. I'd anticipated a pleasant stroll against a captivating sunset, followed by a have-anything-you-like-you're-on-your-holiday excess of Italian food and wine. But at the last moment she had ducked into the loo, and now seemed intent on staying there beyond any reasonable call of nature.

'Come onnnn, Minnie,' I whined through the door.

'All right! – just a minute,' – her voice came back.

But no sight or sound of activity. Just silence, punctuated by birdsong and the crunch-crunch of my shoes pacing the gravel.

That was 8th September, 2008: a lifetime ago. The scene: the ablutions block of a campsite called Dennis Cove on the out-skirts of Padstow in Cornwall. In my ill temper, so at odds with the postcard scenery around me, I was ridiculous. I can see that now. And yet I feel sympathy towards the me that was, I suppose because now I know I was stood at a precipice, that a train of events had been set in motion that was going to shunt me out into cold thin air. On one side of that wooden door my wife was doing something that would later inspire the opening pages of a book I'd yet to conceive of, while on the other I had nothing in mind more profound than pepperoni. All I wanted was food, for Ali to hurry up and finish doing *God knows what*. Which when you come to think about it isn't such a bad name for a pregnancy test.

*

I'd forgotten we were trying if I'm honest, which speaks vol-umes for our relaxed approach to the topic. There had been no concern, no anxious awareness of the lunar cycle or going at it like the clappers during the ovulation window. All that trying for a baby had amounted to was agreeing between us one day to leave the condoms in the bedside cabinet and carry on with life and love as normal. So yes, on some level, I was aware that we were not-not trying, but no more than that. Babies were an abstract, something to be hoped for vaguely but not obsessed over. Just part of the potential of what our lives could be now if we were fortunate.

With hindsight we had probably been preparing the ground since our honeymoon, albeit subconsciously, just by being a bit more sensible – overpaying the mortgage while we still had two incomes, saving a little tax-free: the kind of things you're meant to do to feather a nest. Even this latest holiday choice could be seen in retrospect as part of the plan. Not South Africa, Malaysia or Japan this time – all places we'd visited in our four years together. This time we'd taken a leaky two-man tent, borrowed from Ali's brother, to a sodden field in Cornwall and found to our considerable satisfaction it was very nearly as much fun. As we revelled in the pleasures of cooking our breakfasts al fresco, giggling by torchlight, and the sound (inherently funny to anyone raised on Carry On films) of canvas being zipped and unzipped at all hours, it felt like we were recalling childhood, and against a backdrop of gathering economic gloom, having a high time of it without spending too much, confident we were so in love you could drop us down anywhere and we'd be fine.

That particular day we'd fried bacon and eggs on our portable stove, hired mountain bikes and cycled twenty miles along a beautiful disused railway line and back, pausing now and then for photos or for me to have a pint. I was so preoccupied with pleasure I hardly noticed Ali wasn't drinking. I wasn't tuned in to things like that back then. So when she did finally come out of the bathroom that night, with that smile across her face, and said what she said, it took me completely by surprise.

'Guess what?', she smiled at me.

'What?' I replied, a little snappy, still focused on dinner.

'I think we're going to have a baby.'

*

The feeling, for the first few hours at least, reminded me of the way I felt in the immediate aftermath of proposing to Ali in the summer of 2006. Like then, I knew something momentous had happened. It just took me a while to actually believe it – for my emotions to catch up with the fact. Like many men, I imagine, particularly those at the older end of the progenitive spectrum, I felt some relief that everything 'down there' had proved to be in working order. But beyond that, only mild shock and a characteristic wariness of what felt like unmitigated good fortune. It took until the smallest hours of that night for the news to sink in (and some unlikely messengers to make it do so). Ali and I were huddled together in the tent, laughing at the intensity of the rain battering our hopelessly inadequate home by now, just inches above our faces, when all at once, in choral unison, the cows in the field behind us began to moo: a cacophony so silly, so unexpected, it felt like it had to be meant just for us: our bovine blessing in the midst of the flood.

That's when I started to feel like a dad-to-be.

'We'll name the baby Dennis,' I whispered over the noise.

'Why?'

'Because of Dennis Cove'

'What?

'Dennis Cove,' I said louder. The name of the campsite.'

'All right,' Ali said, snuggling closer. 'That'll do for now.'

And we lay there like that in the darkness, with the bottom of the tent down by our feet already sopping wet, trying to imagine all the wonders life had in store for us.

*

That first photo, the one that begins this chapter, I took early the next day as we were packing up the hire car to leave. Look closely and you can see the line of water around the base of the tent and the last of the storm clouds clearing up above. What you can't see, as Ali wrestled our inflatable mattress back into the boot, is how happy she looked. Or, for that matter, the size of the idiot grin on the other side of the camera as I walked around the campsite taking photo after photo, trying in vain to capture just how extraordinary, how exciting and very new everything seemed to me that contrary September morning.

With Child

Home from home

By late afternoon, after a detour on a whim to see a farm show that turned out to be full of screaming kids (whom we naturally looked upon more benignly now from our new vantage point), we were dry, warm and eating fresh-baked scones with jam and cream at Ali's parents' house on the south coast of Devon. We had last been there just a few days before, when everything had been so different, when we hadn't known our wonderful news, and the urge to share it with them was strong.

But should we?

In favour of no was the risk faced by all expectant couples – that things might not work out. We could be involving them in our happiness only to have to draw them into our sadness later if we were disappointed.

10

In favour of yes, by contrast, was the reception we knew the news would get. It was difficult to imagine who would be more excited. Sally: my mother-in-law, an organiser, a do-er, whom I could picture beginning to buy, plan and cater for the prospect almost immediately. Or Gordon: my father-in-law, likewise animated but more heart-on-the-sleeve: the more likely of the two to show a tear in the corner of his eye. We mightn't even have needed an immediate resolution had they not promised to take us out to dinner that night, where any out of character abstinence on their daughter's part would be sure to raise eyebrows. Conceivably, Gordon could be diverted with a reference to an upset tummy or the do not pass of period pain. But Sally, we were certain, would guess immediately, and thus spoil both the surprise and our enjoyment of it. So with an eleventh hour no-really-we-have-to-make-a-decision-now con- versation in hushed tones in the bathroom before we went out, the two of us decided to go for it. Sort of.

'If you want to tell them, you can,' I remember Ali declaring while she rinsed conditioner out of her hair. 'It's up to you.'

'All right,' I said. 'If you're sure.'

'I'm *not* sure,' she countered. 'It's up to you, I said.'

Which was where negotiations were still resolutely stalled by the time we reached the restaurant half an hour later. When it came to ordering pre-dinner drinks in the bar, I could only wait to see how Ali would play it.

'I'll just have a juice thanks, Dad,' she said.

'Oh?'

'I think I'll save myself for my meal.'

A classic piece of neither here nor there that served only to buy us more dithering time, which I put to good use by sinking two fast pints for courage before the owner showed us to our table – where Gordon immediately ordered a bottle of wine.

'I'll stick to the juice for now,' Ali said this time, holding her hand over her glass as he went to fill it. Which didn't seem to trouble Gordon, but I did detect Sally eyeing her daughter just briefly at that point before turning her attentions to the menu. If our news was to be a surprise, we were on borrowed time I felt sure. So again I turned to Ali for guidance. Every time her parents appeared safely obscured behind their menus, a frantic silent-movie conversation took place between us: variations on a theme of imploring eyes, palms up (me); downturned mouth, Gallic shrug (Ali). It was apparent the final decision was destined to be mine. And so I decided the temptation to pull the pin on our celebratory grenade was too much to resist. After what felt like an unnaturally cavernous gap in conversation, during which the room took on an ethereal, woozy quality, I sucked in a last breath and went for it.

'Before the evening progresses too far –' I began, feeling at once all shy and Victorian as all eyes around the table turned to me, 'you've probably noticed Ali has been steering clear of alcohol up until now.'

At which I could have sworn I caught an almost, but not quite, imperceptible shift in Sally's countenance: just the merest smile suppressed. But I couldn't bring myself to look at her for confirmation. Instead I directed myself exclusively at Gordon, using a ruse I'd adopted years ago when I first started to play a role in business meetings. I concentrated on the bridge of his nose. It makes people think you're looking them right in the eye when for whatever reason you don't have it in you.

'The reason for that –', I continued, 'is that, very tentatively, and it's very early days, but – '

And then, from I don't know where:

'We appear to be with child.'

With child.

And with that our short-lived secret was out. What followed was a blur: a congratulatory hug from Sally, a manly handshake between Gordon and me, a slap or two on the back, and I'll confess it was one of the happiest exchanges of my life. I felt proud, blessed to have arrived at such a juncture. I had a beautiful, loving wife, with a lovely family, and now she was carrying my child. At a stroke it felt like every ill-conceived decision, every misplaced step along the path of my life up to that point had been justified, had been leading inexorably to the here and now of that moment in time. Gordon handed me the wine list. I sank back into my seat. And the rest of the evening passed in the glow that goes with being looked upon favourably and, unlike Ali, having the freedom to get happily hammered.

'With child?' she mocked, when we were back in our room that night. 'Where the hell did *that* come from?'

'I have absolutely no idea,' I sighed – face down on the bed. When I could have kept it simple: 'I'm glad to announce we're expecting' or 'Folks, you're going to be grandparents again', I'd plumped for 'We appear to be with child.' Only my first day as a dad of sorts and already my mind was shot.

*

Wisely, as far as spreading the news went, we kept our mouths shut after that. Almost entirely. I told my mum, which felt like the appropriate thing to do after telling Gordon and Sally, and my middle-of-three brothers, Dave, because he and I are close, he has a child of his own so he could empathise, and I wanted someone to confide in man to man.

I can still see him now, shaking his head.

'Oh, Matty-boy,' he said, with a broad smile across his face, 'your life will be so different now.'

*

Otherwise, for Ali and I, there was nothing to be done except be as patient as possible while we waited for the scan at twelve weeks: the first milestone of consequence, when the peak time for miscarriage would be past and we'd get to see our child for the first time. When the day came for that, Ali was giddy with anticipation. I was sick with nerves. Which tells you something about the two of us. She's the optimist: the one who leads with a smile and is sometimes disappointed. I'm the pessimist: the one who expects the worst and is mostly pleasantly surprised. At least that's the way we were back then, and certainly the way we were that day.

We'd opted not to have the scan in Brighton where we live. In the run-up to the day, we were offered the chance to be part of a sample test group for Down Syndrome at the same time if we travelled to King's College Hospital in London. So thinking we may as well as it was free, we took the day off and went up on the train – Ali squeezing my hand all the way, trying to keep us close. I knew she wanted it to be an adventure, a memory in the making for us to treasure later, but all I wanted was to get to the part where they tell you everything's okay.

In the waiting room, with a dozen other couples and mums-to-be, we watched footage of Barack Obama (on a tiny screen on the wall) addressing the American people and indirectly the world on the morning of his first election victory. It felt auspicious: a signal to feel hopeful about bringing new life into the world and grateful George W was gone.

'Alison Cunningham.'

We were still newlywed enough for that to sound strange.

'If you'd like to come this way.'

I drained the last of my coffee and we followed the nurse to an examination room where I sat on the chair meant for dads. Ali lay on the bed beside the monitor, pulled up her blouse and undid her jeans as instructed. Then the nurse smeared gel on her belly, pressed her Lost In Space gun down into it to find the image. And boom! There it was. I'd expected a little fishing around, a warning to brace for impact. But no. At once, on the screen in front of us, was Dennis, large as life.

Immediately Ali pulled me closer to her. But though I edged nearer I still sat stiffly, not knowing how to be or what to feel. The detail, the extent of development at only twelve weeks astonished me. I had no idea. Every finger, every toe distinct. The entire vertebrae of the spine, the stomach, the beating heart. It was all so clear, so unmistakable, I worried I'd see something I wasn't ready for, something indisputably male or otherwise. *Is it too early for a willy?* In my ignorance I peered obliquely at the monitor, ready to avert my eyes at any moment – I didn't want the surprise ruined. But I watched intently when it came to the various measurements they took: the length of the foetus, the circumference of the head. And finally, the scary one I'd heard about, the thickness of the cortex at the back of the neck: a key indicator for Down Syndrome.

'Can you confirm your ages?' the nurse asked at that point.

'Twenty nine,' said Ali.

'Thirty nine,' I said, sheepishly, suddenly feeling every night and day of my four decades: every one-last-pint, every drunken smoke, every decision to sidestep exercise and pick up a book. Then as quickly as we were in, we were out again – back in the waiting room to sit nervously while they reached their findings. Above our heads, Obama was repeating himself on a 24-hour news loop: the same promises for a brave new world over and over until, after what felt like an eternity, our name was called again. We were shown into another room. An office this time. A doctor in place of the nurse. *Should we read anything into that?* He sat us down at his desk in front of a computer monitor on which I could see all kinds of data pertaining to us but none of it comprehensible to me. The heartbeat, the number of fingers and toes, I'd been able to see for myself. But I knew there were other things – things that wouldn't be obvious to the untrained eye. That was the part I wanted to reach. And sure enough, after what felt like a legion of irrelevant preliminaries, the doctor appeared to be coming to the crux.

'Based on the factors we have assessed today,' he began – a strong Middle-eastern accent which he balanced by enunciating each word meticulously, 'including such considerations as your ages and so forth –'

Spit it out, man.

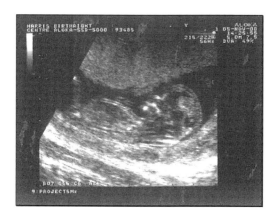

Twelve weeks

'We have calculated the probability for Down Syndrome for this pregnancy would be – one in twenty-seven thousand, three hundred and twenty four.'

At which point (with pun intended) there was what can only be described as a pregnant pause, during which I believe I nodded sagely as if I knew what that meant.

'What does that mean, exactly?' Ali had the presence to ask.

'Well,' he said, 'it means that with these test results and other data taken into account, only one woman out of this number would have a child born with Down Syndrome.'

I looked at him closely. 'That's pretty good then, yes?'

'Yes,' he agreed.

Then he explained that there were ways to find out for sure: chorionic villas sampling at twelve weeks, amniocentesis a little later, but that both involved a life-threatening risk to the baby which, given our excellent results, would be close to pointless.

And there and then, I relaxed finally. I breathed a sigh of relief, thinking that was it. We were in the clear.

*

On the train going back to Brighton it was Ali's turn to be pre-occupied, distant, and I didn't need her to explain to know that it was my fault. I'd let her down by being uptight all through an experience that should have been a joy. I had to work hard to convince her I'd spent the time not uninterested, as she imagined, but afraid; my fear had got the better of me and, not for the first or last time, made me cold. She softened then, and for the rest of the journey we looked at the small black and white photo of Dennis they'd given us as a memento. It was easier to see it now for the miracle it was. My pessimism was quietened, leaving only a feeling of wonder that something so incredible, and so easy to achieve, could have happened to me.

*

The atmosphere surrounding the second scan at twenty weeks could not have been more different. Instead of being the focus of an entire angst-ridden day, it was Brighton-based and sandwiched between two bouts of last-minute Christmas shopping. I showed up at the hospital clutching armfuls of presents, feeling frivolous and playful. I'd had time to get used to things by now. I was eager to count fingers and toes again, to get another photo. Dennis, however, was more coy this time: disinclined to face the camera, indifferent to all coaxing.

Though not to sugar, as it turned out.

'What you two need is a bar of chocolate,' the nurse said.
'I'll have a Toffee Crisp then,' I cut in, making myself laugh. 'As in mother and baby,' she continued, pointing a brief but withering glance in my direction. She knew her stuff though. After a quick detour to the hospital shop to buy a bar of organic, fair trade, 75% cocoa solids (nothing but the best for our foetus), which Ali refused to give me even a piece of because it was 'for the baby', Dennis was wired for action: an established life now, halfway to being born, and more than happy to perform acrobatics for the picture.

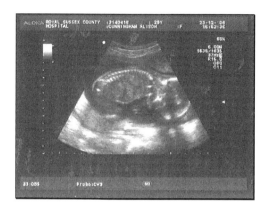

Twenty weeks

As for the scan, it was more in-depth than the first. We saw the baby in much greater detail, moving down in cross-sections from head to toe through each of the major organs in turn. All functioning perfectly, and all so clear this time I was convinced we'd see a willy. Even Ali was being careful where she looked.

'Are you wanting to find out the gender?' the nurse asked.

'No!' we barked at her in tandem.

We were sticking to our guns, wanting it to be a surprise. So despite the nurse's assurances that there'd be no obvious give-aways, we averted our eyes when the scanner passed over the hips and groin.

We learnt a lot that second time. But the biggest single difference from the first outing was simply that Ali and I enjoyed it. We smiled and joked our way all through that appointment. In the eight weeks since our trip to King's College, our confidence had grown, the worry that attended us that day had faded. After all, why *wouldn't* everything be all right? (Of all the babies born to my siblings and friends, every single one had turned out fine.) And besides, it was Christmas Eve. If we weren't going to feel excited then with a baby on the way, when were we?

Happy

Christmas stockings

I don't remember exactly when or why we decided to host that Christmas at ours. I think it had something to do with wanting to ensure my mum had an easy time of it. Maybe an idea that Gordon and Sally too would welcome a year off. But mostly I think it was about us feeling pleased with ourselves, proud of our happy state of expectation, as well as our home, which was on its way to becoming a family home like the ones Ali and I grew up in. Whatever the reasons, those few days proved to be special, a unique amalgam of circumstances and people. It even felt that way at the time. Just Mum, Gordon and Sally to entertain, and Ali and I so untroubled, so ripe with what-might-be at the cusp of parenthood.

We didn't own a car back then, so I'd done all the shopping

on foot: one rucksack on my back, another worn in reverse on my chest and two bags minimum on the end of each arm. Under the load I could only plod along like a tortoise, but a happy tortoise all the same, out of his shell and loving life. It's remarkable how happiness can make light of hard work.

Christmas Eve night I made seafood chowder for everyone. Then Ali and I walked Mum down to the church at the end of our road for the candlelit mass, which (though my forays to the church are rare) felt good: the benevolent warmth of the congregation around us, the pleasure of seeing Mum put her hand on Ali's belly more than once, the smiles they exchanged. That would have also been our first encounter with Father John: a man we'd come to know and appreciate in the months to come though we had no idea of that at the time.

Christmas morning we had scrambled eggs and smoked salmon for breakfast and drank Champagne. Even Ali had a small glass while we watched our parents opening the stocking fillers we'd wrapped for them: a pair of drinking-straw spectacles for Gordon, a grow-your-own priest for Mum.

'I don't think I've got room,' she said, misunderstanding the instructions, thinking he'd grow by four hundred times when it said four hundred percent. 'I'll have to keep him in the bath.'

With such an intimate number and no children to keep amused, we were free to please ourselves. So I messed around in the kitchen with pigs in blankets, goose fat, a turkey of prehistoric proportions; Sally pottered in and out to give me a hand; Gordon regaled us with quotes from the autobiography of his home town legend, Dean Windass; and Mum got cosied up by the fire with a book and a festive G&T. Even without the context, it would have been joyful. But what held it all together, what made that Christmas feel like so much more than the sum of its parts, as we all knew, was Ali's bump: no more than a pot belly to behold back then but bearing so much hope for times to come.

More than once that day, when she and I found, or contrived, a few moments to ourselves, we played at trying to imagine 'this time next year' (God help us if we'd known). Then later, I took a photo of her standing by the tree with her sweater lifted just enough to hint at her precious cargo: things that helped me to feel connected to something that until then often felt like it was happening only to Ali. While she'd been whipped up in the hormonal magi-mix of early pregnancy, my concerns had been more mundane: how we'd cope with one income, how in years to come we'd handle childcare, schools, university, or whatever it was that mattered at the time. But now, with the tinsel-tones of Christmas around us, a touch of sentiment to get me up and running, I began to feel the magic, to want to touch Ali's bump without being prompted, to rest my face against it, to whisper and sing to the little life inside. The instinct, the compulsion, to place myself physically, emotionally, like a layer of bubble wrap between Ali, the baby and any harm, took root in me. But I've learnt since there is only so much you can do.

*

By the time we got to Fuertaventura in February for a blast of sunshine before D-Day, Ali was much more obviously expecting – near the end of her second trimester now – the peak time for difficulties long past. And with modest expectations from a no-frills last-minute deal, we settled gratefully into what turned out to be one of the simplest, most pleasurable holidays we'd ever had together. Ali made picnics for the beach; we lost ourselves in books; at night we hunted out less touristy restaurants away from the main drag; and wherever we went we were noticed, acknowledged by parents who could see we were soon to be joining their ranks. Even the restaurateurs vying for trade paused to fuss over Ali and offer up commentaries from their own life experience, wistful and otherwise.

'Ahh – my oldest is away at university.'

'My youngest is *this* high now.'

Larks in the sun

'I have three girls. I love them – but they make me crazy.'

Men became more gentlemanly around Ali. Women reached out to touch the bump as though it were a holy relic or a good luck charm. And I began to appreciate more that faraway look, that inimitable blend of pride and turn-your-hair-grey tiredness you see sometimes in the eyes of fathers. As Ali sipped her half glass of wine each night at dinner and I downed the rest of the bottle, it was more than the grape making me glow.

*

Over the next two months we both celebrated landmark birthdays: thirty for Ali, forty for me. I was four decades long in the tooth and about to become a father for the first time. Gordon had three children at home by the time he was my age. My own dad had five, not counting one lost. In fact most of the men I knew, the straight ones anyway, were further down the parenthood path than me. All of my siblings too. Which might have bothered me subconsciously once upon a time, but not anymore. Now, from the perspective of thinking everything had worked out, I could even congratulate myself discreetly on hav-

Me – on my 40th birthday

ing made a good stretch of my youth, on having lived well on the other side of the coin: the side those young dads must have pined for once in a while as they navigated those early years. Now or later. Now or never. The dilemma that runs under every life. I felt like I'd gambled and won – just.

*

Then, with the last of the April showers, with both the end and the beginning in sight, came the first dent in our best-laid plan. Only four weeks before her maternity leave was due to begin, Ali was made redundant, which felt like a major setback – at a time when our standard for major setbacks was so much lower. It was tough on her though. She'd put a lot into constructing a life as conducive as possible to becoming a parent: a well-paid job, in her field of expertise, in Brighton – it was the holy grail. But just months after promoting her and giving her a pay rise, shortly after she announced she was pregnant, they made their decision. We were angry. And with two barristers in her family (her mum and brother) and a dad with a Human Resources expert on his payroll, the appetite to take it to tribunal was shared between us. We got as far as taking legal advice. But when Ali started to lose sleep over it, and to feel more and more that her life should be focused on her baby now, she chose to let it go. And despite my reservations and desire for justice, supporting her in her decision felt like the only thing to do. She'd been in the job over a year, so her maternity payments were assured, that was something. And the bottom line was she was right: her health and the health of our child did come first.

The Countdown

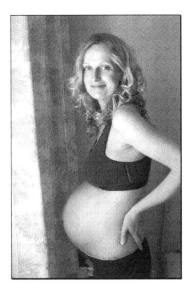

One day to go

With little more than a month to go, we took a last trip to Devon so Ali could soak up some TLC from her mum and dad and celebrate her birthday with them. She was slowing by now, yet still looking glamorous to me, unrealistic in her pregnancy, like a soap opera actress with a pillow up her top. There was none of the hip-holding-huffing-and-puffing I'd been expecting. Ali was composing herself in her own quiet way.

With the extended family down from Hull for the weekend,

Gordon and Sally treated us to dinner out again, where I took photos of the various family combinations: dad and daughter, mum and daughter, brother and sister, sisters together. We all knew it was good luck time now, that next time we met, God willing, there'd be a new member of the family.

*

Back in Brighton our National Childbirth Trust classes got up and running: three evenings and two days over three weeks to consider all things labour and baby related in the lead up to the birth. I had no idea what to expect, but from the off those sessions were a riot. Informative no doubt, good for camaraderie in the face of the common goal and all that, but mostly a riot. It was like being back at school.

Our teacher and guide was a sweet-natured hippy-grown-up called Rose: a mother of three herself, with a remarkable talent for acting out birthing pains. And our fellow mums-and-dads-to-be a fairly homogeneous bunch of Brightonians (and thereabouts): Sinead and Dave, Vic and Simon, Anneka and Chris, Laura and Will, Sara and James, Kath and Trevor. Seven couples including us heading out into the unknown via group tasks like arranging drawings of wombs and vaginas across the floor in ascending order of agony, and brainstorming ways to get the dads more involved in the pregnancy: foot massages, shoulder rubs, perineal moisturising for the more intrepid. Our education even extended to warning us men that our ladies' shapely figures might not survive the birthing experience, and that we weren't to be unkind about it. We needed regular time-outs for tea and hobnobs to take it all in.

By the time the classes ended, Ali's due date was less than a week away and still she stayed calm on the surface. Thinking ahead to the labour brought waves of anxiety but always tempered with wonder, and a stoicism that must have been growing inside her those nine months alongside the baby. I felt humb-

26

led, full of admiration, as we passed the time as recommended: eating curry, making love uncomfortably, trying to be patient.

*

It was the following Friday night when things started to get interesting. We were watching a film, eating chicken madras, lamb passanda, chapatis and onion bhajis with an extra order of mint sauce when Ali had what we assumed had to be her first contraction. (Though as she'd had no more contractions in her life than I had at that point, we were unsure how to react.)

Certainly I came to learn that night that a contraction is an unusual thing; at least it is when you're enjoying an Indian takeaway and the person beside you is having one. One moment Ali would be in full conversational flow on the phone with her mum and the next she'd freeze mid-sentence, hand the phone to me and double over, grimacing and groaning, until it passed as abruptly as it had come. At which point she simply took the receiver back and picked up the conversation where she'd left it. Intense discomfort, then absolutely fine, over and over.

It took a while for me to find my niche in proceedings. The first couple of times I leapt to my feet, primed to call a cab and grab the overnight bag. But taking my lead from Ali I soon settled into a greyer area somewhere between action and inaction, being sure to acknowledge her at every surge, to adopt a mien of sympathy and offer my free hand for crushing purposes; just without necessarily lowering my forkful of madras.

'Are you all right, sweetheart?'
'No.'
'Will you yell if you need anything?'
'Yes.'
'Do you think it might be Braxton-Hicks?'
'No. Shut up.'

*

27

That night, we just about slept. The contractions became more intermittent, less intense, settling into a pattern that would provide the physical and emotional structure for the coming three days. Saturday came and went. Sunday and into Monday, things gathering momentum slowly, until just before 11pm that night Ali felt sure the time had come. I called a cab and minutes later we were on our way.

Thank God, I remember thinking to myself as we pulled into the grounds of the Royal Sussex Hospital, the driver negotiating the last of the speed bumps as carefully as he could. And again, *Thank God*, as Ali and I crossed the threshold of the delivery unit to find just one of the nine birthing rooms in use. We could even have the birthing pool if we liked. No mad dash to Haywards Heath or Worthing. No home delivery. *Thank God*.

The delivery unit itself was nothing like I'd expected. There were no nurses rushing from room to room; no PA announcements telling doctors where they needed to be quick smart; and most surprising of all, not a hint of wailing and screaming. Instead roughly half a dozen midwives were hanging about by the front desk looking bored and in need of something to do. The moment Ali and I came through the doors, they descended on us like too many cabbies for too few fares; which I should add was fine by me. Though not fine by Ali, it seemed, because as soon as we were settled in our new surroundings her contractions came to a halt almost completely, and I've pondered since whether that might simply have been because the next midwife waiting in line was a man. Not that a man isn't capable of delivering a baby with aplomb. I just don't think that's the way Ali had it pictured in her mind and something inside her clammed up and put everything temporarily on hold.

The longer we waited the more her body calmed, until the contractions wouldn't come at all while the midwife was in the room. It was only because he could see the spiked tremors on the paper printout that he believed she was having them at all. In short, whatever Ali was going through wasn't deemed to be enough. They gave her sleeping pills, told us to pack up and go home. So I called another cab and that's what we did.

What followed then back at the house was the most absurd and ineffectual attempt at sleeping either of us had ever managed. At first Ali suggested I take the spare room –

'So at least one of us can rest.'

But as all I did was prop open the doors between the rooms and rush to her each time I heard a surge, there was little point. Soon enough I was lying by her side, her hand gripped around mine, the idea of sleep an unfunny joke; until just before 2am, with Ali certain that things were progressing now, I phoned for our third cab of the night.

Barely three hours had passed since our previous arrival, yet the scene that confronted us at the hospital was unrecognisable – something had clearly happened in the interim to the expectant women of Brighton: a maternal green light must have been shone because now there very nearly more fares than cabbies. We were shown to the one and only available room. And I resolved, the moment I put our bags down, that we weren't going anywhere until there were three of us.

Thankfully, once Ali's dilation had been measured, her temperature taken and the heartbeats of mum-to-be and baby monitored, we were given the nod and I set about preparing the room as I'd been briefed over the preceding weeks. I scattered pillows and cushions across the floor. I softened the lights with coloured scarves and dripped lavender oil on anything that looked like it could take it. Then I arranged our snacks and drinks (juice cartoons with straws for easy drinking mid-labour) along the window sill, and finally found a plug socket for our decrepit CD player, the one we use for decorating, and set Ali's Meditation Mantras CD playing for the first of I can't say how many times. It was to play on a loop for the next thirteen hours.

Though by then it was more than three days since Ali's first contractions on the Friday night, the usual rules governing the passage of time didn't count for much. The midwives came in and out, remarking on how fragrant and tranquil our room was compared to the others; Ali tried to breathe the way she'd been taught; and the hands on the clock went around and around.

I remember our first midwife telling us her shift was due to end at 8am and how she was determined to meet our baby. But 8am passed, the shift changed and Ali had to build a rapport all over again with someone new. In the meantime, all I could do was arrange myself into whatever contortions she needed from me for physical support, try to keep her relaxed, and get her to sip some juice once in a while. Occasionally I'd glance up and note another hour had passed, but always with an acceptance – emanating from Ali and rubbing off on me – that nature would take its course in its own time.

Around 2pm, Tuesday afternoon, induction was mentioned for the first time: hospital policy, we were told, once the twelve hour mark had been reached. The senior midwife was satisfied, however, that progress was being made, and agreed to give Ali another hour, making her all the more determined to finish the job for herself.

By 3pm she was squatting over a birthing mat on the floor, with me on my haunches behind her holding her up. From my vantage point I could see the tuft of hair on the crown of the baby's head as Ali gathered herself for one last psychological and physical push. Yet even then it was twenty minutes before the moment arrived: not like in the movies with the infant held aloft, crying. Contemporary wisdom, as I knew, was to pass the baby straight into the arms of its mother to minimise the shock of arrival. There was no little slap to encourage the first breath, but I could see that our baby was breathing and no-one seem-ed alarmed so I assumed mother and child were safely through. Ali's birthing plan had made it clear we wanted to discover the gender for ourselves, though in the immediate aftermath neith-er of us thought to check, would you believe that? It took a few minutes, and one of the midwives to prompt us, before we peered down at last at all the wrinkles and blood and curled

The first family portrait

umbilical cord and concluded we had a son.

The midwife thought that was great fun.

Laughing at us, she said, 'I think you need to look again.'

So we took a longer, more intimate look this time – and saw that our baby boy was in fact a baby girl. *I always wanted a girl.*

I took my shirt off then (skin to skin for dads too) and the midwife passed me my daughter to hold while they made sure Ali was okay. I looked down at the scrunched up features: her tiny face with just one eye open, glaring up at me grumpily. I counted fingers and toes again. I could feel the warmth of her little body against my chest. I didn't cry. I wasn't overwhelmed. Just silenced, by love, and a great rolling joy that was gathering momentum inside me.

'We're going to call her Molly. Molly May?' I half asked, half told Ali, who looked at that moment like she'd agree to call the child Ermintrude. Then I gave her Molly to hold and went out to the space beside the lifts to call Sally from my mobile phone, our first contact since arriving at the hospital the night before. She was driving. She had to pull into a lay-by to hear the news.

'I wanted to let you know it's all right to come,' I said after

I'd told her. 'I'm already on my way,' she replied. 'I'm just past Exeter.' And with that I knew parenthood proper had begun.

Fifty-Nine Days

Molly's home debut

Once we were home, the three of us, I took the first of my two weeks of paternity leave (my employers allowed me to split it): a week I'll remember always as one of the happiest of my life. More flowers arrived at the house than I'd ever seen under one roof, boxes of cakes, parcels of baby clothes and cards from all and sundry: an explosion of pink, as I'd been warned to expect.

There was so much love surrounding us, I could land upon any minute from that week and find a treasured memory. But the one that sticks in my mind, that epitomises for me the magic of that time, is hardly anything to look at from the outside. I remember the weather was sticky and hot. Ali was cooling off in the bath upstairs. I was stretched out on the sofa watching Humphrey Bogart in The Treasure of the Sierra Madre (one of my favourite films) with Molly asleep along the groove of my lap, tilted towards me so I could see her face, when suddenly I realised I had everything I needed in the world. My wife was at ease; my daughter was dozing peacefully; Bogart had just hidden his share of the gold under a rock. For the first time in a long time, years really, I felt absolutely at one with the present moment: the see-hear-smell-and-touch of now. All because of a baby girl whose names and arrival in this world we registered the next day at Brighton Town Hall. Molly May Cunningham, born to Alison Frances and Matthew Clive, 19th May, 2009.

*

Even back at work, with the pressures of the ordinary day-to-day seeping back, I felt untouchable. I was the newest inductee to the parents' club and its members passed on their good offices wherever I went.

First the mock resignation to the struggles and strain –

'That's it now.'

'Say goodbye to your freedom.'

Or from the more poetic:

'Your heart will live outside of you now.'

Then the heartfelt coda to complete the picture –

'You can't beat it though – seriously.'

'There's nothing better on this earth.'

'Congratulations, mate. I'm so happy for you.'

One day, the man who lives directly across the road from us made a point of coming to his door when he saw Ali.

'Can I just say –,' he said, 'that I believe having a child is the most wonderful thing that can ever happen to a person.'

And it was true what he said. What they said.

Life had become very simple indeed.

I am here to take care of Molly now.

*

34

The first 'official' pic

It was about that time I met up with a friend of mine, Emma, for an Indian meal one night after work. She was only a month behind us expecting her own first child. And as we ate, dipping our naans into little pots of this and that, I shared with her all I'd learnt so far – about pregnancy, labour, what to take to the hospital, what it's like at home in the aftermath, all of it. Only weeks into parenthood and I was blagging the role of seasoned adviser; though for old friends who had seen each other in all kinds of scenarios through the years, salubrious and otherwise, it was a sweet conversation to have. We were able to share our thoughts and feelings, to imagine lives for our children, even to wonder idly whether they in turn might be friends one day. It was the kind of exchange that ought to have become common-place, and surely would have had things turned out differently.

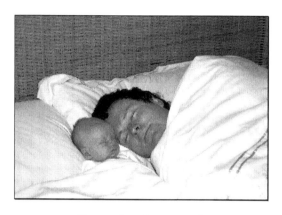

Sleepy time down south

*

Meanwhile, in the weeks that followed (barely any time at all), I began to learn how to be a dad. Not that it was obvious at first what role I'd play. Ali was breast-feeding so I wasn't involved in that side of things and I was gone from the house at work, or travelling to and from, thirteen hours a day.

But a determined pupil finds a way, and a pattern soon emerged that focused my contributions, midweek at least, around bathtime and the task of settling Molly for the night. It became the part of my life I lived for: from lunchtime onwards I clock-watched shamelessly; I ran for my bus; I stood swearing on the platform if my train was delayed, all for the love of those precious minutes when Molly and I forged our first bonds, when I played with her in the bath, then rocked and sang her to sleep.

Soon I added nappy-changing to my bank of skills and was surprised to find, once I knew what I was doing, that I liked it. In fact, many dads I've spoken to since have said the same. To take a little person who is out of sorts and over the course of a few minutes make them content, connecting all the while with gentle words and touch and silly songs, was something I found life-affirming. Could there be any greater antidote, after all, to a man's petty vanities than wiping a baby's bottom at the end of the working day?

Life was like that most of the way through June.

Bathtime. Bedtime. Daddy and Molly time.

I was walking on air.

*

And yet.

And yet even before that charmed month was over, in a way I didn't understand yet or even acknowledge fully to myself, I began to feel ill at ease. So much so, in fact, that by the time I took the second week of my paternity leave (timed to coincide with the second week of Wimbledon), I hardly enjoyed it at all.

Because I'd not been a parent prior to Molly, I had little to guide me as to what to expect of a baby at close quarters, what they should be able to do, how they might be expected to behave. So the idea that something might be wrong took a while to take hold. It ran so counter to our frame of reference (this was our blessing, our celebration, our joy of joys) my subconscious must have dismissed it a hundred times as impossible, an illusion, like seeing a river running uphill or an orbiting planet stop still in the sky. It can't be, therefore it can't be.

But while I'd not been a parent before, I was an uncle seven times over by then, so I'd had my fair share of handling babies. Certainly enough to be aware of how strong they can be – how robust disproportionate to their size. I remembered particularly my first nephew, Stephen (the first baby I played with regularly), having an almighty grip, as well as being an inveterate wriggler from his earliest days. The others too, though all unique in their own ways, were also highly mobile, their movements all jerky and chaotic as they began to explore their capabilities. Yet

Molly wasn't like that. Her grip was gentle, and always fleeting as though she'd quickly lost the inclination. When we lifted or held her, her frame felt floppy. And most disconcertingly of all, as far as I could see, she barely used her legs at all. In the bath, yes, she'd kick out a little with the buoyancy to support her, so we knew there was no paralysis. But the more her body lengthened during those first six weeks the more glaring and undeniable the lack of movement became.

Was there a defining moment?

A starting point for the worry?

Perhaps yes, just as that second week of my paternity leave began. Ali and Molly had been down in Devon for a few days while I worked. Gordon had driven them back. I went to greet them when I saw the car outside, to lift Molly up into my arms. And as I did, her legs dropped down beneath her as limp as a rag doll. I'd noticed it before, of course, but there was something about being reunited after an absence that made it plain, and a voice inside me spoke out clearly then for the first time: *This isn't right.*

Ali raised our concerns with the health visitor and our GP soon after, though neither seemed too concerned at first. They both took the view that because the spectrum of normal baby behaviour is so wide and Molly was so bright and responsive in all other ways, there could be no serious cause for alarm. So we tried our best to make our nagging worries go away. But trying not to worry about something like that is like pretending there isn't a thorn stuck in your foot.

*

That next Sunday we took Molly to Preston Park for a reunion of our NCT group now that the last of the children had been born. Fourteen new parents: seven babies: six healthy boys and one girl. I'd seen a photo I liked of a group of babies arranged like the spokes of a wheel, their faces all together in the centre, so we re-created it and I balanced myself carefully over them to get the shot. It was meant to be one of those landmark images: something for those children to look back at one day and wonder what became of us all.

It was an afternoon of forced smiles for me, of phony bonhomie and empty plans –

'We must do this again soon.'

'Us boys should definitely meet up for a drink.'

I was too worried even to think of it. All I got from that day was a chance to compare Molly as discreetly as I could with the other babies and to see quite plainly that she just wasn't made of the same rough-and-tumble stuff.

*

That took us up to Molly's six-week check-up with our GP: the first routine assessment for a new baby, and the feedback from Ali when I got home from work that night did nothing to allay my concerns. Though Molly was progressing well in virtually every respect (her cognitive responses, her growth levels), she had not responded at all to one of the basic reflex assessments, commonly known as the Moro test.

The Moro reflex, named after the man who first recorded it, is a baby's primitive and instinctive reaction to the sensation of falling – and is thought to be the only unlearned fear in newborns. It can be observed by holding a baby in the sitting position, tilting it back slightly, then just for a moment letting go. The normal response (we are born with the reflex and retain it for the first few months) is to fling out the arms as if trying to break the fall. But with Molly there was no such response, nothing at all, and no encouraging reason why it should be absent. Probably trying to mask her own fear and alleviate mine, Ali took pains to convey that the GP had still not been overly concerned and had stressed that the Moro test was only one of a series of assessments used to build a general picture, and that

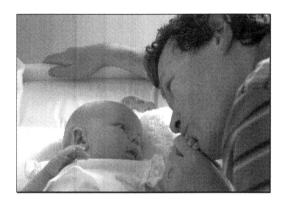

Nappy changing duties

that picture in Molly's case was still good. For each other's sake then, we tried to take comfort from that and make light of the situation as best as we could. But inside now I was scared half out of my mind. I thought about nothing else.

That was Thursday, 9th July, 2009 – the date I started to feel with a forceful, instinctive response of my own, that Molly, and with her my nascent family, was in serious trouble.

*

The next day Ali tried phoning the GP again, but she'd already left for the weekend, meaning more limbo, more anxiety growing inside us by the minute.

Though I didn't tell Ali at the time, that night while I was getting Molly changed for bed, I tried the Moro test for myself. I'd looked it up on YouTube during the day so I knew what to do, and I saw for myself that she completely failed to react. With Ali sat downstairs watching TV I felt guilty, like I'd done something wrong behind her back. I just didn't want to frighten her any more than she was already.

*

My sister, Maria, and youngest brother, Colin came to Brighton that Sunday with their families to meet Molly for the first time. And though Ali and I did our best to entertain and make a success of the day, our thoughts by now had become desperately dark. *Something is terribly wrong. Why can't anyone see it?* So despite reassurances from my sister and sister-in-law that all kinds of things happen with babies that generally turn out for the best, along with tales from their own experiences intended to make us feel better, I grew more distracted as the day went by.

By Monday morning (realising we could barely function the way we were), Ali and I were determined to escalate things as far as necessary to get to the truth; which is when we discovered we weren't the only ones to have spent the weekend worrying. When Ali went online to contact the GP, she found an e-mail from her already waiting. Dr Jarvis too had been unable to get Molly out of her mind: something seemed amiss: she'd lost sleep over it. So between them they arranged for Ali to bring Molly back to the surgery that afternoon to consult a different GP (who'd previously been a paediatrician). And yet, almost unbelievably, he too wasn't especially concerned and tried to soothe Ali into accepting an appointment at Brighton's Royal Alexandra Children's Hospital at the end of August: more than six weeks away, Molly's entire lifetime again to stew in our hell – I'm not surprised Ali refused to stand for that. And by now Dr Jarvis shared our view that Molly needed urgent, expert assessment. With the collective sense of alarm cranked up at last, a call was made, strings were pulled. An appointment was arranged for that coming Friday at 10am.

*

The four days of waiting in between were abject. Neither of us slept more than a jumpy, nerve-shredded hour here and there.

We ate next to nothing. Without resolution, no possible use of time made any sense. Ali suffered with the evidence in front of her eyes all day. I suffered trying to function at work somehow with my mind so achingly preoccupied.

My first day back, keeping up only the barest appearance of work, I did what most people do these days when confronted with something they don't understand: I turned to the internet. At the Google home page I searched with the only word I had to go on: the symptom that seemed to be at the heart of the issue: *hypotonality*: the medical term for muscular weakness – and what was to be the first place name on the map of our journey. And from there I searched for hours, unearthing all kinds of unimaginable possibilities. With my workmates coming and going around me, an ordinary day in flow, I studied the extremes of Cerebral Palsy. I pored over the symptoms and first indicators for conditions like Motor Neurone Disease – the prognosis for which left me feeling faint and sick. But as scared as I was, nothing, none of the other signals associated with those conditions, the hypotonality aside, applied to Molly. She was as responsive and alert as any baby I'd ever seen. She followed sights and sounds like a bird of prey. Her capacity to concentrate was actually striking. It didn't add up.

So I kept at it, following each lead, trying every conceivable combination of the things I found. Yet remarkably, amazingly in fact, knowing what I know now, not once did I chance upon even a reference to what the problem turned out to be.

What I do remember is reaching another word: *milestones* – a word that for whatever reason had an especially powerful effect on me. Specifically, what I read was this:

It is likely that children exhibiting hypotonality will experience significant delays in reaching their milestones, though this can often be remedied with physiotherapy enabling them to catch up later in life.

That's when I stopped reading, stopped searching. Quietly I

got up from my desk and, walking as quickly as I could without drawing attention to myself, I went to the bathroom out by the lifts and locked myself into a cubicle. My mind was in torment now, racing with the harshest images of my child struggling to walk, unable to keep up with other children, having to sit off to one side and look on in pain at things she couldn't do. And in the fire of that moment, I felt there would be no way I could bear that. Not for Molly, not for Ali, not for me.

Looking down I became aware that my body was shaking – convulsing as if freezing cold. I could feel tears running down off my cheeks, see them dripping onto the floor one by one. For half an hour I sat there, with people coming in and out just the other side of the door, trying to keep the sound of my sobbing and sniffing as quiet as I could.

*

When the day itself arrived: Friday, 17th July (*I wish I'd gone with Ali to the previous appointments now*), she and I set out as positively and brightly as we could, as if somehow we could fool the day into being kind to us. It felt very unreal: the way I imagined the world might feel to a condemned prisoner on the morning he is scheduled to die –

The sun still shines. The birds still sing.

So it can't really be happening, can it?

Sat in the cab on the way to the Royal Alexandra, literally a stone's throw from where Molly had been born just fifty-nine days before, Ali and I were superficially calm. We had worried ourselves full circle, I think, all the way through hell and back to a point where again we half expected to be given a straightforward, benign explanation for the way things were.

How we'd sigh with relief when we heard the good news –

'Children can be complicated,' they'd say, 'but you've got a little fighter there. Give her a month and she'll be right as rain.'

As we neared the hospital we even shared a hollow joke. Ali

43

had mistakenly noted the paediatrician's name as Dr Trout instead of Dr Trounce.

'Don't worry, he'll tell us there's nothing fishy going on.'

We actually said that.

We tried to picture ourselves an hour into the future when we'd know everything was all right. Only sometimes, no matter how hard you pray or hope or beg or bargain, things just aren't all right.

*

The first thing I noticed about Dr Trounce was he had a slight disability of his own: a curvature of the legs that had obviously done little to slow his progress through the world or to prevent him from having a successful, meaningful career. I took that as a good omen. I thought he must have been sent to us as a sign that Molly was destined to be wonderful – one way or another, that we should try to be positive because things would still turn out well, just differently from the way we imagined.

He showed us into one of the consultation rooms and, once we were settled, began by asking us to explain our concerns, to tell him what we'd observed ourselves and why we felt worried. Then after we'd done so, he asked about our family histories. Had either one of us or anyone in our extended families ever exhibited similar muscular weakness? The answer was no. But was that good or bad? *Would it be better if one of us had?* I'm certain now that even before he examined Molly, Dr Trounce had a clear idea what was wrong.

At his request then, Ali took Molly over to the couch where we undressed her before taking a step back to give him space to work. And for the next few minutes we looked on while he observed first the movement of her chest as she breathed, then tapped at the joints of her elbows and knees with a miniature mallet, looking for reflex reactions that should have been evident but patently were not, even to our untrained eyes. Then he

44

told us we could dress Molly again, and moments later we were sat around his desk together as before.

There was the briefest pause at that point: an almost audible drawing of breath as each of us prepared to go where he knew, and we feared, we had to go next.

When Dr Trounce spoke at last, his first words were:

'I think you are right to be concerned.'

*

For the next few minutes inside that room, two very different worlds moved in parallel: interdependent yet entirely separated from each other, each according to its own parameters of time. On the outside the seconds must have passed as they always do: measurably. But inside, it felt like I had forever to contemplate the precise import of every word spoken.

Hypotonality – milestones – you are right to be concerned –

Now, as we listened to Dr Trounce, one by one there were more names for our map, new territories charted. From an outpost called *concern* we arrived at a harsher place: *condition*, where, for the first time, I was to hear three familiar words spoken in sequence: Spinal – Muscular – Atrophy.

Atrophy. I knew what atrophy meant. It meant wasting away – the room swirled. And with barely a pause, still another indistinct form loomed up and over us, until Dr Trounce gave it a name. *Progressive*. I felt my chest tighten, my consciousness flicker and judder like a videotape held on pause. Whatever breakfast I'd managed turned inside me as I saw the comprehension taking shape on Ali's face.

But still, what exactly was he saying? Was Molly going to be disabled? Profoundly? Was she facing a lifetime of wheelchairs, round-the-clock care? Slow decline? Pain? And what about Ali and me? Yes, I thought about us. About me. Were *we* facing a life of relentless, aching responsibility now? Until that moment I wouldn't have believed it was possible to have so many distinct strands of thought running in tandem.

And not one of them close to the ultimate truth.

With Ali and I sat there side by side, our hands gripped together as we tried to absorb the gravity of what we were hearing, Dr Trounce gave us the last destination for our map. Not with a word or name that stood alone this time, but with a sentence.

'I have to tell you,' he said, 'that a child diagnosed with this condition so early in life, would not be expected to live beyond their first birthday.'

There was silence.

I felt like my guts had been exposed to the air.

Beside me, very quietly, Ali began to cry.

It Can't Be True

Hung out to dry

Afterwards one of the nurses called for a cab to take us home. I have no recollection of waiting for it, nor of being told it had arrived. My memory jumps straight to being aware of Ali sat in the back seat behind me with Molly (fast asleep now, oblivious to her role) while I sat beside a driver who was to give me my first lesson in concealing unspeakable pain.

'That's where we had *our* two,' he said, pointing up through the windscreen at the hospital as we pulled away.

I nodded just the barest acknowledgement. I had nothing to say to the man, yet he talked at me all the way home.

'You lived in Brighton long?'

Please, not now.

'Been here since I was a boy.'

Leave me alone.
'Forty-seven years.'
Spinal Muscular Atrophy.
'Probably die here too.'
My daughter's going to die.
'Up here, mate?'
She's not expected to live beyond her first birthday.
'That's very kind of you, cheers.'
Molly –
'Mind how you go now.'
Darling, darling Molly.

*

When we got inside I set Molly's carrier down in the lounge to leave her sleeping. Then Ali and I sat on adjacent sofas, mostly in silence, too shell-shocked to be of comfort to each other yet. Anything we might ordinarily have done: switch on the kettle, use the bathroom, make a sandwich, felt like an affront. So we sat there staring into space with no idea how to get through the next few minutes let alone the coming months.

We probably knew we should call for help: spell SOS in the sand in oversized letters. But it took some time to pluck up the courage. To expose such a wound, even to loved-ones, was intimidating, more than I could bring myself to do initially. It was Ali who bit the bullet first. She called her parents and spoke to her mum while I stood close by, willing her to be clear about what we'd been told. I didn't want Sally, Gordon or anyone to be left in doubt and in need of clarification later. I wanted the plaster ripped off. It seemed like the only way.

'They want to come,' Ali turned to me with her hand pressed over the mouthpiece. 'Dad's there too; they want to know if it's all right to come.'

'Tell them yes,' I said. I knew at once I wanted them with us. Looking at Ali, at the agony already etched into her face, I felt woefully out of my depth.

Then: 'I'm taking Molly to the park,' Ali announced suddenly after her call. 'It'll give you some space to speak to your family.' And without another word she attached the carrier (with Molly in it) to the wheels of the pram, pushed it down the hall and out through the front door. I couldn't tell whether she wanted time alone or time with Molly or she just couldn't stand to hear me make those calls.

Should I go with her? Will she be all right?

'Don't worry,' Ali said, reading my thoughts. 'We'll be fine.' Then she lowered the pram onto the pavement and closed the door behind them.

*

Alone then, I went to sit at the foot of the stairs by the phone. My first thought: *not again* as memory took me to a night more than twenty years before when it had fallen to me to call my siblings one by one to tell them our dad was dead: it had been sudden, his heart, at our family home in Rickmansworth. Then another decade, another crisis: Mum this time, felled by an aneurism (not permanently, thank God) and again I was the only one at home and the calls came down to me. Now mine was to be the voice of doom a third time, and I honestly didn't know if I had it in me. Not with this. Not with something so far out of its natural place in time.

But *rip the plaster off*. Allowing myself no time to back out, I keyed Mum's number quickly, steeling myself not to fall apart. I'd start at the head of the family and work my way down.

She picked up on the second ring, surprising me –

'Mum,' I said. 'It's Matt. Are you okay?'

And right off she said, 'No,' sounding miserable. And then, over the crackly line, completely throwing me, *she* broke down, for all the world as if she already knew. But I'd told her next to nothing about Molly, not wanting to alarm her until we knew

49

what we were facing.

'What is it, Mum? I asked, panicking slightly now, trying to imagine what could have possibly happened to make that dark day even worse (Mum's no complainer without good cause).

And that's when the banal everyday came rushing back in.

'I've had the most horrible time at the dentist,' she said.

And with a jolt I realised how close I'd come to telling her our news over the phone and how thoughtless that would have been. Though in rude health, she was seventy-eight that year, living alone; and more than either she'd lost her own first born, Stephen, to leukaemia, when he was five years old. She would feel our pain as her own.

She pulled herself together then, explained that the anaesthetic was starting to wear off and apologised for being dramatic. I felt for her. I reassured her I'd stay in contact and in the end said nothing about Molly. I phoned my brother, Dave, at work, gave him the facts as calmly as I could and asked him to tell the family for me. I didn't have the stomach for it after all.

I lay on the sofa instead and found some comfort thinking about Dad and Stephen: our family's departed. I tried to recall the feeling of Dad's arms holding me, and wished I could hold young Stephen too and tell him I was sorry for what happened to him. It had been a good while since I'd thought about Dad and I'd never thought of my eldest brother that way. But their company for that hour made perfect sense and I stayed with them peacefully until Ali and Molly got back.

*

It was just us then until Gordon and Sally knocked on the door towards the end of the afternoon. As Ali went to let them in I hung back in the hallway, unsure of what it would feel like now to face our families with this awful reality a part of us.

While Sally held her daughter, I looked down at my feet.

Then she came to me while Ali went to her dad.

50

Until finally there was just Gordon and me.

He looked undone, as lost in his grief as I was lost in mine, and desperately sorry for the pair of us. He gestured me to him and we gave each other a hug: something we'd never done before that day, though we have a close bond. It was plain, I suppose, that the old ways didn't matter anymore.

*

We tried to 'carry on regardless' the following day. Ali went for a walk along the promenade with her parents and Molly while I met an old friend from Sydney who was in town for a day. We sat in the Old Ship Hotel drinking Bloody Marys, talking about the situation with Molly, about Ali, about his girlfriend, books, history, whatever came to mind. And in some ways it was like old times, so that for minutes at a time it was possible to leave my anguish aside and find things to laugh about; though I sensed even then I no longer belonged in a situation like that.

Back at home that night, once Molly was asleep, the four of us ate a lamb casserole conjured by Sally with her unerring eye for what's needed in a crisis. And later, after the girls had gone up, Gordon and I sat up talking. We drank a second bottle of wine. We even poured ourselves a glass of whisky each: a drink neither of us likes. It was just that kind of night: really the only kind that made sense to me thereafter. If I wasn't with people who were part of it, or close to it, then I wasn't where I wanted or needed to be.

*

And I hadn't even considered Molly yet. The situation, yes, but not the person: the living, breathing wonder that was the focus of our love now more than ever. It wasn't until the next morning that I had my first moments alone with her since the news.

Back then she still slept in a cot in our room, so we always

51

knew the moment she was ready to start the day. At weekends that would be my cue to rise too to give Ali a chance to lie in. But this time Ali was restless and wanted to get up. And Molly (an unheard-of luxury this), once she was propped between the pillows on our bed and Ali had gone, drifted back to sleep. So I turned onto my front as quietly as I could, to gaze at her for a while and drink her in. Then slowly, so as not to wake her, I lay back down and rested the side of my forehead gently against hers. And for what must have been only twenty minutes or so, we lay there together floating back and forth between dreams and the waking world, her delicate hand in mine. I was just aware of the scent of her hair, the rise and fall of her frame as she took and surrendered each breath. I was so enraptured I could have stayed that way forever.

But too soon Molly declared her readiness for the attentions of her grandparents. Ali came in and scooped her up and away. If all that had been was one of my first wonderful experiences as a father it would have moved me to the core. As it was I was left breathless, almost traumatised by the sudden absence, and I wept for the next few minutes there in bed.

That was my first real clarity, I think, when I absorbed fully that Molly was going to die, and realised that that cold fact was going to strike anew every day. There was going to be nowhere to hide, or duck, or do anything other than face up.

*

That afternoon Gordon had to fly from Gatwick back to Plymouth to pick up his car and some papers he needed for work, while Sally was to stay on with us for the foreseeable.
'I'll be fine,' she reassured him, as they said their goodbyes in the hall. 'I'll drive myself back later in the week.' And what he said in return has stuck in my mind ever since.

'Don't speed,' he blurted out, almost sharply.

Which sounded strange coming from him: out of character.

Sunflowers

Sally isn't the kind to go haring down the motorway and neither of them are undue worriers. But still I felt like I understood. I believe his mind had been doing to him what mine had been doing to me all weekend: making him see that we have no right whatever to keep hold of the ones we love.

Later I learnt that such awareness can be a blessing, a call to action to express what we keep inside. But at the time, and for a long time afterwards, all it did was make me afraid to let anyone I cared about out of my sight.

Blood

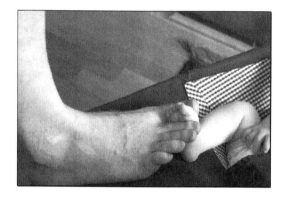

Playing footsy

The end of that first weekend also marked the end of the brief time when our circumstances remained a private family matter. By Monday morning I knew the demands of the outside world would soon be upon us, so I tried to write an email to work to explain what had happened. Yet in the same way I'd struggled to pass the news to family, I faltered again, dwelling (as absurd as it sounds) over the phrasing, searching for a way of making things clear without laying ourselves bare. In the end I settled for the basics: diagnosis, prognosis, the fact that I'd need time out for Ali and I to take stock. Then I sent it to the member of the management team who I knew would deal with it with the least fuss. I felt embarrassed almost, as if I'd been hit by a car and was lying broken and exposed in the street.

While I waited for a reply, Ali and I read through the first messages of condolence arriving already via email from extended family on both sides.

'We can't begin to imagine how you're feeling – '

'I know there's nothing anyone can say – '

'You are in our thoughts and prayers – '

'If there's anything at all we can do – '

It was striking to see the same phrases again and again: the set language we call upon in times of grief: formulaic, yet comforting too in its familiarity.

Then minutes later, word arrived from work: the immediate, unequivocal support I anticipated. It was reassuring to have no worries on that score at least.

*

Sally drove us all to Rickmansworth later that morning, aware that Mum would be anxious to see us. I wanted to see her too, though it pained me that Molly's first visit to the house I grew up in should be under such tragic circumstances.

Arriving outside I'll bet we looked the epitome of proud parents come to show off our first-born to Grandma. That must have been what Mum's neighbours saw as they waved to us from their windows. Had they been closer they might have taken in the faraway stare on Ali's face or the bloodshot eyes on mine: the details at odds in our otherwise lucky-them scene.

Still there were comforts to be had in familiar surroundings: homemade soup, crusty bread, homemade plum crumble too – all served with motherly words of apology for not having got much in. And for a couple of hours we did what little we could to soothe one another. Sally even took Ali and Molly out for a while to give Mum and I some time alone. But though the tears nearly came when she put her arms around me and told me to let it all out, our roles had been reversed too long. My instinct was to protect *her* now and I held myself in check.

Mum and Molly

'You two will have to put up with so much,' she said, when the others were back and we were sat in a line along her sofa – Mum holding Molly with Ali and I either side. As the only person we knew who had lived through anything comparable, she was inclined to give it to us straight.

'I remember once,' she began, taking Ali's hand into hers, 'I was shopping in the Co-op with my little Stephen.'

I knew what was coming. I knew this story.

'It was at the time of his chemotherapy and the poor little thing was exhausted. The drugs they were giving him had made him put on weight and sapped all his strength. So I'd rearranged my bits of shopping in the pushchair to give him a place to sit down. And as I was standing in the queue to pay, one of the women there looked down her nose at him and said: "What's a big boy like you doing in a pushchair? You should be up helping your mum." '

I get angry when I hear (or think about) that story, probably because it's just the kind of thing any one of us might think, in an unkind mood, should we happen to see an overweight five-year-old being pushed around in a pram.

Look at that lazy fat kid.

We might imagine, with that nasty thought, we were getting at the truth, when the truth would have been:

Look at that brave little boy who's going to die soon, and that courageous mother who has to carry on somehow in spite of that.

I reached my arm around Mum to stroke Ali's hair.

'I could have killed her,' Mum said, finally. 'But I didn't say anything, because you don't, do you.'

I knew her lesson for us was simple: people will be ignorant, foolish. Not all, but some. The world would go on being what it was: usually kind, often insensitive, occasionally cruel, and we should try not to let that draw from our strength.

For a while then I left the four girls together and went for a wander around the house and garden. I looked into each of the rooms in turn, sifting through their histories in my mind, the random memories: ping-pong up against the front room wall; Mum and Dad dancing to Nat King Cole; football matches and cricket in the garden; all the hundreds of books devoured with my feet propped up on the piano stool; Dad being taken away. Now there was sorrow under the roof again, for my daughter.

On the way home I sat with her in the back making videos of the two of us on my phone. Then after she'd fallen asleep I tried to read, but it was pointless. Every few lines I realised I'd taken nothing in. I kept looking back across at Molly (her head bobbing with the motion of the car), wishing with all my heart there was something I could do.

*

Not even a week had passed since our first fateful visit to the hospital but the next day we returned. They were keen to take a blood sample from Molly to send for testing so the diagnosis could be formally confirmed. A mean and sad day for us: Molly having needles put into her: her first experiences of pain. And for Ali and me, a first taste of the helplessness we would come to know well in such situations.

'I'm so sorry for you,' the nurse said to us more than once. She had seen the diagnosis and knew what it meant. I thought that was kind of her. Yet kindness aside it still took her a long time to take that sample (it wasn't easy with someone so small). And after, there was a bruise on Molly's hand: her first wound of any kind, not counting the nick Ali had made the first time she'd tried to cut her nails. Ali had felt bad about that for days, and in the same way now we felt miserable that Molly had had to endure discomfort, as if it was our fault – big clumsy giants with big clumsy hands, too coarse for such a delicate task. It made me think of the elephant in Horton Hears a Who! trying to protect that speck of dust from the wind: a whole world in his hands. The sample was biked up to London that afternoon.

*

Ali and I both needed solace after that, so she and Sally took Molly and went shopping in town while I stayed at home, taking my usual path of turning to the bookshelves for comfort. I began reading Things Fall Apart by Chinua Achebe and not far into it I came to a reference to a character, Ekwefi, losing nine of her ten children, mostly before the age of three. Maybe it was inevitable in the circumstances that I should pause over that passage now. I could see the potential it had for offering perspective; for reminding me that suffering is the daily bread for so many; for perhaps even helping me to accept that a crumb of that quotidian had found its way to us. But I was kidding myself putting my mind up against my heart. The sadness was impenetrable that way.

I had better luck seeking solace in less high-brow ways that afternoon. The second I heard Ali and Sally arriving back from the shops, I set the book down and went to gather Molly up.

'Now then, Molls. How was shopping?'

I crouched down and put my ear to her mouth.

Multi-tasking

'What's that? The shops were okay, but you couldn't wait to get home for a dance with Daddy?'

Which earned a smile from Ali, a mother-in-lawly roll of the eyes from Sally, and the look of part-trepidation-part-adoration Molly often aimed at me as I whisked her upstairs to the stereo on the landing and our rectangle of 'dance floor' there between the bookcase and tumble dryer.

What started (our dancing together) during the first days of her life began to change that day into therapy for the two of us. For her the thrill of motion, of being able to move in ways she couldn't manage for herself. And for me the counterweight of dancing in the face of fear and pain. It was funny to note her earliest musical preferences (the contentment that went with I Want Your Love by Chic; the choice of Ooh La La La by Kool & The Gang to fall asleep to) and uplifting to picture the outside world looking in, expecting to pity us and finding us dancing instead, stepping and twirling in our pocket of happiness.

Confirmation

With Dave in our garden

I suppose that until we knew for sure, there was still hope for a miracle, still leeway to leave our heads in the sand if that's what we wanted to do. The temptation was certainly there, aided and abetted by the fact that superficially at least our lives still seemed so charmed. Molly was happy, bright-eyed, as keen mentally as any baby you could wish to meet; the weather was hot; the roses in bloom. In the diary I began to keep at about that time, the loose record that later served as the basis for this book, the first entry scribbled at the top of the page is *The illusion of bliss* – followed by the unremarkable events of a single day –

The lounge: Sally colouring Ali's hair in little twists of silver foil, the two of them in relatively good spirits. The bedroom: a rare explosion of laughter when I walked in to find Ali sat up on the bed, topless, with Molly sucking noisily on one of her breasts and the express machine chugging away on the other; an impromptu fart from Molly at that point had us in stitches. The kitchen, towards the end of that day: a splendidly eccentric meal as we tried to use up all the leftovers from our fridge and freezer in one go. The bathroom: Molly loving her time in the water; the warmth; the splashing and toys. All the simple ingredients for well-being in place, until –

'Matt! Matt! Quick!'

Ali was yelling for me to hurry upstairs.

'What?' I shouted back, jumping to my feet. I could hear the excitement in her voice. But elation? Panic? I couldn't tell. Was there a crisis with Molly? Had we reached a reckoning already?

'Quick!'

I took the stairs in twos, adrenalin pumping, my heart in my mouth (I know what that means now). *Keep your head, whatever it is.* Yet when I reached them all I could see was Molly lying on her changing mat, looking just the way she usually did: quizzical, serene, content.

'What?' I snapped at Ali, angry with her now for scaring me that way for no reason. But she was wide-eyed, staring at me –

'Molly moved her legs,' she said. 'She kicked out her legs.'

So I looked at our daughter more closely: as playful as ever, all the wonder of the world in her eyes and the faintest glimmer of movement in her legs as before; and in doing so caught just a glimpse of how hard the months ahead were going to be.

'Ali sweetheart, come on.'

I pulled her to me. And feeling rent in two, we stood there together like that in the nursery, with our first-born gazing up at us, the sweetest, dribbly smile on her face. *The illusion of bliss.*

*

We took Molly back to the GP the next day to put her through what seemed like the pointless discomfort of being given jabs to ward off illnesses she'd surely never face. I wondered whether the doctor thought it was pointless too, whether it was just part of the pretence of carrying on as normal until we had confirmation. Regardless, the apparent senselessness had Ali and I on short fuses, curt with each other as we made our way home; though neither of us took the bait, both backing down before it turned into a fight. We knew instinctively there was nothing we needed less.

*

In the meantime our news had filtered all the way out by now to family, friends and beyond. So in spite of ourselves Ali and I began to be aware of who had reached out to us, and who, for whatever reason, had not.

She was shocked, I knew, to find that more than one person she thought of as a friend had stayed silent. And though I remembered the same from when Dad died (people get paralysed by uncertainty until it's too late), I was shocked too by the silences, and angry to see further needless disquiet heaped on Ali.

You think this is hard on you?

But then maybe an equilibrium of sorts was reached via the many acts of kindness that came our way, often from the most unexpected places: people we hardly knew who struck just the right tone with things they said and did. Many called their faith into play. We had messages of support from Christians, Jews, Muslims and Buddhists, all saying strikingly similar things. But what mattered was simply that so many: close family, relatives, friends, colleagues, bare acquaintances, stood up to be counted. And whether they did that with a letter, a phone call, an email, a quiet word, even a text, didn't matter at all.

*

62

I was grateful for the weekend when it came. Not that a weekend meant much when I hadn't been working during the week, but this time I knew Dave was coming to stay, so there would at least be company to lighten the load and brighten the darker tones for a day or two.

The weather that Saturday was exceptional, so beautiful that Ali and I pushed ourselves out early to take Molly for a walk by the beach. We stopped in at the Meeting Place Café for tea and bacon rolls. And later, once Dave had arrived, we indulged in a lazy afternoon in the garden, barbecuing, soaking up some sun, singing country songs to Molly. More or less we felt all right, which by the standards of the time was good.

The mood held into Sunday too. Dave helped me to mend the overflow on the bath and to do the Sainsbury's shop (by strolling behind me reading the Racing Post) before I cooked a roast dinner for the three of us. It was sweet relief, a breather, and all over much too quickly.

For the hour before he left, we watched TV: Will Ferrell out in the wilderness with Bear Grylls. Ali was beside me with her laptop open. I could see she was reading through the website for The Jennifer Trust (the support charity for Spinal Muscular Atrophy), and in particular the case studies: the what, how and when, described in detail by those who'd gone before.

It was too soon for me though. I tried to avert my eyes, fix them on the TV. But the more I tried the more I was drawn to the screen beside me, to the words and phrases written there – *Respiratory difficulties. Naso-gastric tubes. Risk of aspiration.* Reality was yanking me up by the hair, forcing me to confront it when all I wanted was to rewind that weekend and live it over and over until I felt ready to go on.

*

But Monday came nevertheless (*Mondays With Molly*) and again we returned to the hospital; though not for her this time; it was

63

Ali's turn to be examined and told by a grave looking young doctor that any damage done during labour had now healed to their satisfaction.

'You may now resume sex,' she announced in a stern monotone, making it sound like something unpleasant but required for the war effort. Still it gave us a laugh and a new catchphrase at home. And we were glad of the news, of course, even if sex seemed like something from a very different world.

After that, with the Royal Alexandra being part of the same complex, Ali decided to call in to have Molly weighed (to save herself a separate trip during the week). She took Molly to the bathroom to change her when we got there, and while waiting I saw Dr Trounce passing and stopped him to say hello.

'Dr Trounce,' I said. 'It's me. Molly Cunningham's dad.'

'I know,' he said, with a gentle smile. 'How are you?'

I hadn't been sure he'd recognise me, which was silly. Why wouldn't he? Only ten days ago he'd told me my daughter was going to die. He'd diagnosed Spinal Muscular Atrophy just half a dozen times in his career, he'd said.

As a courtesy then, he invited me through to a consultation room and asked if there was anything he could do to help. So I enquired after the results of Molly's blood test and asked whether, given the certainty, it would be necessary for us to come in again to hear the news. Though Ali still held out a glimmer of hope, I had none and I said as much.

'I think you're right,' he said. 'It would be unwise to expect good news.' But recognising that even with apparent certainty the wait could hardly be good for us, he offered to do what he could to hurry things along. He left the room and returned a few minutes later with word that the laboratory had agreed to fax the results within two hours, if we had time to wait.

If we had time to wait.

Even in the circumstances, that made me smile.

And so, once Ali and Molly had found us, we were shown to a 'quiet room', soothingly coloured in shades of purple. And there we waited, quietly – Ali turning the pages of a magazine mechanically, while I did nothing more than follow the second hand of the clock on the wall and get up now and then to pace the room. I felt hollow, emotionally half conscious until, a little over an hour later, Dr Trounce came in. At which point I just happened to be sat opposite Ali, so he took the seat beside me, probably so he could address himself respectfully to her.

He said: 'It isn't good news, I'm afraid.'

Which, keeping in mind the conversation he and I had just had, confused me for a second. Could things be *worse* than we thought? *Was* there a worse? All I knew was I didn't want Molly to suffer and certainly not to the point of self-awareness. But no, as it quickly became clear, he was only confirming what we were expecting.

As he spoke to Ali I looked down at the sheet of fax paper on his lap (he followed my eye-line and momentarily made as if to conceal it before realising there would be no point). At the top of the page I saw Molly's names and her date of birth, and in bold letters in one line across the middle:

The clinical diagnosis of Spinal Muscular Atrophy has been CONFIRMED.

We sat on for a while then, discussing the various people he felt we should see now to help build our knowledge and ability to care for Molly as best as we could: a respiratory specialist; a dietician; the experts in Spinal Muscular Atrophy at the Evelina Children's Hospital in London. Then later still, if and when we were ready, we could meet genetics counsellors who could help us understand where we stood in regard to having children in the future. It was a lot to take in. But it helped that Dr Trounce was straightforward with us, that he paid our intelligences due respect, and we liked him, both of us, and for some reason that seemed to matter.

Outside, as we pulled away in a cab, I reasoned to myself that at least now we knew for sure: the diagnosis and more crucially the prognosis were facts I could begin to assimilate. That was the way *I* saw it anyway. It was different for Ali. I recognised and respected that. She'd carried Molly inside her for nine months, endured thirteen hours of labour to bring her into the world. Sitting with her coming home that day, seeing the loss, the pain, the rage in her eyes, I knew she was a million miles from accepting anything.

Facing Facts

The Y-fronts chair

That night, after Ali had gone to bed, I sat up to read through The Jennifer Trust website for myself: the basics on Spinal Muscular Atrophy, its various forms and anticipated life spans, as well as the stories of those who'd been through the experience. Based on what I found there, on what Dr Trounce had told us, and on what I already knew about genetics, which amounted to having read Genome by Matt Ridley a couple of years before, what follows are the essentials of what I came to understand:

Spinal Muscular Atrophy (SMA hereafter) is a degenerative condition that limits the capacity of the anterior horn (the connection between brain and spine) to relay muscle movement signals – as a consequence of which the muscles remain largely unused and begin to waste away (atrophy).

The *prognosis* depends primarily on the age of the person when the condition is diagnosed. If that's within the first six months of life it's defined as Type 1 SMA – considered to be the most severe – with an average life expectancy around seven months. When the diagnosis comes later but within the first two years, it's defined as Type 2: a different condition, sufferers of which usually live into adulthood, though with profound physical limitations. And finally Type 3: diagnosed later still, which can usually be managed towards a normal lifespan. Ali has always disliked the coldness of Molly being referred to as a Type 1 baby, but in plain medical terms that's what she was: a terminally ill child with roughly five months left to live.

Likely cause of death was not easy to predict. The most probable scenario would be a slow decline in Molly's respiratory strength compromising her ability to fight off a chest infection; though other possibilities hung over us, the most frightening of which went by the name *aspiration*: the deceptively optimistic-sounding medical term used to describe the inhalation of fluid.

And finally, your rough guide to the genetics. SMA is inherited via what is known as an 'autosomal recessive' pattern, meaning that Ali and I contributed equally to the problem. If you don't know about such things, here's how it works:

Each of us carries two sets of our chromosomes (our genetic make-up) which, though similar to each other, are not identical. At conception one set is passed on by each parent to form the basis of the two sets that make up the child. Which, as Ali and

I both carry one set with the potential to cause SMA and one set without, means three possible outcomes for any pregnancy between us:

1. We both pass on our non-affected set: the best case scenario, leading to a child who is neither a sufferer nor a carrier. The likelihood of that: 1 in 4.

2. We both pass on our affected set: the worst case scenario – though I hate to think of it that way, leading to a child like Molly with Type 1 SMA. The likelihood of that: 1 in 4.

3. One of us passes on our non-affected set, the other the affected set, producing a child like Ali or me. Not a sufferer, but a carrier. The likelihood of that: 2 in 4.

In the UK about one in forty of us carries the gene deletion for SMA. So first you have to calculate the likelihood of two of those one-in-forties meeting and conceiving. Then multiply by four for the probability of SMA. Already the odds are up in the stratosphere, the kind of risk any gambler would accept in the blink of an eye. It works out at approximately one new case in every twenty thousand babies born.

Twenty thousand to one. And the one was Molly.

*

None of us slept well after that. I lay awake restless, thinking about all I'd read. Ali was unsettled beside me. And Molly, perhaps picking up on the newly intensified anguish in the house, remained fractious long into the smallest hours. Like any first-time parents we had little idea what to try beyond the obvious, but with a whole added layer of never knowing what was due to Molly's condition and what was just normal for a baby. I felt

69

especially bad for Ali, destined, as I knew she was, to bear the greater share of the strain. Even for me, the sleep deprivation coupled with the psychological trauma felt fundamentally exhausting and I wasn't the one breast-feeding every two to three hours around the clock. She had all that debilitating workload to face and none of the happy expectation that would normally be there to make it bearable.

We knew what was coming: that was the worst of it. We even had a fair idea of when: sometime in December or January probably when the weather would be at its coldest and Molly's life expectancy would have been reached. In our cosy world of central heating, log fires, hot water on tap, to fear the winter felt dreadful, a shadow over-hanging from an age long past.

*

Tuesday morning, knowing that theoretically I was due back at work, I emailed a half-hearted offer to contribute from home. But I was in no fit state. They knew it as well as I did and had kindly arranged cover for a second week: some breathing space for Ali and I to collect ourselves.

And so it was that later that day, instead of being sat behind a desk in London, I found myself sat beside Sally (with us again after returning home to prepare for a longer stay) driving to Shoreham-by-Sea down the coast to look at second-hand cars. We'd decided the time was right to buy one to help with hospital appointments and emergencies, and to make it easier to be with family or friends when we wanted to be.

It should have been routine: an arrangement of conveyance from A to B (I cared no more about it than that). Yet the hour we spent in that showroom was unexpectedly hard. Childhood memories (*Can I sit in front? Can I do the gears? Bagsy the window*) that started out sweetly seemed to sour in the knowledge Molly would never know the same.

Then later that afternoon, as if to underscore the point, we had our first significant scare. Molly had been upstairs with Ali, crying inconsolably for fifteen minutes or more, when abruptly she came to a point where she couldn't summon the strength to clear her throat and began to struggle to breathe. As she had before, Ali shouted down the stairs to me to get there fast, and this time there was no mistaking the fear in her voice. But by the time I reached them, Sally was there. Reacting quickly she'd placed Molly face down over Ali's feeding pillow, head lower than her feet, enough to enable her to clear the blockage for herself. And with that, exhausted by the episode, Molly fell asleep at once with the three of us stood around her breathless, and Ali and I terribly shaken. *God help us*. Was this what life was going to be like from now on? Had we to stay vigilant every minute, every hour? I felt so inadequate in the face of the task, I wanted to drop to my knees and howl.

Sensitively then, Sally left us alone to take some time to recover ourselves. And gradually, watching Molly sleeping peacefully, we calmed. We lay on our bed side by side, cuddled close; and shortly after, seeking reassurance or solace or simple tenderness, Ali pulled me to her, and for the first time since before Molly was born we made love, clumsily, reaching out to each other like inexperienced teenagers. It felt awkward, too soon. I couldn't rid myself of the picture of Molly in trouble, nor my awareness that this was only the beginning.

Survival Skills

Dave, Brian and me

The immediate prospect, however, was something very different, something with the potential to be fun. As incongruous as it sounds in the circumstances, along with two of my brothers (Dave and Brian) I was booked in to attend an Introduction to Bushcraft weekend down in Somerset. It had been my fortieth birthday present from Ali and between us we'd decided I ought to go and try to enjoy it as intended. She and Molly would return with Sally to Devon while I was gone.

It was our first separation since the news and at first I made a complete mess of it. Watching Gordon and Sally's car backing down our road, disappearing from view, was hard enough. But coming back into the house, the silence and stillness after all those weeks of family life: what could I have done to prepare for that? Instead of pulling down a book, opening a beer, toasting my temporary freedom, as I know I'd have done in the past, within minutes I was stood at Molly's cot with her pillow held to my cheek like a child clutching a security blanket.

I tried to clear my head by getting outside. I cycled down into town, but if anything the dazzling sun made my mood even darker. Weaving slowly through the throng of afternoon shoppers, I found myself staring at people's faces, trying to guess at which of them might be suffering too. Is *he* terminally ill? Is *she* lost in mourning? Suddenly it seemed possible, even logical, to view everyone in that same grey light. And had their eyes happened to alight on me? Would they have thought me lucky to be out at my leisure on my bike on a sunny Thursday afternoon? Or later, looking at camping gear (a melamine mug and bowl, a head-torch), luckier still to be off on adventure somewhere?

Home again, with my anxiety threatening to overwhelm me now, I did what I'd once read Woody Allen used to do to keep him from obsessing over the deeper issues of health and mortality. I chose topics at random to consider in detail: the precise layout of the playground at my old primary school; my first and last recollections of various friends over the years; the minutiae of long-forgotten holidays; the personnel of football teams. It didn't matter what. It wasn't the details I needed but the process, whatever it took to keep me from myself for a few minutes at a time. It was a long, lonely afternoon. By the time I opened the door to Dave that night, I was so relieved to have company again I almost broke down when I saw his face.

*

The following morning, and into afternoon, he and I drove for hours through the densest traffic to rendezvous with Brian at a pub in the Somerset village of East Coker. And from there, having been advised by the locals that the nearest all-day pub was in West Coker, we passed a charmed afternoon drinking cider, recounting tales (true and apocryphal) of when we were young, and meandering between the two villages getting stoned.

In the evening we dined back at our pub, fuelling the fires with red wine and whisky, before dressing up in our 'bushcraft outfits' for drunken photos upstairs in our room – the Family Room I'd booked so we could talk in the dark like we used to when along with our other brother, Colin, the four of us shared a bedroom and two sets of bunks.

It was escapism the whole day, pure and simple, and despite the sadness running just below the surface, *because* of it probably, perfectly timed. I felt the way I imagined a soldier might feel on leave, a mile behind the trench with a beer in his hand and a girl on his knee. What would be would be, just not yet.

*

When morning came, notwithstanding hangovers and here-to-stay rain pouring outside, morale was high as we drove the last leg to nearby Beaminster to meet the instructors and the others on the weekend. We drove a few more miles in convoy before hiking deep into woodland, further and further off the map, at least in our minds: no phone reception or contact with the outside world for the next thirty hours.

Instead, from the first moments we were drawn into a boys' own world of useful, or useless, skills (depending on your point of view): how to kindle fires from scratch in both wet and dry conditions; how to make tent pegs from branches of ash; how to identify which antiseptic plants could be used to make poultices for dressing wounds; and how to recognise and steer clear of the poisonous varieties. We mastered the various knots needed to hang tarpaulins up between the trees, and all beneath a dense forest canopy that was fragrant, ethereal and hauntingly beautiful even in the rain. In fact the more it rained the more our daily lives receded and the less we felt defined by them.

Brian and Dave were as caught up in the make-believe as I was. Within the first hours we'd nicknamed the stream running between the campfire and the tents the Congo River; the treacherous marshy undergrowth either side of it, in a leap across continents, the Mekong Delta; and from another continent still the drop-toilet deep into the woods became simply the Dunny. All the corners of the earth had arrived in Somerset and given three grown men the liberty to be boys again.

My temporary sense of well-being was threatened only once and briefly. I'd just been back to the tents to collect my head-torch in preparation for nightfall when I bumped into the one woman attending the weekend (there with her husband) as our paths crossed in the fading light.

'It's my daughter's,' she said, pulling a face, rolling her eyes up to direct mine to the daisy-patterned head-torch strapped to her forehead. To which I offered a grunt of acknowledgement, a polite, bare-minimum smile. But without even breaking stride I kept walking, knowing at once I'd ducked a conversation only because she'd mentioned her child. I knew that had Molly been well I'd have given her a wider, more inviting smile and shown an interest –

'So how old's your daughter?'

And she'd have told me, adding one or two brushstrokes to the portrait perhaps, before inevitably getting around to asking me, 'How about you? You got any kids?'

And I'd have smiled that coy smile new parents reserve for when they know they're about to be oohed and aahed –

'Actually, yes. We've just had our first one.'

'Ooh – how exciting! How old?'

'Nine weeks.'

'Aah.'

All of which would have been true.

But I trudged on because I couldn't bear to have to pretend, or worse get cornered into telling the truth, then pressured into saying something brave or philosophical when I didn't feel brave or philosophical at all. It was a no-win exchange that left me feeling despondent, like I'd denied Molly, and by the time I reached the others by the fire I felt like a bucket full of holes with all the weekend's accumulated strength draining out of me into the mud.

Most of the group had reassembled by now: maybe a dozen or so sat on upturned logs around the flames, trying to dry out socks and boots. I took the space Brian and Dave had kept for me in between them, and for a few minutes more I struggled, reflecting on how much I'd opened up to people in the weeks before the news, and how bleak it was, now I felt so scared and sad, to feel the old walls-up me taking control again. That woman probably thought I was rude, no more, too wrapped up in myself to bother with her and hers.

In time though, the fire soothed me, the buffer of invisible protection my brothers provided did its work. And later, when the time came to turn in, sensing that a gesture of grand futility was called for, the three of us decided to forgo our tents and sleep out under the tarpaulins. Which on a dewy late summer's night was a cold, uncomfortable experience. Brian snored loudly throughout; there were millipedes sharing my sleeping bag in the morning; I know for a fact I didn't sleep a wink. But still I loved that night out in the open, listening to the life all around us, waiting for the sun to rise. It was just what it needed to be.

*

Sunday was brighter. As dawn broke, the sun poked shards of light down through the trees making the woodland look like a scene from a fairytale. We stoked up the fire again, deep fried Navajo tacos for our breakfast and took a last hike through the woods. It was captivating: so other-worldly I knew even then it was the kind of place (had my fatherhood been more blessed) I'd have paused to reflect on my good fortune, just as I had at several points in my life when fate had seemed to be smiling on me: starting at university; getting a job in Soho; moving into London; finding myself living and working in San Francisco; marrying Ali; holding Molly for the first time. At each juncture I'd taken a moment alone somewhere to listen to a voice inside me. *Look at you. Look where you are. Breathe it in, Matt, this is incredible.* Now I could hear that same voice again, but with the self-belief shaken from it. *All right Matt, this is the other side of life now. Take a deep breath, go home and do the best you can do.*

Back To Work

Waiting at home

The last day before starting back at work I felt positive, cautiously hopeful as a few things conspired to give me courage.

First, Sally and I returned to Shoreham to test drive a car: a gold Vauxhall Meriva and this time it didn't get me down at all. It made me think about holidaying with Ali and Molly, getting sand and surf between our toes. Unless we were really unlucky, there would still be time for that.

Then when I logged into my work emails to prepare myself, I found a dozen or so messages of support, people saying they were looking forward to seeing me back: simple things like that that meant a lot to me and helped me to feel more assured.

And finally, Gordon made an impromptu appearance on his way home from watching Hull City in Beijing. I was glad of his presence that night especially, Sally's too. It gave me a few precious hours to feel as much a son as a father before I had to go out to face the world.

*

Nevertheless, when it actually came to returning to work and how difficult that would be, I couldn't have misjudged it more. For some reason I assumed I'd be tough enough to take it, that I'd snap back into 'work mode' somehow and keep it separate from my personal life. But I was wrong. And wrong principally because I'd braced myself for a polite, sympathetic, but ultimately cold environment, and what I walked back into was wave upon wave of human kindness.

Though I managed the early exchanges with the simple momentum of determination, it got harder as the minutes passed. Only an hour into the day, with alarm, I realised I could taste blood in my mouth. My teeth had cut into my cheeks on both sides with the grim effort of holding myself together.

Those who got it right from my point of view were the ones who acknowledged me, who just said 'hello' or 'welcome back', or another I recall who did nothing more than rest her hand on my shoulder momentarily before leaving me to get on. Others, and I don't blame them, had no idea how to handle my return and avoided me with greater or lesser degrees of subtlety. And last, the brave ones I suppose, those who came right up to me at my desk to tell me how sorry they were. That I found almost impossible.

I made it as far as lunch. Then I took a bus to Waterstone's over on the King's Road to look for a book on trees (I'd found it comforting being surrounded by them over the weekend and wanted to learn how to distinguish one from another). And after half an hour there, browsing the shelves and reading, I felt better on the bus going back, more confident I'd be able to handle myself: a feeling that held right up until the moment I ran into one of the guys from work as I was walking back into the building. A newish dad himself, a nice fella: all he wanted was to say he was sorry and I had to stop him mid-sentence. Why then, I don't know, but very suddenly: *I can't do this. I can't.* With a mixed-up gesture, part hands, part facial expression, I tried to convey that I understood and was appreciative but I found it too difficult to talk: a lot for a gesture to accomplish. Then I turned and darted between the traffic on the Battersea Bridge Road and down onto the path by the Thames, with all the day's pent up tears spilling out of me now like a riot breaking through a police line.

I found a bench a reasonable distance away, sat down to try to compose myself. And gradually, as the world went by (jogging, cycling, multiple-dog-walking), I calmed; until at length I found I was laughing quietly to myself, all at once self-aware of how I must have looked to passers by: a middle-aged man in tears, staring into the River Thames, like a training assignment for the Samaritans. *Your challenge today: identify the potential suicide and make a timely intervention.* Within minutes I'd gone from 'man crying his eyes out' to 'man crying his eyes out, laughing like an idiot', which in the circumstances felt like progress.

*

Feeling marginally more in control then, I went back into the office and arranged that for the duration (and all parties understood what that meant) I'd leave early enough to be home each day for Molly's bath and bedtime: something to look forward to at least, and with that in mind I got through the afternoon.

In fact by the time I reached Brighton my mood was much improved. I felt relieved to have cleared the hurdle of returning to work and excited to be seeing Ali and Molly again; so it was especially joyful when I saw them up ahead unexpectedly as I was cycling home from the station, as if my thoughts had come to life before my eyes. Ali was pushing the pram along on the other side of The Level, with the sunlight (filtered through the trees) flickering on the path around her feet. It made a stirring picture: a keepsake of all that's best about being a husband and a dad, and I held back a few seconds to take it in before cycling quietly up beside them.

It was Molly that saw me first and let out a yelp of delight.

Then Ali turned with a smile, a spontaneous hug.

And from there we set off home: six wheels rolling along in the evening sun, and me thinking how lucky I was to have the two of them to come home to, even with our troubles.

*

Indoors that night we went through a sequence that over time would solidify to become our weeknight routine: as important eventually to Ali and me as it was to Molly. Before then routine had always seemed such a settling-down-and-giving-up kind of word. Now it felt like a blessing: a reservoir of reassuringly predictable rhythms and pleasures.

Playtime –

The thick sheepskin spread on the floor, the games and songs, the talk and togetherness, from the time I got home until Molly tired, sometimes sooner, sometimes later. Ali taking her to the nursery then to undress her while I ran her bath: always deeper than I should to give her more buoyancy, and warmer too to give her more time to enjoy her freedom.

Raspberries –

Going back to collect her then, pausing to blow raspberries on her tummy, to pretend to eat her toes and find them tasty, to whizz her legs up and down fast (as if she was running) while I sang the theme tune to Bod. A touch of the tip of my nose to her lips, the tiny lick she always gave it, making me laugh aloud like I was being tickled.

Six stairs –

Carrying Molly in my arms (like a newborn, the way her condition demanded, supporting her neck and back) along the landing towards the bathroom, down the half-flight of stairs, counting them under my breath as I went, six down to one, to make it impossible I should ever lose my footing and hurt her.

The number 7 cup –

Lowering her into the small blue chair she had to support her in the bath. Then out with our favourite bathtime toy: nothing more than a plastic cup with a number 7 printed on its side and small holes in its base so when I filled it and held it up I could make warm water fall like rain. It was one of a set of ten cups, though we never bothered with the others. Number 7 was the Goldilocks cup: just right. Just the right amount of rain.

Phwoar, Molly! –

Ali washing Molly then with the baby sponge, taking good care to get between her toes, sniffing them as she went – pretending they were smelly.
'Phwoar, Molly!' and over again: 'Phwoar!'
Molly never grew tired of that.
But eventually the water cooled and we were done. Always a melancholy moment: an unspoken and unanswerable question: how many more bathtimes would we get?

Sing, Sing, Sing –

Molly fed and cosy now in a sleepsuit (always the zebra-pattern if it was clean and down to me) and me dancing her to sleep, humming the tune and drum-beats of Benny Goodman's Sing, Sing, Sing: Molly's counter-intuitive sandman song: all percussion and rhythm and jiggling about until gravity won, her weight shifted just perceptibly in my arms and I knew she was gone.

Daddy loves you –

Then last, setting her down in the cot, her blanket tucked in around her, a kiss touched gently to her forehead. 'Good night, sweetheart,' and a few moments more to watch her chest rising and falling. 'Daddy loves you.'

In time those rituals would become family history, that plastic cup more precious than a jewel, that frenetic piece of music impossible to hear without pangs of longing. But that night we were only beginning to understand the power of such things.

Leaving Molly asleep then, I crept from the room (stepping over the creaky floorboards) and pulled the door to behind me. I went back along the landing and down the six stairs, without counting them this time; and on the small mezzanine floor beside our bathroom, for the second time that day I sat and wept. Not the tidal wave of desperation that had struck me at lunchtime. This was softer, sweeter even: a kind of thanksgiving for being home and loved and safe. *Thank God today is over.* Within seconds I felt the towelling of Ali's dressing gown against my face as she wrapped herself (still wet from the bath) around my shoulders. And I heard the conviction in her voice as she told me, 'It's all right, darling. We'll get through this. We will.'

Part
Two

Dear God

Communing at Devil's Dyke

'I don't mean to pry, but have you thought about baptism?'

It was Mum who posed the question (in her very Mum way) in one of the regular letters of support she sent us throughout that time. Always well written, frequently sage and very funny, their content was generally a tonic for Ali and me both. Yet the moment I read that question I saw its potential for causing upset, even conflict, between two people I loved very much.

On the one hand, Mum: an every-Sunday-and-at-least-once-during-the-week church-goer, a woman of faith, with just short of eight decades of Catholicism in her blood. If she was asking about baptism, it wasn't out of concern for catering, how many vol-au-vents we might need afterwards. She was thinking about the after-life: Molly's safe passage from this world to the next. I knew she wouldn't try to force the issue. Her relationship with Ali was too strong for that; our decision to have a secular wedding she'd accepted with equanimity as none of her business ultimately. But baptism was fundamental to her world view, to the way she was raised. If we chose not to have Molly baptised it would be deeply troubling for her. I understood and appreciated that.

And on the other hand, I had Ali: my wife, my first point of loyalty, and the person at the very epicentre of our crisis as far as I was concerned. For her (and I agreed) this sudden addition to her concerns was unreasonable. She was brought up without religion so she had no ready frame of reference for it. She felt pressured by what Mum had written, pressured by the urgency surrounding the issue, and both at a time when she was justifiably angry (I believe she'd have taken a swing for God had they come face to face) as well as uncertain of what she'd feel comfortable with in that regard, for her or her daughter.

As for my viewpoint, it was an unholy ragbag when I came to look at it closely. I'd been taken to church every Sunday as a child. I made my first holy communion at eight, was confirmed in the Catholic faith at fourteen. But by sixteen I was estranged from it, already at the point where I found confessing so-called sins to a priest ridiculous and my church-going soon dwindled to nothing. I got into books instead: literature, philosophy, history, science: a process that gradually stripped away any lingering respect I had for the church, though never entirely my affection for it. It was too closely associated with a happy childhood for that, and many grown up pleasures too: choral music, ecclesiastical architecture, Graham Greene novels. If I had to write it on a passport, I'd put Catholic-agnostic. No firm convictions about God or faith, but a definite weakness for the bells and whistles.

*

Ali and I agreed to shelve the issue, at least while I settled back into work. And certainly by the time the weekend came around again, it was far from mind. We had a car now, of course, and the novelty of that alone was enough to lift our spirits. By late morning Saturday we were driving out of Brighton, heading up onto the Downs, gratefully anticipating a change of scene.

We parked at the promontory near Devil's Dyke and passed a few minutes taking in the fresh air and watching the paragliders suspended in the sky above and below us.

'I want to learn to do that,' I remember Ali saying.

'You should,' I told her.

Then we set off walking, taking turns to push the pram, talking and singing to Molly and pointing out things of interest to amuse her, until in time we found a pretty spot to sit and enjoy the view. Beneath us a breathtaking panorama fanned for miles to east and west, and as far as the eye could see looking north. Sussex villages in midsummer: a cricket match in play, thatched roofs, church steeples. It all looked much too good to be true. And sure enough, it wasn't long before the idyll below struck a more sombre chord in Ali.

'Do you think we'll be all right?' she asked, after we'd been sat there for a while in silence.

And the first part of my reply I got just right –

'Of course we will,' I said – a show of confidence, belief, of we'll-get-through-this-we-will. And I meant it – I *did* feel confident about Ali and me, certain that we wouldn't fall prey to the average, the mean, and allow ourselves to be pulled apart.

It was the second part of my reply that let me down.

'Why wouldn't we be?' I said, much too defensively – a contrasting show of fear and inadequacy that can only have sounded harsh and insensitive to Ali. We were barely a hundred yards from the grassy incline where I'd proposed to her almost exactly three years before, where after two bottles of Cava and a bag of cherries we'd agreed to join our lives together for better or worse (though we didn't expect worse so soon).

Now Ali was asking me, 'Why us?' And I didn't know.

'Why Molly?' And I don't know that either.

I knew that things like SMA had to happen to someone, but what was the good of saying that? All I seemed to have at my disposal was fatalism at one extreme and impatience at the other when I sensed I wasn't getting through. It would take a lot more ineptitude before I saw that all I really needed to do was hold Ali, tell her I was sorry and that I loved her. She knew I couldn't solve things any more than she could.

Fortunately, at least, the elements were on our side that day: a cool summer breeze teasing the grass around us; an equitable share of clouds and blue sky making the sunlight especially enchanting. Ali lifted Molly onto her lap. And just as I had that first morning at Dennis Cove, I circled, camera in hand, trying to capture the moment. Click after click until I had it: the photo at the start of this chapter: that play of sunlight on Ali's hair; her body a perfect arc of protection around Molly; the sublime communion of mother and child (my child) against a backdrop so timeless. I'll never take a picture more beautiful, not to me.

We went driving after, through the villages of Poynings and Fulking and beyond, discovering places with the car we'd never seen: horses running free in the fields, sheep and cattle grazing, rabbits popping up along the side of the road. We were out less than three hours in all, yet our excursion was all we could have wished for. Molly had felt the warmth of the sun on her skin, and Ali and I had beaten back the gloom.

*

That night though, the religion thing resurrected itself (pun intended again, I'm sorry). Though we'd tried to put it out of our minds, unsure of what to do, or whether to do anything at all, it was evident the genie I'd stuffed into the lamp two and a half decades earlier was out now and demanding attention.

It was my fault, squarely, for insisting that we watch something 'intelligent' that night, which turned out to be the recent film adaptation of Brideshead Revisited. I'm a devotee of the book as well as the eighties' TV version, so I should have been prepared for what was coming. But even I was taken unawares by the degree to which the full gamut of guilt-ridden Catholicism was explored in all its dubious glory: damnation, purgatory – even a death-bed repentance thrown in for good measure. As inured as I thought I was to all that, for Ali it was new and very uncertain ground and as we watched I could see she was finding it disturbing. What, she must have thought, was she considering letting her daughter become part of? I began to wish I'd agreed to watch Desperate Housewives.

Afterwards, though we both agreed we'd enjoyed the film, Ali was clearly troubled. So I tried to explain that not all Catholics are so ardent in following the tenets of the faith and that members of my family were unlikely to be found weeping together in their private chapel. Personally I was more Father Ted than Vatican II. And even my mum, my sister and sister-in-law, the more notable church-goers in the family, were not without humour on the subject and would have much to say about the community feeling that goes with being part of the church. But the truth was we both had our doubts. Ali because religion was unfamiliar to her, even frightening. And me because I resented circumstances opening a door I'd closed decisively and without regret many years before. And what were we talking about anyway? Doing it for Molly? To appease Mum? The hellish perils of the afterlife? Seriously? When Molly was diagnosed I expected challenges, but a reckoning with the church wasn't one of them. It caught me off guard, especially as I began to realise that when all the cynicism was stripped away, I actually wanted Molly baptised. Not as an act of faith, I can't say that. And certainly not as an act of fear. But an act of love? A gesture of family continuity? A bright occasion in the midst of dark times? Either way we knew a decision had to be made, and we didn't have forever to make it.

Quality Of Life

Brighton beach – with Dave and Georgie

Meanwhile, the merry-go-round of medical appointments we'd discussed with Dr Trounce was about to get underway. It was time to start discovering what life was going to be like now, for Molly, and for Ali and me.

– Home –

The day before the first appointment we spent just the three of us. I cooked a Sunday roast with all our favourite components: smoked gammon, thyme-roasted potatoes, parsnips, cauliflower cheese, carrots and green beans finished in butter. And it felt reassuring, the cooking and the eating: an emotional anchor for us. Ali must have been thinking the same –

'It's incredible what a difference it makes,' she said, looking down at the plate I'd set in front of her.

'Yeh,' I said, half-word-half-sigh. Nothing more was needed – we understood each other. Our lives had become so concentrated now around our child, something as simple as a lovingly home-cooked meal could have an impact on morale out of all proportion.

'Thanks for doing this, darling.'

'You're welcome, sweetheart.'

– Hospital –

When the morning came Ali and I set out in determined mood. For the fourth time in as many weeks we made the ten-minute trip to the Royal Alexandra (the Alex, as it was already known to us), aware that we were entering a new phase now. Whatever we could learn in the next few weeks might make a life-or-death difference to Molly. There could be no greater incentive to concentration.

We were set to begin with a respiratory consultant, Dr Seddon, to have Molly's breathing patterns examined, the strength of her lungs estimated, and to pick up some advice (we hoped) on how to counteract the threat of chest infections: our enemy number one. His prior appointment ran over by nearly an hour but it didn't faze us. We knew the parents and child causing the delay could easily have been us, grateful for being treated with sensitivity, however long it took, so we settled in for the wait.

I tried to pass some time by strolling the corridors, first one way then the other, taking the chance to familiarise myself with a place that had already played (and would go on playing) such a pivotal role in my life. And despite the circumstances my impressions were positive. The architecture and layout inside felt fit for purpose, airy and light, sensitive to the feelings of people in pain. Each consultation room bore the symbol of an animal on its door: a giraffe, a lion, a monkey and so on to make the place less imposing for the children; which absurdly made me want to discover which animal had presided over us during our first fateful meeting with Dr Trounce and so would be forever associated in my mind with our trauma (I'm a sucker for a symbol). It was unusually quiet there that day so I was free to poke my head into each of the rooms until I found the configuration of desk, chairs and couch I remembered so well. And the animal on the door? Hardly the nemesis it might have been. I smiled when I saw it, recalling the film Happy Feet. It isn't easy to take umbrage with penguins after all.

With the mood lightened then, for me anyway, the consultation that followed wasn't too bad. Now Ali and I were familiar with the basics, though never entirely at ease, we were composed at least. It helped that we both took quickly to Dr Seddon. I appreciated his manner, the tenderness with which he examined Molly and the courtesy he showed to us. Like Dr Trounce before him he had me wishing I'd done something more meaningful with *my* working life, something that made such a difference to the people *I* met.

I wondered too, as I watched him work, what it was like for him (and for all the other doctors and nurses we met) knowing that Molly was going to die. In less than a year in all likelihood, regardless of his efforts. Did that make it difficult emotionally? Or was it just work? Certainly I sensed that day – and became certain later – that Molly reminded more than one of them of why they'd followed their calling in the first place. Dr Seddon knew he was there not to cure but to care this time, and he did so with the utmost regard for the value of Molly's life, no matter how short it might prove to be.

– Visitors –

We felt dejected afterwards in spite of the doctor's tender care. It was still a hospital, still a reminder, after all, even on the easier occasions. So it gave us a lift when we turned into our road to find Dave and his daughter, Georgie, parked up outside the house. She'd not met Molly before; she was the last of the first cousins to do so, so to mark the occasion and ignoring the gale now gathering force, we crammed into the Meriva and I drove us all down to the beach.

I found a space to park on the front across from the Grand Hotel and (we forget, living in Brighton, how exciting it can be to see the sea) the moment Georgie was free of the car she set off at a sprint down the steps onto the beach, and on over the pebbles towards the shore, with her dad running close behind. I hung back with Ali, helping to get Molly into the baby carrier, watching them up ahead, at the water's edge by now, skimming stones up off the waves, laughing and calling out to each other.

I should have seen the thought coming.

I'll never get to do that with Molly.

Coming straight from the hospital, as we had, it was almost too obvious, the contrast too plain. But even so, as that simple thought struck, my legs nearly fell out from under me. It would have looked like I'd stumbled merely on the pebbles, but to me it felt like dying and clawing my way back to life all in the space of a fraction of a second. Not even long enough to fall.

Ali slipped her arm through mine. Perhaps she'd seen what I'd seen, read it the way I'd read it, I don't know. Whatever the truth, she kept me on my feet. Then Molly joined in the cheer-up-the-old-man act, blowing tiny bubbles from the corner of her mouth, gloriously unperturbed by the force of the wind giving us all a real battering now. Her determined little expression made me laugh out loud. And with the sound, the darkness was dispelled, the here and now took precedence again.

– *Work* –

Meanwhile, work was anything but peaceful. The office was in the early stages of a pitch for a major new marketing contract: a process in which I would normally play a prominent part. But this time no-one knew what to expect of me or even what was reasonable to request. Twice already I'd contributed ideas from home and both times what I'd done was no longer needed because things had moved on and they hadn't had the heart to tell me. So while I knew they were only trying to shield me, and themselves while they got the job done, I felt frustrated. It was worse than doing nothing at all.

From rumour, and one or two things I'd seen coming out of the printer, I gathered one of ideas being considered centred around an image of a pregnant woman. It looked interesting (I didn't make any connection) but when I tried to get involved it became obvious an agreement had been made to keep that line of work from me – in case I found the associations upsetting. Suddenly people I knew well were being evasive, visibly embarrassed when I came too close. It was unsettling to realise that good intentions were at work, that discussions were being had about what might or might not be best for Matt.

Later that week when the team returned from the first pitch meeting, everyone was called to the boardroom to be thanked for their hard work so far. And as always I was sat there among the main players. Only this time I'd done nothing: nothing that counted for much anyway; which depressed me, forced me to acknowledge that my working life was more closely linked to my sense of self-worth than I'd imagined.

– Ali –

What life was like, really like, for Ali, while I was out at work, I could only guess at, or try to piece together from the things she told me at night when I got home. Unlike me she had no projects to distract her mind, no workmates with whom she could share a little banter, no hour each way on the commute to read, sleep, calm herself. Even with my reduced workload I was still gone ten hours a day, four days a week: a long time for Ali to keep Molly diverted with all that anguish circling inside her.

The only counterweight, if you can call it that, was the same thing viewed in reverse: the fact that she got to spend so much time with Molly when time with her was so very precious. Only in that sense could I see Ali as fortunate in any way; her burden otherwise seemed unbearable to me. Not just the glaring things like continuing to breast-feed (a show of enormous emotional bravery by any standard), but the countless superficially lesser trials that also called for courage. How hard must it have been just to go for coffee with the other six NCT mums? No matter how kind they tried to be.

I was glad when I got home the following night to find her relaxing in the company of her brother: another Dave, and her sister: Samantha. They'd been for a long lunch, just the three of them, for the first time, they realised, in nine years. It was good to see them coming together in adversity like that. Like me, Ali was turning to the people she knew best and she looked better for it. She was smiling and laughing for the first time in weeks, and anyone who could help her do that through that impossible time was more than all right by me.

– Another hospital –

The midweek ended, as it had begun, with a hospital appointment: a physiotherapist this time at the other major local hospital: Brighton General: the gloomy Victorian pile that glowers over the town from beside the racecourse looking every bit the workhouse it was built to be. I'd arranged to work from home again so Ali and I could continue to learn together.

It was eerily quiet when we got there. We shared the waiting room with just one other woman, a girl really, and her two children, the younger of which appeared to have Down Syndrome. Her face was an uninterrupted beatitude of smiles as she played on the floor around our feet.

'She's an independent little thing, isn't she?' said Ali, smiling across at the mum, sensing a kindred spirit probably – another woman for whom motherhood must have been an isolating experience sometimes.

'Oh yeh, she's into everything,' came the reply, mixed with a sigh and just the traces of a brave-face smile. It seemed such a weight of responsibility for one so young, and I hoped I wasn't patronising her by wondering where the dad was and whether he'd stood his ground to help take care of them: Mum as well as the children.

Then our name was called and our brief appearance in each other's lives passed. We were shown through to a room where the physiotherapist began by spreading a large blanket over the floor and scattering it with various toys and tactile stimulations. And from there she showed us one or two useful things: methods of massage, gentle stretching exercises we could try to keep Molly mobile; but essentially she repeated what Dr Seddon had told us, namely that Molly's limited movement would make her vulnerable to chest infections.

'Because germs gather in still water,' I said aloud, recalling something I'd read about drinking water in Africa.

Ali gave me a weary look. The physio smiled politely.

'Yes,' she said. 'The same principle.'

Then for a few minutes she showed us how to mitigate that risk by patting Molly's back and chest regularly (with either our cupped hands or a small plunger-like device she offered us) to produce downward pressure and stimulate movement.

'Most babies love this', she said at the outset with misplaced confidence. Ali and I knew better, having already tried an identical device at the Alex and found that Molly disliked it with a passion. She'd cried from start to finish each time we'd done it. And not just her normal cry either, but a tortured lament it was impossible to listen to without wanting to scoop her up and do something fun instead.

Like it or not though, from that day forward we tried to do the patting thing every day, twice if we could face it (five minutes on her chest and five on her back), though it never got any easier, despite Ali and I adopting different tactics. I worked fast and firmly, blocking out Molly's tears, trying to get it over with as quickly as I could for her, while Ali went more methodically, with constant soothing words, trying to make those encounters less traumatic overall. Molly, I'm sure, weighed up the pros and cons of both and found them equally objectionable.

– Football –

That Saturday the new football season got underway (always an early harbinger of the colder months) and with it came an invitation to join Gordon, Ali's Dave, and a contingent down from Yorkshire for Hull City's opening match at Chelsea.

We met up at the pub in Paddington station just before ten, began drinking in earnest the moment the staff opened the bar, and continued in the same vein until a much vaguer hour near tea-time with a football match tucked hazily in between. It was TLC as administered by men: all-day drinking, non-stop banter and piss-taking, and it did me a world of good. They knew the deal with me but it wasn't mentioned. It was assumed, rightly, I'd prefer to forget my troubles for a day.

Even so, by the time I was sat on the train back to Brighton I was pining for home, looking forward to being with Ali and Molly again. I phoned ahead and asked Ali to order me a curry, which I gobbled down without ceremony as soon as I got in, hiccupping throughout, before clambering my way up the stairs to gaze at my daughter as she slept. When Ali came to bed two or three hours later she found me asleep on the floor, curled around the base of Molly's cot. Even the drunken, smelling-of-lager-and-curry me knew where he belonged.

– And home again –

That day and the next were an island of respite – Sunday lunch again providing the emotional glue. Michael, a good friend, got in touch just when I was hoping he would. And Tess, another friend and ally to Ali throughout, was with us for the weekend. So I cooked, and the five of us passed a put-the-world-on-hold afternoon around the dining table, with Molly's chair plonked on top in among all the plates and glasses where she could feel part of the conversation. She looked happy. I think we all did. The occasion demonstrated to Ali and me that we could still be sociable and host well, for a few hours at least. But the respite, as I said, was mercilessly brief.

We've Had A Difficult Day Here

My mum's favourite photo

Early the next morning, as agreed, two of our local community nurses came to the house to introduce themselves and explain the various ways they'd be able to support us in the months to come. For Ali and me it was a first chance to meet people with first-hand experience of children with SMA: people who'd held the hands of the dying and their loved-ones many times. Reluctantly then, we braced ourselves to go deep: to push the boundaries of our knowledge to the limit by asking *all* the questions we had inside us now.

How was the end likely to come? What scenarios were possible? Would it be obvious to us when the end was near? Would I have time to get home if I was in London? What choices had other parents made? Would the approach to Molly's passing be distressing or painful for her? Could we choose to have her last hours at home? Would drugs be available to help her through? There was no dressing any of it up or pretending it wasn't what it was. We asked our questions in whatever order they occurred to us and soaked up the answers, which the nurses gave in sensitive but straightforward language the way we needed them to.

'Yes, that can happen.'

'In our experience that tends to be the case.'

'The truth is we just don't know.'

Having them there with us took a bit of getting used to. Before Molly I'd have known of their existence only as abstracts. Now I knew their names: Sheena and Jill. They were sat in our lounge on our sofa, having tea and biscuits, trying to guide us through the worst thing that ever happened to us.

Neither Ali nor I showed much emotion during our discussion. We were concentrating too hard to get upset, determined not to miss anything that might help later on. Even after they'd gone, Ali just got on with things around the house and I cycled into town in a kind of daze (I had a notion to get the photo of Ali and Molly at Devil's Dyke printed and framed for Gordon and Sally). Perhaps I really thought I could shake off the meeting, retain its content but duck its emotional fall-out somehow. While the frame shop did its work I spent half an hour strolling in the sun. It might almost have been a happy day –

Until I saw the photo again. In a simple wooden frame now, as heart-stoppingly lovely as anything in this world could be to me: my wife playing with my child in the summer sun.

Cycling home across The Level I felt tears welling up in my

eyes again, only this time they didn't take me by surprise. I was beginning to understand how these things worked. The discussion with Sheena and Jill in the morning and the framed photo in the afternoon had moved together to form the two halves of something whole. I cried because the things we'd talked about were agony to me, but it took the photo to make the tears fall.

*

Then came the longest day of all: a Tuesday that began for me in the humid early hours with a vivid dream. I was out walking somewhere along a cobbled road when up ahead I saw a young boy staring down at what appeared to be a wounded animal on the kerb. When I drew closer I saw that it was indeed an animal but something fantastical, impossible. I caught a glimpse of a tortoise shell and the damaged wings of a bird: two creatures conjoined because (and I intuited this in the dream itself) only one of them could eat and one could fly. I awoke disquietened, disturbed. Was it meant to be us? Ali, Molly and me: each contributing something to a whole that just about functioned?

Downstairs I made coffee, trying to rid myself of the image. But that eerie phantasm held, making me nervous as I contemplated the day ahead. At least that was the only excuse I could find for the way I lost my rag with Ali minutes later over something as unimportant as some spilt water.

Arriving in the kitchen after a near-sleepless night of worry she had gone to pour a drink from the filter jug I'd just refilled. So the lid came off, the contents poured out over the worktop. Nothing. Yet I flew at her. And the fact that she was too tired and incoherent to clear up properly annoyed me even more. It was disgraceful of me, and poetic justice was done immediately as in my anger I cracked my head hard on the metal corner of the cupboard not once but twice. Livid now, cursing under my breath at Ali, and more at myself for being so powerless over our fate, for one desperately pathetic moment I came within a whisker of punching my fist through the back door window – never mind the repercussions or the fact that Sally was on her way downstairs for breakfast. It wasn't the best start to the day.

*

Of course my anger had very little to do with my dream. It was fear more likely: an impotent pre-emptive strike at the prospect of yet another appointment at the Alex, this time to discuss the likelihood that in time Molly would lose the strength to be able to swallow safely. Which raised two uncomfortable issues: the challenge of ensuring she didn't become malnourished; and far worse, the very real danger that she might inhale fluid (milk, or even vomit potentially). *Please God, I don't want to have to do this.*

At the hospital, even before the swallowing issue was broached, there was a first course: a taster to whet the appetite. I saw the piece of equipment under one of the chairs as soon as Ali, Sally and I went into the consultation room where Dr Trounce and Sheena were waiting. About the size and dimensions of a car battery, I knew what it was because we'd been warned in advance: an oxygen monitor for us to take home to measure how Molly was breathing at night when we might not be aware if she was struggling. It looked hideous, industrial, something meant for a mechanic's garage or a factory, not a child's sleeping place; just seeing it there made me clench my stomach like I was bracing to take a punch. But still I listened intently while Sheena explained how it worked, how to hook it up to Molly at bedtime and set it running.

Then we turned to the crux: the question of swallowing and feeding. Molly was managing well enough on her own for now (feeding was tiring for her but not impossible) yet the harsh reality was she was already three months old. With her life expectancy reckoned at seven months, we knew we didn't have long to decide on our tactics, and the options available to us hardly made it easier.

Option one, as we both understood from our own research, was the standard provision made in such circumstances, namely to provide Molly with a naso-gastric (NG) tube: a thin length of rubber, running (as the name suggests) via her nose down to her stomach: a semi-permanent arrangement that would enable us to feed her but would need to be taped to her face constantly and changed once a month for as long as she lived.

Sheena dipped into her pocket at that point and pulled out an example –

'You can see it's quite slim,' she said, 'and smooth, to minimise any discomfort during insertion.'

So we paused to examine the tube. Me, then Ali, then Sally. For what? To give it a little roll between finger and thumb, as we all did, and conclude it was okay? Instinctively I knew if I had a tube like that running up and through my nose, it would make me panic, feel claustrophobic and desperate to get it out. So why would Molly be any different?

'Most babies get along with them quite well,' Sheena said.

Most babies again.

'Once they're in place,' I qualified.

'Yes, once they're in place.'

'Can the insertion be traumatic then?' Ali asked.

And right away Sheena conceded that was the part *most babies* didn't like at all; and it would need to be done several times potentially, every four weeks until –

'It *is* the usual approach in a case like this,' she said.

Yet somehow, though Sheena made the case for the naso-gastric tube honestly and fairly, I got the feeling neither she nor Dr Trounce favoured it. We spoke about other drawbacks then – the fact that such tubes have been known to become dislodged, to curl their way out of the stomach into the throat or even lungs and cause fluid to be inhaled. The risk, though slight, was real, and would mean Ali or I having to draw up a sample of Molly's stomach fluid prior to every feed to test it on litmus paper to confirm the tube was correctly placed; which was hard enough to think about let alone do. And what if Molly caught a cold? If she was struggling to breathe? If she vomited – with a tube blocking her airways? There were considerations too that hadn't occurred to me: psychological aspects I was glad we had the candour to discuss. For one, as Sheena explained, the tube would always be on show: an invitation to strangers to pry, to offer sympathies that might not always be welcome. Nor will I deny that the thought of corrupting Molly's beautiful face with something so foreign offended me to the core.

I hoped option two would sound better.

It did and it didn't.

The alternative was to opt for something called a gastrostomy: a surgical procedure to make a direct link to Molly's stomach via a small fixture attached to her tummy, through which we could feed her. Like the NG tube, it would allow us to bypass her mouth and throat and thereby reduce the risk of inhalation. It would also remove our concerns about the trauma of inserting a tube, along with the irritation for Molly of having one in place constantly. (And yes, it would mean she wouldn't have a tube taped to her face for the rest of her life.)

But. And there was one hell of a but.

Because Molly was notably weaker than average, there was a real chance she'd lack the strength to come through the general anaesthetic required for the surgery. So in trying to safeguard her quality of life for longer we'd be running the risk of losing her sooner and having to live on, knowing the choice had been ours. Even the comfort of prolonged consideration was to be denied us. With Molly weakening slowly but steadily our window of opportunity was closing fast. If we delayed too long, the chance to help her would soon be gone altogether, the risk posed by the surgery would become too great.

Dr Trounce, Sheena and Sally all contributed to the debate. But the decision clearly rested with Ali and me. And the decision we made (though it weighed heavily on us), on the proviso that we could back out later, and acknowledging that red tape would have to be got through anyway, was to set the wheels in motion for surgery.

And with that our meeting was over. We said our goodbyes and left: Ali holding Molly, me carrying the monitor, both of us feeling like we were losing all over again.

*

Back at the house, drained emotionally and dog-tired, Ali went upstairs to lie down as soon as we got in, leaving Sally and me to watch over Molly. And as she and I sat talking, for the first time with anyone, I raised the question of how to manage Molly's passing when it came. The practicalities, I mean: how to go about arranging things. I know it sounds cold to have done so with Molly so very alive there in the room. But I needed to begin exploring how I felt about such things, and suspected that Ali wouldn't be ready for that particular conversation. Sally and I talked about cremations, woodland burials, Funeral Directors, our recollections of various memorial services down the years, and whatever else came to mind. And it felt necessary at the time, our conversation, albeit dreadful to consider once it was done. I felt sickened, ashamed of myself to have spoken about Molly that way.

*

Sally went out to buy groceries soon afterwards, leaving me alone with my thoughts: thoughts too dark to be lightened with a book or hot bath this time. I thought I'd be better doing something practical and proactive, something to help us. Little did I know I was about to make that day of all days even worse.

With Molly asleep across my lap I decided to tackle head on the issue of baptism. I went to the internet, found an email address for the priest at our local Catholic church, St Joseph's at the end of our road, and started to write. All I wanted was to ask for advice, to test the church for sensitivity perhaps before committing. I thought I could rattle something off in a minute. But an hour later I was still there struggling with the facts, still searching for a way to reconcile my twenty-five year absence from the church with this sudden, extremely ambivalent cry for help. And by the time I was done, I was done in: the unnerving portents of my dream; my loss of temper at Ali in the morning; the hospital with its talk of oxygen measurement, life-threatening surgery; then funeral arrangements for a child; and last my troubled re-engagement with a long-abandoned faith; it felt like all those disparate elements had coagulated, lumped themselves together into one malignant ball of hurt.

*

Even then it looked like the day might be saved. Molly awoke from her afternoon nap full of fun. And shortly after, Ali and I gave her a long and playful bath. As she pushed her legs gently through the water, I sang to her. And I honestly thought the pain had dissipated again.

While Ali got Molly ready for bed I warmed her milk. Then I settled myself into the rocking chair on the landing (the one I'd assembled in readiness for Dennis). Ali lowered Molly into my arms, left us to it, and for the next few minutes I sank into the heaven of cradling her, looking into her eyes, listening to the suckling sounds she made as she drank. When she drifted off to sleep with the teat still in her mouth, I knew I ought to wind her before letting her settle but I couldn't move for the love of having her warm little body (in her zebra-pattern sleep-suit again) held against me. I only realised I was crying when I saw the teardrops landing on the black and white stripes.

Presently I became aware of Ali beside me and for a minute we locked ourselves together the three of us, just rocking back and forth with the motion of the chair; until Sally came up, and she and Ali took Molly through to our room to get the oxygen monitor connected and up and running.

I needed a moment for myself then. I went into the nursery, took hold of Molly's man-in-the-moon toy and sat on the floor until I'd calmed and I'd heard Ali and Sally go back downstairs. Then I got up, checked in to see that Molly was asleep and the monitor was working, and followed them down, knowing that the worst had passed now, that I had hold of myself again.

When I walked into the lounge, Sally was talking to Gordon on her phone. 'We've had a difficult day here,' I heard her say.

Here And Now

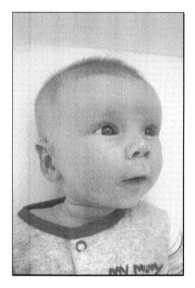

Molly, aka Mollington, Molls etc.

There were days like that, when Ali and I felt the full weight of despair, when the dark side of what was happening dominated. And even on the better days, the invisible underlying strain was formidable: enough to keep Ali from sleeping, sometimes at all, so that much of the time she was running on empty, worrying to the point where she feared being unable to cope; enough to keep my skin in a state of near constant rebellion, with patches of eczema around my eyes and in painful swathes down both sides of my body. And that was without beginning to acknowledge the pressure on us as the two halves of a marriage, each of us trying to keep the other standing when our own legs had been kicked out from under us. We could have been forgiven for sinking into the ground. But what I hadn't reckoned on, or even considered, was Molly herself coming to our aid.

When she was eight weeks old, when we were told she was going to die, I anticipated only decline: a slow, inexorable declension to the end. I had no idea that first Molly would thrive, blossom, delight us in so many ways. Physically, aside from her lack of strength and limited mobility (which both became only slightly more apparent as she grew), her condition gave no sign of progression at all. The expression on her face in the photo at the start of this chapter was the way she looked the greater part of each day: bursting with life and enquiry, fascinated with everything and everyone around her. There were even magical things that came from the condition itself: the gossamer gentleness of her touch; the way she channelled her physical limitations into intense periods of concentration: so deeply affecting if you happened to be the subject of her gaze. She was finding her voice now too, experimenting with a world of new sounds, responding brightly to her name, recognising and jumping into gaps in conversation.

It was around that time that I overheard one of the girls at work talking about visiting her family in South Africa because her sister had just had a baby.

'I think I'll leave it a while,' she said, unaware of me, 'babies don't have much character for the first six months, do they?'

And for a second I thought about setting her straight, telling her it depends on how closely you observe, on how much love you bring to bearing witness. But of course I didn't. Grief is so personal at a moment like that, unfathomable from the outside.

On the inside Ali and I were left taking photos (mostly me), making movies (mostly her). And more than either, just trying

111

to stay rooted in the present, aware of the wonder of everyday things: things as simple as the feeling I got coming in at night, calling 'Hello?' through the house, hearing Ali's voice directed at Molly in return –

'Who's that! Is that Daddy? Is that Daddy, Molly?'

Crawling into the lounge on hands and knees then so Molly could hear but not see me; popping up to surprise her; seeing her look to her mum for reassurance, then back at me, breaking into her all-my-boats-have-come-in smile.

Be aware. Here and now.

Each time she did that, every minute I worked, every mile I commuted, every bruise I earned in the big bad world was justified. Even the end itself became something I could face.

*

Meanwhile, three days had passed since my email to the church and still I'd heard nothing back. I began to feel aggrieved, then increasingly angry, and the more I obsessed over it the worse it got, until I'd worked myself up into a blaze of indignation.

You rise to this Now, or I'll never set foot inside a church again.

It was a Friday. I was sat at my desk at work, turning over in my mind all the things I'd say if my plea was ignored, the denouncements I'd hurl at the churchgoers in my family, when suddenly, as if God himself had heard me raging and decided to chivvy his people along, the screen on my phone lit up: Father John. For a moment I was taken aback. For a couple of rings I froze, trying to collect myself, before walking quickly out to the corridor to be alone. I thought the call might be difficult. I had no idea what to expect of him.

But a woman's voice –

Instead of Father John it was a clerical assistant called Celia – who was so faultlessly kind, respectful and apologetic for the delay in getting back to me, I was instantly and completely disarmed to the point where I felt overwhelmed and I struggled badly not to break down during our conversation, the line between wrath and desolation was so fine. She explained that Father John was away on holiday and promised to get him to contact me urgently upon his return. Then she said, 'You do know you can baptise your daughter yourself in an emergency?'

'Yes', I said, I knew. And just for a moment as I stood there in that sterile corporate corridor in the middle of the working day, I pictured myself doing just that, in an emergency, and my heart groaned and ached in my chest.

Then seconds later, as if nothing had happened, I was back at my desk. From grief-stricken father, speaking the unspeakable with a member of the church, to working man, donning his strained how-can-I-help-you face: a switch of countenance that was becoming second nature to me. I came up with something good too later that day, something that made a difference to the second part of the pitch. Which might sound preposterous: to have cared, I mean, but to me it felt like a tiny personal victory when victories of any kind were few and far between.

*

On the way home that night I met Dave at a pub in Blackfriars. We had three pints together in exactly fifty minutes: 6.25pm to 7.15pm to accord with my train time back to Brighton. Not so long as to leave Ali feeling abandoned in the face of our tasks, but long enough for me to let off steam and feel I was getting a break of some kind, no matter how short. So while Ali grumbled the first few times, later she began to encourage it, seeing the disproportionate difference it made to me to take that time with my brother once a fortnight or so.

'I've been in a bit of a mess about all this,' Dave said to me that night as we began our third pint and the end of our time together came into view. 'The other night, for no reason at all, I started blubbing into my fish fingers.'

Blubbing: a word from our childhood, levelled then at anyone unwise enough to show feeling during the sad bits in Little House on The Prairie. Now, more than thirty-five years later, a word to show familiarity, sympathy, solidarity between siblings.

I told Ali what Dave had said later that night at home while I was cooking fish fingers for us too on a whim, with chips and baked beans – a kids' dinner. And while we ate we talked about the various ways people around us were coping with our news: how it was comforting sometimes to see how much they cared, and yet oddly irritating at other times to hear them speak about their grief, as if they were talking out of turn about something that belonged to us. After which we sat quietly for a while, eating dinner, watching TV. It hadn't been an especially emotional conversation, so I was surprised when Ali came to a stop out of the blue, set her knife and fork down, put her head into her hands and started to cry.

'What is it, darling?' I asked, taking her hand. 'What is it?'

'Nothing,' she said. Then after a second or two: 'Just *this*.'

We were silent for a moment, then we both went to say the same thing at the same time, our words crossing over in the air, 'It must be something about fish fingers.'

*

That night proved to be our toughest with Molly so far. Until then, one or other of us had always been able to find the touch to get her to feed and sleep. Now, for the first time, the magic deserted us. Molly fought her way into the vicious cycle of too-exhausted-to-feed-too-hungry-to-sleep until there was nothing we could do to console her.

Was it just a bad night with a new baby? (The kind any parent would recognise.) Or something more sinister? (The condition itself tightening its grip.) Certainly in the loneliness of the smallest hours, as Ali and I took turns, I believe we both feared we'd arrived at the limits of our influence, the beginning of the end maybe. Unable to sustain or comfort our child, it was hard to see it any other way.

It was past 9am before any sunshine broke through, literally as well as figuratively. Downstairs, slumped on the sofa, staring blindly at cheerful Saturday morning TV (with Molly on my lap and her bottle still in my hand), I gave it one last try. And this time, as hungry as she had to be by now, out of nowhere she guzzled down five ounces, barely pausing for breath; which for Ali and me, faced with a prospect so grim, was little short of a miracle. We were fighting back tears watching her: something as unremarkable as a baby drinking milk. Maybe things weren't so bad yet after all.

*

Shattered but buoyed we decided to make the most of the sun, to get out of the house, out of Brighton. We drove north then west through the first few villages on the Downs as far as Edburton where we found a pub with a garden; and Molly, as she often did, attracted an admirer: another mum this time looking to compare and contrast. How old was she? Was she doing this or that yet? How did she feed and sleep? And to her credit Ali fielded the questions with an appearance of ease, staying polite, friendly and just evasive enough to avoid difficulties, though it can't have been easy chatting casually like that.

It was strange how those everyday challenges were so simple to negotiate sometimes and at other times desperately trying. I had one such situation preying on my mind as we drove back to Brighton after lunch. As silly as it sounds, I was fretting about having a haircut later that day. I knew Jonathan, the salon owner, well enough to have to tell him, and the thought of going through that revelation again had me dreading what would normally be the pleasure of his company. I didn't want to risk breaking down in front of him; or to see his expression change as he registered what I was saying; or to have to manage him then through the awkwardness of comforting me, and in a situation where there would be no ready escape.

As it was though, I'd worried for nothing. As I approached the salon on foot later that day, braced as well as I could be not to get upset, I saw him leaning against the wall outside, plainly waiting for me. With a gentle smile he offered me his hand and said simply, 'I've heard your news. James told me.' A mutual friend. And that was all I needed, just knowing that he knew. It made it easier to talk and, with that barrier gone, enjoy my escape the way it was meant to be. The only departure from the norm was the glass of Stella he put in front of me in place of a coffee before he set to work.

Professional Opinion

Shoreham-by-Sea

But it would take more than a haircut and glass of beer for me, more than a drive in the country for Ali, more than five ounces of milk for Molly to keep us afloat. The fortnight ahead was set to bring still more uncomfortable appointments in quick succession, with all the stress that went with them, and it was draining even finding the strength to begin.

Much of it came from Ali's insistence that we should try to live as normally as possible, have the same outings and adventures as if Molly had been well. That Sunday for one, when I'd have opted to rest at home probably, she had us out walking by the estuary down the coast at Shoreham-by-Sea amidst a scene so pleasing I knew I'd have been a fool to pass it up. In the sky above us (a chance discovery) an air show was in full flight, the azure criss-crossed with the tail smoke of Hurricanes and Spit-fires: right up Molly's street, all that deafening noise and jolting about as we pushed her along the rocky path by the water, her eyes fixed to the sky, mesmerised. People I presumed to be locals were settled in for the day with their blankets, wine coolers and hampers, looking practised, like they'd honed their pleasure to perfection over years. There were children zigzagging every which way, dogs doing figures-of-eight around the pram as we craned our necks up, shielding our eyes. It was playful and picturesque: very England-at-its-best. And though Ali and I knew there should have been hundreds of days like that with Molly, and it was sad to know we'd be counting them in double figures at best, just this once we didn't let it get us down. We were still children ourselves at heart. We knew how a day like that was meant to feel, so we tried to make it feel that way for her.

*

Then on Monday we came back down to earth. The first of the next round of appointments arrived early in the morning in the shape of a counsellor from The Jennifer Trust who'd come all the way from Liverpool to see how we were and whether we needed any help. I was impressed, grateful to her, and Ali and I were determined as always to gain whatever we could from the encounter. Not that either of us necessarily *wanted* to talk. With so much of what could happen with Molly beyond the realm of prediction, I was beginning to think we'd do as well just to care for her, play with her, have as much fun together as we could, rather than invite still more subjective views on how to manage her time with us. But I knew too that we had to remain open to anyone who might offer fresh insight. And this was, after all, someone who'd worked for many years with families affected specifically by SMA.

Again then I found myself making tea, setting out a plate of

118

biscuits, offering whatever contributions came to mind, as our conversation slowly became another of those in which all subjects are broached, no matter how unpalatable, Ali asking most of the questions this time –

'Could that happen?'

'Might that be the case with Molly?'

'Do children sometimes die that way?'

And the counsellor, Maggie, did her best (as the community nurses had before her), answering honestly and delicately as Ali posed question after question, pushing for anything that sounded like certainty. I can understand her determination now, but at the time it wasn't long before I felt frustrated, then irritated, that all we ever seemed to do was cover the same ground, just with different people.

'Is that a possibility?'

'Is Molly at risk of that?'

'Yes!' I felt like shouting. 'Of course she is!'

I thought Ali wasn't getting that none of the people we kept seeing knew anything for sure. Nobody did. But of course she knew perfectly well and was right to keep asking her questions. It was hard to see her banging her head against a wall like that, being hurt over and over, that's all.

Inevitably our talk turned to the feeding issue, the now familiar NG tube versus gastrostomy debate, and here Maggie was surprised to hear we'd been given the choice.

'A gastrostomy would be very unusual,' she told us, though she conceded there was a school of opinion in favour, that believed it should be standard procedure for children with Type 1 SMA. That was our first indication that a consensus had yet to be reached on the subject within the medical profession as well our first awareness that the view proffered at the Alex was at the more progressive end of the spectrum.

After that, I knew that Ali wanted to talk woman to woman for a while, to ask Maggie how relationships, how marriages in particular, tended to fare under such strain – a topic they could approach more freely without me, and about which, rightly or wrongly, I didn't care much for the opinions of a stranger anyway. I made myself scarce. I took Molly upstairs for a dance instead. *Most* babies. *Most* marriages. Not mine. Misguidedly perhaps, I never lost faith we'd be okay.

∗

I didn't meet the next professional waiting in line. Ali's sister had come with her husband and children to stay at a campsite on the outskirts of Brighton: a chance to combine some family time with support for Ali while I was at work. When it came to consulting a dietician then, the two sisters took it on together.

Ali told me about it that night in bed: the fact that the dietician had been young, hadn't appeared to have been confronted by a terminal condition before and seemed unsure how to help; though she had been able to confirm one thing we already suspected, namely that Molly wasn't gaining weight at all now, at a time when a healthy baby would be gaining rapidly.

If she doesn't want to eat, leave her alone.

That was my first reaction if I'm honest. I was beginning to feel belligerent, to tire of the endless interference with my family. But of course it wasn't that Molly didn't want to feed, just that she found it too tiring to maintain for long enough to get the sustenance she needed. So I was pleased to hear she'd been prescribed a high-calorie formula to replace the one we'd been supplementing Ali's milk with; the added positive being I could help out more at night now: something I was happy to do to give Ali a chance to sleep. It was just the kind of tangible job I felt best equipped to handle.

Sam had found the appointment hard, Ali told me: the emotional impact of it had shocked her, I think (her sensitivity acute as a mother of three herself). Which made me think of that phrase we kept hearing at the start: *We can't begin to imagine how you're feeling.* There was Ali still getting used to the situation, and Sam with all that experience on her side. Yet for once fate had cast Ali as the veteran and her sister as the rookie being led through the muck and bullets.

*

Throughout it all, it was remarkable to me that Ali and I always took turns to crack or crumble, as if subconsciously we realised that was the only way we'd be able to survive.

A tortoise shell. The damaged wings of a bird.

Her struggle with sleeplessness was becoming more serious now, more destructive; though it was *my* dysfunction that took next to the stage, exemplified by the fact that I was downstairs the next Saturday morning at 5.30am working anxiously on my idea for the pitch at work. Now that one of my contributions had counted for something, in my fractured state of mind I felt responsible for its safe passage, paranoid the process might run aground because of me. It was transference, plainly enough – I can see that now. There was nothing I could do to save Molly; next to nothing I could do to help Ali (or so I thought). So I was up at that ridiculous hour, obsessing over the only thing I believed I could influence.

When Ali brought Molly downstairs for her first feed of the day, I told her there was a good chance I'd have to spend the coming Bank Holiday Monday at the office in London, that I really needed to be there in person, because what I was working on was important. *Important.* I actually used that word. And that, thank heaven, was the trigger for Ali (my wife of not yet two years, there on the sofa in front of me, exhausted, noticeably thin now from the stress) to speak her mind. With a calmness of tone that wasn't easy for either of us to find consistently back then, she helped me to see what was happening to me and understand it for what it was. Yes, I was being rock solid but no-one expected or demanded it of me. It was acceptable to falter, let a few things slide. For those precious minutes she

121

levered aside her own considerable anguish to ease mine. And in the short term at least, that was all it took to make me see sense: to feel stronger, saner, almost immediately.

*

Timing worked in our favour then for once. The weekend took us away from home to be with extended family: a gathering of the tribe on Mum's side. We stopped at Rickmansworth to collect her on the way and pause for an overnight stay. She'd baked a homemade chicken pie, made shortbread, and we passed a peaceful evening in front of the TV. After a tough week it was comforting to sit between Mum and Ali holding their hands.

Then in the morning we drove on to Milton Keynes, where we caught up with family, ate and drank our fill, played rounders in spitting rain. Ali and I had both wondered how it would be, whether a party might be too much for us. But my long-standing, fond familiarity with several there counted for much when it came to how instinctively they knew how to be with us. Ali and I both unwound. Molly got to be part of her wider family, to be part of their lives, while they in turn got to be part of hers. And I liked that. Though the day was bittersweet, as it could only be, I liked that very much.

And yet the disconnection, the isolation of our predicament, was never far away, even in the company of those closest to us. We stayed at Mum's again on our way back and in the morning as we were getting ready to leave she got upset. She had Molly laid out on the sofa. She was playing with her fingers and toes when she got caught up in the moment suddenly, the front fell, and she broke down momentarily. It was the first time anyone other than Ali had cried about Molly in front of me and at first I didn't know how to react. In a slightly awkward gesture I put my hand on her shoulder to comfort her, surprised by my own discomfort. Mum and I are close, quick to a hug, but even with her it didn't come naturally to me to

122

reach out. In fact it was never simple for Ali or me when others grieved for Molly. It just isn't straightforward to console someone who's crying because *your* child is going to die, no matter who they are.

*

And so, with the Bank Holiday behind us, we passed into September, a month that began with still another appointment: this one so intimidating to me I lay awake the night before, praying it would turn out all right.

Not that there was anything especially different about the appointment itself. It was just that it involved taking Molly to London to see the specialists in SMA at the Evelina Hospital in Lambeth: a journey that would mean a train from Brighton to Clapham Junction, another to Waterloo, a walk to the hospital, then the whole thing in reverse. By no means epic, but a long way in a protective father's eyes for one so delicate. I hated the thought of exposing Molly (or Ali for that matter) to the brute manners of the capital, where no-one would know or care how vulnerable we were. The prospect stressed me so much I began to play out scenarios of roughness and rudeness in my mind, obsessively, so that by the time we set out I was as uptight as I would have been had they been real.

Again though, I'd worried over nothing. Both transport and weather were kind: the trains ran on time; the sun shone for us; and Molly passed the journey on Ali's lap, visibly thrilled with the motions of the train, the clouds and the trees rushing past the window. Our anxiety eased then as we made our way there, though Ali and I were sceptical, making the journey reluctantly, wondering what it could really achieve.

'It's just to get the benefit of their experience,' Dr Trounce had counselled us when we'd questioned it. But we were jaded with hospitals now. What else was there to learn? Not much as it turned out, though one or two things.

This time the doctor began by asking if there was anything particular we wanted to know. So I asked her to explain the likely progression of Type 1 SMA, the what and how and when, which she did by helping us to understand the order in which Molly's muscles would atrophy and consequently the probable sequence of the difficulties she'd face. She talked about intercostal muscles, fasciculations of the tongue: our lexicon expanding again, becoming more abstract and charged as the minutes passed (with Ali and I trying to keep Molly diverted, punctuating all our talk of decline and death with sweeter words, fragments of song, raspberries on the tummy).

Inevitably then we turned to the gastrostomy debate and again the lack of consensus was evident. Here, in contrast to the Alex, the view was very plain that surgery would not be recommended for the reason we already understood.

'If it was my child, I wouldn't take the risk,' the doctor said. Which I thought was unfair of her, overstepping the mark; and looking back (though I accept her good intentions) a statement that marked a parting of the ways for me: the moment my confidence as a parent began to override professional opinion.

It isn't your child though, is it?

Then in the wake of that grim conversation, feeling morbidly depressed, immediately afterwards in the street I picked up a voicemail from work. Could I present the creative ideas at the pitch in the morning? My heart sank. After what we'd just been through I wondered how on earth I would make the transition from the one mental space to the other, and to the standard required for something like that. But then I remembered what Ali had said that Saturday just past, about keeping work in its proper place, and I sent back a polite but firm no. I didn't have what it would have taken to do the job well, and to accept that finally and let it be was a big step forward for me.

'Isn't London exciting!' Ali exclaimed as we set off back towards Waterloo, both slowing our stride to absorb the mildly dodgy vista of Lambeth.

'You don't get out much, do you Minnie?'

'No,' she said, 'Not much.'

She had a point though. Even Lambeth looked well-disposed now the appointment was behind us and I'd ducked the involvement at work. Walking up past Westminster Bridge, with Big Ben rising up behind us, felt reassuring. It made me think of the major role London had played in my life: my birthplace, two schools, three jobs, a legion of flings and excesses, all that theatre, music and art. Now here I was with my daughter looking up and around her at the sights of the city, her entire experience of it encompassed in a couple of hours.

*

I breathed a long sigh of relief arriving home that day. Another challenge had been got through, another chasm crossed. I opened a good bottle of wine and Ali and I relaxed just enough to feel human again, though the layer of relief was thin.

Was it possible, after all, in so short a space of time, to see a respiratory specialist, a physiotherapist, community nurses and doctors to talk about NG tubes and life-threatening surgery, a counsellor from The Jennifer Trust, a dietician, the experts at the Evelina Hospital, all under the constant shadow of mortality, and not suffer collateral damage of some kind? Taken in isolation every one of those meetings was stressful, but taken in sequence like that they were barely short of an assault; and the wear on us, on our emotions, our capacity to function, our relationship, was beginning to feel crippling.

It didn't help that the day-to-day for Ali and me was so contrasting. More than ever now, I was arriving home worn out mentally with the strain of maintaining the façade outside: all I wanted was to shut down and recharge before I had to carry on. While for Ali, after long days with Molly, sometimes alone, the need was very different: she wanted to talk at length, to try to come to terms with things by going over them repeatedly: two states that were hard to reconcile. I needed calm, my home to be my refuge. She needed warmth, a sympathetic ear. And neither one of us could get it right for the other.

Related, both cause and effect, was the fact that Ali's insomnia was intensifying week by week, draining her strength at an alarming rate now. Even taking on more of the nightshifts, as I was glad to do if it helped, achieved next to nothing. Ali was still in and out of bed all night, taking herbal remedies, reading, writing, doing crosswords, none of which made any difference. And so inevitably the buck passed back to her while I decamped to the lounge, and an inflatable bed with a not-so-slow leak, just to get enough rest to be able to work.

In the background Sally, living with us as often as not now, continued to play a near-impossible role, doing everything she could to keep us going with healthy meals and wise counsel. Ali and I were lucky to have such reserves of love between and around us. But there was no denying that individually and collectively we were starting to crack. We had to bring ourselves to a complete stop to find a new way to go on.

Holiday

Bovisand

Molly was an old hand at Devon by now. She'd been there as a four- or five-week old, then again at the time of my bushcraft weekend. But with a week off work secured, this would be our first time staying with Gordon and Sally as a family, and the relief as we set out was palpable. It would be a safe haven for us, with willing hands to help with Molly, as well as a chance for Ali and I to spend some less-pressured time together. At least that was the theory. In practice, stress of that magnitude wasn't easy to outrun. It hitched a ride in the stomach, the chest, the space behind the eyes, and it took an effort of will and several false starts to break even partially free of it.

*

Things began auspiciously enough with the unheard-of heaven of a Saturday afternoon in the pub. With Sally and Sam marshalling a children's party at Sam's home in South Brent, Ali and I snuck out with her brother. And though guilt got the better of her after two quick halves and she went back, it was enough to get her looking and sounding more like herself again.

Dave and I stayed on meanwhile to sink a respectable number of pints, not enough to give offence but sufficient to leave us sated, and I was glad of his company. He and I seemed closer than we were before Molly, more inclined to share our time. And nor did that apply just to him and me. Bonds were forming and re-forming all around us. Ali and her sister were closer again; my sister and I were talking more often; she and Ali had taken to calling each other sometimes; Sally and my mum had upped their exchange of occasional calls and cards. Now Dave and I were taking a tactical draught during a lull in proceedings. It was as if we were all taking pause to view the world through each other's eyes.

Our visit to Plymouth Aquarium the next day was less successful, though I attach no blame to the facility. It was just one of those occasions where my mood was defined by Molly who remained resolutely disgruntled throughout. Nor was the scene outside any brighter: a zero-visibility pall of fog: Jack The Ripper weather. Ali and I even managed to lose Max, the family dog, while walking him later that afternoon. We had to split up to search. It was fifteen minutes before he found me; another ten before we found Ali again. Even with her silhouette in view I couldn't make her hear me, no matter how loudly I called.

By the following morning, however, the fog had lifted, taking with it much of the doom and gloom, and we relaxed into the rhythms of an unremarkable but mercifully soothing family day. A snapshot around 11am would have featured Dave and me sat in the kitchen bemoaning the perils of the man-boob while he filed his taxes; Ali snuggled in the chair in the corner; Molly asleep in the pram beside her; Sally building a fire for the day in the wood-burner in the lounge; Gordon coming out of his office periodically for companionship and sustenance; and last, but not least, Max, crouched in front of the fridge in the hope that someone would throw his ball or push the button on the ice-maker for a mouthful of his eccentric favourite snack.

Into the afternoon, a rare treat indeed: the freedom to read for several hours. I'd been saving John Reader's *Africa: A Biography of the Continent* for the holiday ('You boring bastard' – Ali). Then after dinner that night we took our drinks through to the lounge to watch *2001: A Space Odyssey*, with the lights out to crank up the atmosphere; though all that did was encourage Ali and Sally to giggle, particularly through the killer ape sequence at the start. Gordon had us laughing too, recounting the tale of his elderly dad being taken to see it at the cinema, falling asleep then waking during the psychedelic scenes near the end and thinking he was dead.

It was simple, leisurely time, and I needed it desperately.

I didn't know how much until the end of the film when Ali spilt the last mouthful of my wine and momentarily I was cross with her for breaking the spell.

*

And yet it was never possible to know how long a good mood would hold. One of us might manage it for a day or night, only for the other to plunge into despair. There was no consistent pattern, no clue as to who would rise or fall. All that was certain was that pressure would force its way to the surface, and it began to do so again as early as the following morning.

Doubtless thinking we could do with airing out now the sun was shining, Sally drove Ali, Molly and me to a nearby National Trust site called Saltram: an attractive Georgian house, pretty grounds, game birds milling through the car park, that kind of thing. And there we passed an easy enough hour ambling with the pram along the pathways outside before stopping in at the café for a bite to eat.

It wasn't until after that that things began to go awry. Sally offered to sit with Molly for a while so Ali and I could go for a wander by ourselves. 'Why don't you look around the house?' she suggested, 'Molly will be fine here with me.' And though Ali wasn't much bothered, I nudged her into it (Saltram House is the kind of place that would normally distract us. We'd find artefacts to admire, fellow patrons to make fun of discreetly) – but from the moment we went inside it was evident Ali wasn't interested at all, and I watched in increasing alarm as she walked through the rooms at a pace, not pausing once, just trying to get it over with as quickly as possible.

To recall any instance of anger with Ali back then pains me now but at the time I just couldn't see why we had to brutalise ourselves on top of everything. I caught up with her in one of the upstairs rooms and took her arm, forcing her to face me.

'Why can't you try?' I implored her. 'It shouldn't be impossible for us to take a few minutes for ourselves.'

And right away she replied: 'Yes, you're right. I'm sorry.'

But it didn't sound like her. Her voice was hollow, dispatched to appease, to reassure me she was okay, that *we* were okay – when patently both she and we were not.

For a few seconds longer we stood still, locked in that awkward blend of embrace and entanglement, my inability to reach her screaming at me, until 'Come on,' Ali said, taking my hand, pulling herself up from somewhere very low, 'Let's try again.' And for the next twenty minutes or so, that's what we did – we tried again. We looked at Victorian toys; at chinoisery familiar to us from Brighton Pavilion; at faded love letters penned by the former mistress of the house: things we'd normally lap up. But as hard as we tried the two of us were as good as dead now inside, so depressed and beaten down suddenly it felt like we were running out of air. A new nadir had been arrived at, unexpected and as lightless as the rooms around us.

'So how was it?' Sally asked brightly when the two of us arrived back at the café. And just as brightly, in tandem, we both said 'Fine.' Because that's what people say, isn't it.

*

Part of the trouble, as Ali managed to explain to me that night, was she thought everyone was coping so much better than she was. Me, Sally, Gordon, everyone. Which was a cruel irony, because all 'everyone' was doing was putting on the brave face we assumed Ali would need to see around her. What she perceived as wisdom, fatalism, emotional calm, was usually nothing more than what I (and I suspect her mum and dad too) had cobbled together to try to project a reassuring presence. Starting to appreciate that was important for me. It helped me to see that Ali needed to be the one doing the caring sometimes. By allowing my frailties to show I could help her find strength.

*

I read a good deal throughout that week and in my book about Africa I found some interesting, unusual words that were new to me: *Aegyptopithecus, Kenyapithecus, Australopithecus*: the scientific labels of our evolutionary ancestors. I enjoyed the sound of the words, the gymnastics they demanded of the tongue; and from then on I took to whispering them to myself sometimes, under my breath, like a mantra, to calm myself when I got too stressed or afraid. *Aegyptopithecus – Kenyapithecus – Australopithecus*.

I had the book in my bag as Ali and I set out with Molly for the beach the next day. Deep into September now, we'd been surprised by the strength of the morning sun and had packed right away, thinking it might be our only chance to give Molly a classic summer's day on an English beach.

I felt every bit the classic dad too, staggering back and forth across the beach at Bovisand, loaded down under the weight of parental kit: the pram, the picnic box, rucksack, National Trust foldaway chair (courtesy of Sally) along with all the equipment for changing and feeding Molly. Throughout the day I saw several men doing the same: the donkey work, while the women issued instructions, and every time it made me laugh out loud – the faux grumpiness of put-upon fathers. It was warm enough for shorts, for Ali to wear a bikini: the kind of day I'd had in mind when we'd first looked at cars that day in Shoreham. We could have fun with Molly and each other and, more than anything, feel at peace with ourselves for a few hours.

While Ali undressed I took Molly down to the water's edge. And what a feeling: the sun hot on my back; the waves falling around us; the thrill of the cold wet sand on the soles of my feet; and Molly enraptured, looking left-no-right-no-left to take it all in. I walked her along beside the shore, kicking up the surf for her to see and hear, overdoing it so the water splashed over her head, little droplets running down her cheeks. It felt like everything it means to be alive and happy was held suspended in those few golden minutes by the shore.

Then I walked back to where Ali was stretched out by now in the sun, got Molly settled for a nap, and took a beer and my book from the rucksack. Before reading, however, I closed my eyes for a while to listen to the seagulls, to the sound of children at play carried on the breeze – close one moment, far away the next – and it felt like balm. Ali and I were doing something that had always worked, always touched the soul. Not only in our time together, but all the way back to our own childhoods, our own parents and siblings. If only – *If only it wasn't true.*

In my book I'd arrived at a fascinating and (to me) beautiful part of the story of life on Earth: the discovery in the 1930s of the earliest known footprints of humans walking upright, preserved in volcanic lava at a place called Laetoli in Tanzania: two adults with a child walking beside them: a moment of ordinary family life from thousands of years ago. And from the moment I read about the discovery, it caught my imagination. I began to daydream about it, to turn it over in my mind, until those ancestral footprints led all the way down through time to us: two adults with a child, and I was taken by a desire to press Molly's footprints into the sand beside ours, to make-believe that our moment too might be preserved for all eternity. As soon as she woke up then, we did it. We pressed our feet into the wet sand, three sets in a row. *Mollypithecus*. Planet Earth. 2009AD.

Then Ali decided Molly ought to be dipped in the water too for the experience. But Molly drew the line at that, howling her indignation (had the temperature not been tested first with her father's elbow and topped up with warm?). Ali wrote MOLLY MAY in the sand in huge capitals instead. Then we took turns to feed her in the shade of the cliffs as the tide began to retreat (I felt a bit desperate watching it go: one of those last-time-for-Molly moments), after which she slept, content in her soporific surroundings. Now and then I stretched out a toe to nudge her cot around a few inches to keep her in the shade. And that's how she stayed, lullabied by the lapping waves, the ocean breezes, for hours, as if she knew just how much her mum and dad needed the time.

We didn't pack up until gone five in the end. Four hours of sunbathing deep into September: we felt kindly-looked-upon as we made our separate ways back to the car, Ali taking the safer, circuitous route with Molly while I clambered goat-like a more direct but perilous path up through the rocks with all the stuff. Arriving first I opened the car doors and was transported back to childhood by the unmistakeable smell of a car interior after a day parked in the sun by the sea. A rolling canvas of memory: the colours of the seventies (bleached slightly like the photos); our Vauxhall Victor, my Auntie Pat's Austin 1100 (the pull of cars again); her dog, Joe; my brothers and sister; the beach at Fairbourne in Wales; sandwiches with one ingredient: cheese or ham or tuna. And in that sentimental flight I ached to be a child again, an age away from the sadness that beyond this lone summer day there'd be nothing I could do to conjure for Molly the magic my parents made for me.

'Molly May' with me in the background

'You've been gone a long time,' Sally called out, coming out onto the drive when she saw the car pull in, 'I was beginning to worry.' But she could see by our faces we were fine, really 'fine' this time, Ali tanned, me freckled, and both full of good cheer. In a way I was glad we'd been gone long enough to cause some concern. It meant we'd underestimated Molly. She'd needed no more looking after than any other child playing a part in a fam-ily day by the sea.

I found sand in the bottom of her bath that night.

I rolled the tiny rough-smooth grains between my fingers.

Three sets of footprints in a row.

*

Later that evening, when Molly was settled, Gordon drove Ali and me out to a country pub half an hour away, with a promise to return for us later and the needless reassurance that Molly would be in safe hands while we were gone.

I felt excited. It was months since we'd been free to have a date like that, just the two of us, and with the momentum of a successful day behind us, all boded well. We had drinks first in the bar and placed our orders from there. I opted for comfort food: a bowl of moules, a sirloin steak, a bottle of red: it was all set up perfectly. And yet somehow we couldn't find a footing that would hold, the momentum refused to carry. As I'd seen happen to us several times now, a taste of pleasure was only a prelude to more pain. The ambience failed to soothe; the wine flowed freely but miserably; and Ali would brook no subject aside from Molly no matter how hard I tried to divert her with anything to stoke the embers of the day.

Can't we pretend? Just for one night?

And so at length I gave up. I sat back in my chair, withdrew, my mood realigning into the push and pull of frustration with Ali and guilt at my feeling that way. I knew she was losing her child, that she had a right to unmitigated tenderness from me. But all I felt sat opposite her that night was morose, and very afraid now that if we couldn't take the smallest comfort at that comparatively bright hour then our outlook really was dire: unremitting sadness for as far into the future as I could see.

'So kids, how was it?' Gordon asked, reminiscent of Sally at Saltram House, when we got back into the car. What could we say? It'd been good of him to drive all that way twice in an evening and I felt like we'd messed it up. Probably Ali did too.

She lay awake all night after that, restless and agitated, despite Sally having taken Molly for the night to give us a chance to rest. And with too much beer and wine inside me, I was neither as kind nor as patient with her as I should have been. It was horrible what fear was doing to us.

*

I'm aware it must have been hard for those around us to know how to help and it's to their credit that they kept on trying. The following night, for example, was it the strain showing on my face that made Gordon so determined he and I should go for a pint? I went along knowing he was offering me a chance to talk man to man if I wanted to. And another day, at another hour even, I might have jumped at the chance. Yet timing can count for so much with something like that and I found I had little to say. I imagined he'd think I was bottling things up, out of pride or misplaced machismo or something (I knew one or two of my friends thought as much). But if I was, it wasn't in a way I understood yet or could rationalise into even the roughest sentiments. That night I was beyond even the kindest reach. I felt hungover and depressed, as well as bloated and dyspeptic after an earlier takeaway curry. As we made our way home in almost pitch darkness along the country lanes, my heartburn mirrored my thoughts. I had to rub my chest constantly to ease the pain, pretending I didn't hurt as much as I did.

*

Our day on the beach at Bovisand had been so blessed, so idyllic, I'd assumed it would be one of a kind. So it felt odd, when Saturday came bringing more hot weather, to set out again with our bags and towels and a picnic. I almost didn't want to go. I was worried something might happen to spoil the memory.

Self-consciously then, we chose a different beach: the other side of Bovisand. Otherwise everything else was replicated: the time of our arrival, our books, even the items in our picnic. But it wasn't the same. Molly didn't settle as well; Ali and I weren't so at ease with ourselves or one another; the weather wasn't as fine. Though we gave it our best there was no escaping the fact that our brief summer holiday, the only one we'd ever get with Molly, was drawing to a close, and neither of us had the heart to jolly that up into anything other than what it was.

Towards the end of the day, I walked up to the café behind the beach to ask for hot water to warm Molly's bottle. And as I went I wondered idly whether they'd regard a non-payer like me as an irritation on a busy weekend. I hadn't learned yet that other parents (they had their own children there) almost always help if they can, because they've been there and know how it is. Except that this time, of course, they wouldn't know exactly. They'd think all they were doing was pouring hot water into a cup for a random dad to take to the beach for his child. They wouldn't know that I'd remember the moment, or record their cameo role in the one and only time I'd run that should-have-been-nothing errand.

'Thanks folks,' I said to them, chirpily.

'No problem,' they chimed back. 'Mind how you go.'

And off I went, with my paper cup in hand, putting a front on things the way Ali and I had to sometimes a dozen or more times a day.

Later I was glad of the chance to give Molly her bath: it was calming to spend time with her. Then leaving Ali to top up the water for herself, I got Molly into a sleepsuit, cuddled and sang her to sleep, and set her down in the cot in Gordon and Sally's room. In the background the radio was playing softly: a piece I knew: Clair De Lune, but arranged for strings. And for a while longer I knelt there just looking at Molly, the sweet refrain and my love for her melding into one. Then I crept from the room, walked along the corridor to the bathroom and knocked on the door, knowing I was about to fall apart, not even caring much, just wanting to be with Ali when I did. Kneeling by the bath I let my head drop, felt her arms enclosing me, her fingers tender in my hair. And that night she slept peacefully in *my* arms, for the first time in weeks, all the way through until morning.

*

As things turned out I spent much of the last day with Juliette, Sam's youngest: firstly in the morning on the touchline at her brother Billy's football match, then later again when we took two car-loads to Bigbury Bay for a last afternoon on the beach.

While Gordon rocked Molly back and forth and the others

137

sunbathed or played, Juliette and I set off for what she would call a 'splore'. We walked, and ran intermittently, over the sand, in and out of the surf, talking and laughing at things along the way. I cautioned her (in loco parentis) on how far was too far, how deep was too deep. And even at the time I sensed there was something for me to learn in those minutes there with her, something to help me, though I couldn't say exactly what. All I knew was it felt therapeutic to be running this way and that in the company of that bubbly little girl, even if (in an impossible play of situation and time) I wished it could have been Molly chattering away beside me, Molly splashing through the water, Molly wanting to 'splore until the last of the sunlight was gone.

The Priest And The Sandman

Pub lunch

Though the holiday had brought lows along with the highs, the impression left was still positive. We'd rested, had a change of scene, after all. And consequently Ali and I both felt blue at the prospect of going home. There was an unavoidable sense that our pause for breath had passed, taking with it time for further procrastination over the two issues playing on our minds: the surgery and the baptism. And they were just the glaring things. Beneath the surface lurked anguishes I hadn't even considered.

After the long drive back to Brighton, and accustomed now to the relative order of Sally's domain, Ali started to stress as soon as we got in about anything she found out of place: an unwashed cup, a homeless sock, the vacuuming left undone. It wasn't like her. I almost had to make her come to a halt to tell me what was wrong, aside from the obvious. And at last, slumped down in her familiar place on the steps between our hall and kitchen, she did. She explained that because Molly was feeding exclusively by bottle now, her breast milk had diminished almost to nothing, and she was finding the symbolism of that tough to bear. It was the end of a chapter for her, a fundamental life experience come and gone, an additional heartbreak that went largely unnoticed. What could I say? It was Ali's turn to cry, mine to hold her, that was all, until we heard Molly waking and had no choice but to get on with what needed to be done.

*

The next day though, Ali was in an altogether different mood: one I recognised and had learnt to be wary of: a surly go-slow she adopts like a work-to-rule trade unionist whenever she has to do something she doesn't want to. And all because we were expecting a priest, Father John from St Joseph's at the bottom of our road, to call in for a cup of tea.

Fortunately I was still off work, my last day of holiday, so I had time to help out around the house and soften her up a bit (because rightly or wrongly I felt responsible that Popish Rome was about to manifest itself in our home, despite the fact that I was none too comfortable with it myself). Unlike Ali, I knew what Catholic baptisms were like, that at a given point, for example, the congregation would be asked, 'Do you reject Satan?' Which always struck me as a hell of a question to fire at a roomful of random relations cooing over a newborn. Actually I had always found the question funny. If Mum was within earshot when it was asked, I'd whisper to her, 'I've been to a few of his parties', she'd tell me to be quiet and all would proceed peacefully thereafter. But what would Ali make of it? Wouldn't it seem incredibly weird and archaic to her? And more, nothing whatever to do with Molly? The only part of that tense afternoon waiting for Father John that made me smile at all was the frenzy of vacuuming and toilet cleaning that preceded the visit-ation as surely as it always had when I was a boy. Priests must think the faithful all smell of Toilet Duck.

We even fixated over drinks and nibbles. What would be an appropriate offering for a man of the cloth? Tea? Wine? Gin? Though the answer in Father John's case turned out to be sim-ple enough. His poison was a cup of peppermint tea and the better part of a bowlful of Minstrels, consumed with an earthly zeal that endeared him to us right away.

About sixty years of age and vigorous looking, he'd arrived at our door in regulation black trousers and jacket, clutching a striped umbrella: a look that put me in mind of Patrick McG-oohan in The Prisoner. He reminded himself of the facts in a slightly scatty what-meeting-is-this way, namely that Molly was the one up for baptism and I was nominally the Catholic. Then seeming satisfied he settled in and proceeded to address him-self almost exclusively to Ali for the duration of his visit, whe-ther out of compassion, an eye to conversion, or in acknowl-edgement that she might need to be put at ease, I had no idea. Nor did I care particularly. I was grateful not to be called upon to explain my errant quarter of a century and glad Ali appeared to like him. That felt like enough to be going along with.

Only once during our conversation did my hackles go up –

'Surely, Alison,' he said in response to a question of hers, 'If there isn't a God, then life just isn't worth living.'

And like one of hell's hounds, I felt the urge to bite –

That's like denying the sea because you're afraid of drowning.

But I kept my mouth shut. The important thing for me was that Ali took something positive from the meeting, even if that amounted to no more than a clearer conviction that the church wasn't for her (or her daughter). Instead I sat back, resolving to listen, while Father John reflected on the meaning of baptism, on the concepts of heaven and hell and, most intriguingly, his own meandering path to faith. I was quite taken with his story. It seemed a far cry from the cloistered path I imagined (probably wrongly) many a priest taking.

By the time he got up to go a couple of hours later we were all at our ease together, though there was still an awkward moment when he paused in the doorway between the lounge and hall and lifted his hand to shake mine – or so I thought. I even put out my hand in return before realising his intention was to pray for us, to pray *with* us. So the three of us joined hands in a small triangle there while he asked God to watch over us, help us find some peace in our sorrow. And if I'm honest, I liked it. And just as the smell of the car at Bovisand had brought back memories of childhood, another lost memory resurfaced now: of a very minor role I'd once played in a passion play, the story of Easter, at the church hall in Wood Green when I was a kid. Mum was Mary. I was one of the mob used for crowd scenes, except for at one point in the production when I had to sit at the feet of the man playing Christ, his hand gripping my shoulder as he spoke passionately to his disciples. I was eight or nine and it made quite an impression on me, as if Jesus himself had had hold of me. Now here I was, forty years of age, a lot less impressionable, but with just the same feeling because a priest in prayer was holding my hand. I suppose that's what Catholicism does, even to the ones who walk away.

More than anything I was satisfied that if God was indeed watching over us, he'd sent a good emissary in Father John, an ally for the toughest times. He'd been sensitive, uplifting, and Ali and I were both surprised at how much we'd enjoyed meeting him. 'Perhaps next time I'll come for dinner,' he said at the door. Then with a wave of his umbrella as he set off down the road, 'I never say no to a meal.'

*

More than faith or the consolations of the next world, however, what we really needed was a good night's sleep in this one for Ali. After seeming to improve down in Devon, she'd struggled again as soon as we were home. And for her it was a short step from losing sleep to beginning to lose confidence in herself as a mum. All I could do was remind her of what I saw to be true: that she was wonderful in the role and doubly so in the circumstances, caring for Molly with imagination and warmth in equal measure. But the more exhausted she became, the less she'd entertain the notion that her agony was the natural, even rational, response to what was happening.

Nor by now was my own mental state any paragon of adjustment. Sensing my inability to get through to Ali, seeing the carnage written over our lives, I could feel myself withdrawing more by the day, to silence, books: *Aegyptopithecus, Kenyapithecus, Australopithecus*. Those words even appeared in my sleep, while beside me Ali stared into the abyss. I wanted to be able to help, but with the best will in the world I didn't know how.

*

At minimum I avoided going to London the next day and we did get to meet Colin Farrell. Okay, not the actual Colin Farrell but the anaesthetist at the Alex to get his opinion on the risk of surgery for Molly. But he looked like Colin Farrell. So much so that even as he was detailing the life-threatening procedure intended for my only child, I was sat there thinking:

'You look like yer man Colin Farrell, so you do.'

Like I said, we were a little cracked at the time.

He had the voice too: soft-spoken and lilting; a kindly, respectful way about him; and Ali and I both liked him instinctively – something that mattered disproportionately when it came to entrusting Molly to his care.

The viewed proffered by the doctor at the Evelina Hospital had shaken our resolution, I can't deny it; especially as, independently of one another, we'd both begun to lose our conviction that what we were doing was right. Could we live with ourselves, after all, if we chose to put Molly through surgery and

143

lost her? Did we have any right to play God? But in time, after more deliberation and discussion between us, we'd returned to our original way of thinking: to opt for the surgery. We were of one mind: that counted for something: the responsibility would be shared whatever the outcome. But it *was* intimidating all the same. All the contrasting opinions over the months had come down to this: to Ali, me, and the man whose job it would be to send Molly to sleep and, God willing, wake her up again.

And how did he rate Molly's chances? I'd had my fill of vaguely loaded half-predictions. I looked him in the eye and asked him to give me odds.

'Well,' he said quietly, 'If you're asking me to put a number on it, I'd say maybe one in twenty wouldn't come through.'

'So that could happen?' Ali asked, casting for certainty again where there was none. 'We could lose her?'

'Yes,' he said.

And one last time that other doctor's voice spoke inside my head: 'If it was my child, I wouldn't take the risk.' Then I put it away. The decision was made.

*

And so we came to the weekend of the baptism. Gordon and Sally arrived on the Friday. I cooked us a prawn and pineapple curry, lit the first log fire of the season. Then on Saturday we drove up to the Downs again, to the pub Ali and I had disc-overed the last time out, so Molly could enjoy the late summer colours and the cooling breeze on her skin. It felt subdued, the way things often did then even at the best of times, but still pleasant enough. Coming home in the car we sang Hello Molly to the tune of Hello Dolly. We had a gathering to look forward to after all.

The positivity carried into Sunday, the sense of occasion gi-ving us all a lift: a reason for the girls to be trying on dresses, for the boys to be shining our shoes and putting on ties. Late

Golden girl

morning Mum and Maria (Molly's Godparents) arrived and just before 1pm our mini-procession wound its way down the road to St Joseph's – Gordon and I suited and booted, the ladies in their finery, Molly in gold for the day, keeping her counsel until she had a handle on things.

Father John had kindly accepted our preference not to have the baptism during a mass but straight after instead. Ali and I had wanted more intimacy, unsure of how we would feel. So we made our way inside just as the last of the congregation was filing out (saying hello as they passed, fussing over Molly), then down to the font where Father John was waiting to meet and greet. And what followed was a simple enough, pleasingly understated rite, neither sombre nor encumbered unduly with hellfire. We did reject Satan, who we felt had it coming, but otherwise all was light. Mum and Maria, familiar with the order of things, looked on in appreciation. Gordon and Sally beamed throughout (not people of faith, but as attuned as any of us to

Father John

the bittersweetness of the day). And Ali? It wasn't easy to tell at the time, but later she admitted to me she'd found parts of it troubling, perhaps taking the wording too much to heart, even worrying that her doubts might compromise the validity of the baptism somehow. All of which was perfectly reasonable. She hadn't had years like me to dilute all that heady symbolism.

Afterwards at the house saw us all back on familiar territory. I cooked Sunday roast. We ate in one happy congregation, and time slipped away (in chatter, laughter, pampering Molly) much too quickly. Soon Mum and Maria were gathering their things. So I invited them to stay for Molly's bath. She was always glad to have guests, I explained. And so they did, knelt on the floor beside the tub to share in her favourite part of the day.

In the cramped space I stepped back to enjoy the rare sight of the principle women in my life (wife, daughter, mum, sister) all playing together, and to be aware of how lucky we were to have Molly with us, to be close enough to feel the touch of her fingers on our skin. Being with her that day, seeing the way she filled us all with such intense in-the-moment awareness, it was *her* life that seemed mighty and ours so needy and small.

Small Mercies

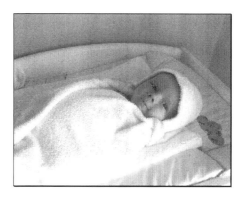

Parcel for Daddy

We both felt sad at the end of that day. One by one the things with scope for being pleasurable: the holiday, the gathering for the baptism, were shifting from what-will-be to what-has-been, leaving only a keener sense of waiting for the worst. Again the light had provided the darkness, and as we lay in bed that night Ali's torment found form in a question:

'Do you think I'm being punished for something?' she said. It was late, gone three in the morning. She hadn't even checked to see that I was awake. She just said it right out like it was part of a flowing conversation. I was shocked: at being hauled up to full consciousness, but more by the brutality of the question.

'Of *course* not,' I said, turning to her, my eyes adjusting slowly to the dark. Then, 'Ali please, don't beat yourself up. There's no reason for any of this: it's just bad luck. Tragic, meaningless, bad luck.'

'But why us?'

The twenty-thousand-to-one question again.

'I don't know, darling. It has to be someone. Why *not* us?'

Which probably wasn't helpful. But it felt like the truth: the only way I could see to try to make sense of it all.

We were still for a few moments. Then I lay back down, slid my arm under Ali and cuddled her to me: the one thing I knew how to do (If we were lucky, I could sometimes soothe her to sleep that way). But, God, we felt vulnerable there in the dark, as if our grief had taken physical form and was starting to bully us now, smash us into the ground while we were just conscious enough to feel each blow. By morning we looked as wrecked as each other. There'd been little sleep for me, virtually none for Ali. And for the first time I did wonder whether things had become too much finally, whether we'd arrived at a point where, with help or without it, we weren't going to be able to cope.

*

Tuesday of that week was our second wedding anniversary: a marking post I'd half expected to taunt us, to cast our lot into even greater relief. Sam was staying for the week and had offered to baby-sit, so we had a chance to go out for dinner. But did we want to? After our last attempt at dining out I was sceptical. If all we were going to do was feel down and argue, we might as well do it at home where no-one would hand us a bill for the privilege. Collective morale really had come to that.

And yet this time the very lack of bright expectation worked wonders for us. Over a leisurely Italian meal, for no reason I could readily understand, Ali and I clicked effortlessly into the most free-flowing easy-going rapport we'd managed in months. We took time over our food, talked about life and love, about faith, our hopes and fears, about death, going deep if we need-

148

ed to, but without once sinking into despair the way we had the last time out. Instead the evening was just what a wedding anniversary ought to be: a time to take stock and be aware of how much you love each other.

It went so well that afterwards outside under the awning we toyed with the idea of going on somewhere for cocktails, thinking we ought to be making the most of having a baby-sitter. And had things been different, had we been Mum and Dad to an ordinary child (if there is such a thing), we might have done just that, gone for Martinis or Bellinis and been grateful to steal another hour. But in the end we chose to head home, not out of guilt or concern that Molly might need us; just because we wanted to be with her more than we wanted anything else.

Back at the house, tipsy with wine, we crept into the nursery and stood beside the cot, whispering to one another, grinning like fools, head over heels in love with the life we'd made.

*

It was always after times like that, those that tugged hardest at the heart, that the contrast with my working life was at its sharpest, the normality of it almost blinding.

On the surface my routine was the same as it had been for years: bike up to the station, black coffee, brown sugar, a book to read; the identical sequence of stations up through Sussex and Surrey, culminating in the Darwinian clamour of Clapham Junction: all those lives merging suddenly, violently: a thousand mountain streams sucked into white water –

'Ex*cuse* me, do you *mind*?'

'Well, get out of the fucking way then.'

'No, *you* get out the way, *prick*.'

London. Rush hour. Mean as hell.

Whenever I heard an exchange like that (and it felt like all the time now) I made sure I had space around me to retreat into if needed. I felt wary of things that would ordinarily mean nothing to me: bustling crowds, loud noises, traffic; and knowing I was just prone to seeing things that way, hypersensitive in my pain, made no difference. The more vulnerable I felt inside, the harsher my surroundings seemed to be.

After Clapham Junction the same bus as always took me up through Battersea to work: the meetings; the banter; the lunchtime walk, time permitting. And later the whole process in reverse: a Stella sometimes from the Turkish shop in place of the coffee. In almost every respect it was a perfect facsimile of my old life. But all wrong somehow. Like the Emo Phillips joke –

'I woke up this morning and everything in my life had been stolen, and replaced with an exact replica.'

I wanted to rewind the clock and not be scared anymore.

I wanted to see the world again the way it looked those first six weeks after Molly was born.

*

Thursday of that week I hooked up with Dave after work, with the idea of spending the night back at his place in Ware. With Sam at ours to keep Ali company, it was an off-the-cuff chance to unwind and do something different.

We met at Liverpool Street station, bought a Stella each for the train, and the tone was set from there. Dave heated M&S pies, mash and beans and we got stuck into the beers and wine; until, inevitably with the two of us, friendly rivals always, we needed competition, and in no time we had the kitchen table extended, the 'floodlights' on (bedside lamps brought from upstairs) and two teams of two pence pieces spread out for a coin football tournament: 'shinies' versus 'dirties', as we had countless times as kids at our old house in Bounds Green. Quarter finals, semi-finals, final; the same exaggerated breathing sounds to replicate the roar of the crowd; the same running commentary from his man and mine, both biased. And most certain of all, the same name for our make-believe stadium – The Citadel.

Neither of us can remember now why we gave it that name. Certainly we didn't know then what it meant. It was just one of those names that sounded enticing, like San Siro or Bernabau. Now though, I knew citadel meant fortress, a place of safety, a last refuge, as if we'd named it all those years ago in readiness for this – a time when a forty year old man and his forty-eight year old brother would feel a need to be leaping about flicking coins across a kitchen table, celebrating with invisible fans, invoking the spirit of childhood to ward off an almighty foe for an hour or two; or until Dave complained his back was seizing up and we slumped into armchairs, sweaty and drunk and done.

I've pondered since how out of kilter with events that night might have seemed to some people.

'It must be awful, Matt. How are you coping?'

'Well, last night I got pissed with my brother Dave and we played coin football until he got backache.'

'Oh. And Ali?'

'Being looked after by her sister.'

Somehow I knew Ali and Sam hadn't spent the night pinging two pence pieces around. But it was just what I needed and at work the next day I felt stronger despite the hangover.

*

That night, however, I came home to find Ali in tears, and still sleepless or as near as made any difference. Like me she'd been glad of the change of routine, but also like me she'd come to – to find the black hole still circling impassively, ready to pull her in when she was done trying to escape. We were lucky the weekend was upon us. We could be together at least.

The weather that Saturday morning was inviting: crisp with a clear blue sky, and warm still, so I drove the three of us along the coast to Saltdean to meet some friends: Damon: best man at our wedding, his wife Bridget and their boys, Alfie and Jake; and another pal, James, there with his daughter, Jess: an outing that would combine the beautiful and piercingly sad for me in equal parts.

Ali had slept well for once. She seemed more relaxed again, thriving in the company she lacked during the week. It was my turn to feel overtired and shaky emotionally after a tricky night with Molly. Certainly I struggled to absorb the day's tableaux – my dear friend Damon splashing around with his family in the sea; and in James and Jess, the inimitable bond between father and daughter that was destined to be so fleeting for me. *I wish I had that.* I knew I could have such a thought without it feeling like envy, because it wasn't the lives of my friends I coveted. I wanted *ours* back, or at least something closer to the path we'd envisioned for ourselves.

Then later, as we strolled beneath the cliffs, James told me he and his wife were relocating to Devon, which depressed me out of all proportion coming on the heels of knowing Damon and Bridget were also planning a year or two in France. I knew people always moved on, that life was in constant flux, so I felt a bit pathetic to be dreading the absence of my friends as much as I was. *Brighton's finished for us now, isn't it.*

But melancholy aside there was still much to appreciate that day, in the way it was possible to appreciate many things if we kept ourselves in the moment: the crystalline sunlight; the deep green sweep of the sea; the banter with the children; and more: the company of friends who knew the deal, who didn't have to be hand-held while they navigated around us. Ali enjoyed our outing especially and for me that alone made it worthwhile.

*

That night Ali slept soundly again: the second in a row: we felt encouraged. So when she suggested we go to the Sunday morning mass at St Joseph's, as we'd half-promised Father John we would, I agreed right away, happy to see her enthusiastic about something. It didn't much matter to me what.

152

Yet by the time I was downstairs pulling on my boots, I was already having doubts. I'd had less than four hours sleep; I had a mild hangover; and Ali's misgivings over the baptism had re-awakened my own long-buried suspicions of the church. I felt ashamed suddenly of my weakness. As I followed her through the front doorway I pictured the books on my shelves mocking me, calling out in snide little voices –

'Oh – God now, is it?'

'Down on our luck, are we?'

'You're too far gone, old son. Too much Dawkins.'

And sensing my last-minute reluctance, Ali paused.

'You don't have to go,' she said. 'I'll go on my own.'

There was no tone. She wasn't baiting me: just offering me an opt-out. But 'No', I insisted. 'I'll come. I want to.'

At the church we found a space at the end of a row where we could have Molly with us, and presently a woman Ali knew from her yoga class spotted her and came over to say hello. As the bell sounded for the start of mass, I heard Ali whisper to her, 'She's not going to be with us very long' and saw the woman give Ali's shoulder a little squeeze before returning to her seat. Another moment. Another shard for Ali.

As Father John made his way to the altar, I wondered whether he'd remember his invitation to us. But as promised, after a few words of welcome, he gestured to us to bring Molly up to the front. So Ali gathered her up and we went to stand beside him on the steps below the altar and there absorb the appreciative gaze of two hundred or more pairs of eyes, along with a round of applause to welcome Molly to the church. And the old ambivalence stirred inside me again: self-conscious and embarrassed to be stood there like that, but flattered and touched too by the warmth of the congregation.

And really I should have allowed that latter feeling to define my mood for the rest of the visit. I should have surrendered to the experience with goodwill without picking too much at the meaning of it. But clearly I was spoiling for conflict now. And the most insignificant semantic slip provided the trigger. Father John's invitation to us to be there that day had been casual (I'm not sure he'd expected us to come). Yet when he explained our presence to the congregation, he said: 'After a baptism I always instruct the parents to bring the child to mass to be welcomed into the church.'

Nothing wrong with that: a harmless enough statement.

But: *instruct*. That one word got stuck on its way into me.

Somewhere along the way an invitation had become an instruction and my distaste for institutional authority was piqued. Not that it was Father John's fault. I was in *his* church, among *his* congregation, in the wake of a baptism I had knocked on *his* door to arrange, but still –

Even then I tried to get into it: to listen actively to the readings, the gospel, the incantations coming our way. But as it had so often in the past it sounded distant to me, even cruel in places, and it wasn't long before my mood began to nosedive. I let myself get irritated by the fact that since my days in church people had taken to praying with their hands in the air, palms to the skies: way too American-evangelical for me: it made me want to scream. Then Molly began to scream, for all the world as if she was doing the job for me, which made me desperate to get out then as fast as we could.

Noticing our discomfort one of the assistants led us into the vestry and let us out through a side door onto the street, where the warmth of the sun struck my skin as sweet relief. We were minutes from home. We'd have Molly content in no time. I'd been foolish to go: the wrong frame of mind, that's all. Within a minute I felt like I was over it –

Until, in the last hundred yards going up to the house, without being aware, Ali pushed the pram through a pile of broken glass, less than a week after we'd replaced a punctured tyre, and something inside me snapped. Right there in the street I seized on that insignificant incident as a provocation to launch at her about everything and nothing: about wasting our money, about not concentrating, about what I perceived to be her endless moods with me. It was bullshit. I was making it up on the spot. But suddenly the church, the broken glass, the strain on our relationship, my vacuous working life, Damon and James leaving, the death of Brighton as our place of hope, my tortured wife, and need I say it, Molly, whose every breath and smile I lived for – hit me all at once. *Fuck this impotence. Fuck this misery.* And for the first and only time that one really obvious, ultimately worthless, question forced its way up into my throat, 'Why us?'

When we got inside, in stunned silence now, between us we got Molly fed and bedded down for a sleep. Then oddly, without exchanging a word, we set about cleaning the house from top to bottom. There was no discussion, no division of tasks, neither one of us took the lead. We just went at it: the kitchen, bathroom and toilet for me, while Ali vacuumed every room in the house, including the stairs, until slowly a kind of solemnity settled over us and we were back talking easily again: Ali on the steps between the hall and kitchen once more (while I peeled the potatoes for our Sunday dinner) with hardly a reference to what had happened. I told her I was sorry, she said it was okay and we pushed on. None of which excused my behaviour, but Ali's better-than-anyone appreciation of its cause at least made it possible to forgive.

*

Later, for the third night in a row, we divided to conquer. Ali chose the quiet of the spare room to continue to recoup some sleep while I took the nightshift: a should-have-been-wearying experience that sat well with me when I knew I didn't have to be up for work. To be waking and sleeping in sync with Molly, mirroring the rhythm of her life that way, felt as natural as rising and falling with the sun.

Her bottle around ten o'clock was my cue to go to bed too, to ease into a part-way consciousness: at peace, but primed for the sounds I expected from the nursery towards two. The restless stirrings first, the little-piggy truffles. And last, definitive to Molly, what always sounded like a car getting started on a cold winter's day: the final approach to the tears. As soon as I heard that, I was up and there to let her know I was on the case. 'I'm on it, Molly. Don't be loud. You'll wake your mum.'

To the kitchen then: a sterilised bottle from the fridge; Infatrini (her high-calorie formula) from the cupboard; a blast in the microwave; a few drops on the wrist; then back to carry her through to our room, to prop up the pillows behind my back; the look from her that seemed to say, 'What took you so long?' And at last (the sweetest sound in all the world?) the moment the crying stopped and the bubbly whisper of drinking began: when Molly and I really got to eye-ball each other, when I looked at her for longer than I've ever looked at anyone.

When she was close to full, she pushed the bottle from her mouth with her tongue and I pushed it gently back in again –

'Come on, Molly, get it down you.'

'That's it. Good girl.'

'All right. Fair enough. We're done.'

Then rubbing and patting on the back, pacing and songs to help her back to sleep: easy at ten, unpredictable at two, all but impossible by six. By then she knew her dad could be prevailed upon to carry her downstairs, play some tunes, even muster a dance move or two, if she was lucky. If *he* was lucky.

'So what's it to be, Molls? Ian Dury and The Blockheads?'

The dawn of another precious day.

That Kind Of Person

The Ben Nevis boys

It was around that time Ali's brother, her brother-in-law, John, and a handful of others signed up to climb Ben Nevis in aid of The Jennifer Trust. It was good of them, practically supportive, and had my responsibilities been less onerous at home I'd have liked to have gone along, for the release of physical exertion as well as the camaraderie; though as it was, my sole contribution was to send out an email at work asking for sponsors.

I felt self-conscious doing so, to be drawing attention to my vulnerability, as well as concerned people might feel railroaded by their knowledge of my situation (which some of them did probably). But regardless, my request set in motion one of the more uplifting experiences in the time Molly was with us.

Within minutes donations began to flood in from all corners of the building: literally hundreds and hundreds of pounds from the ordinary rank and file, along with dozens of messages of support (often from the most unexpected places). Alongside close friends, people I barely knew were being incredibly kind, as if they'd only been waiting for the opportunity, a green light from me, to show that they cared.

The money was coming in via the Just Giving website and throughout the day I followed progress, delighted of course to see the boys' target reached then surpassed but as much to see what people had written. Every word helped me to feel less isolated and alone and I went home that night feeling good, with something bright to say for once when Ali asked, 'So how was your day?' When they were needed most, the good-hearted had stood tall and I'll never forget what that meant to me.

*

At home meanwhile, after another false dawn, Ali's battle with insomnia began to rage again, entering a new, even less forgiving phase. Sleeplessness had established itself as the norm now. She was losing weight fast, becoming worryingly thin, weaker and absentminded; and this applied to both of us: increasingly incapable of making even the most inconsequential decisions without endless deliberation and self-doubt. Should we stay up or go to bed? Read or watch a film? Cook at home or order in? Mundane, everyday choices were eating up minutes at a time.

Thursday of that week, after three nights in a row had gone against us, with growing concern I phoned the office first thing and arranged to work from home: another attempt to keep two worlds turning when maybe I should have backed out of work altogether for a time. It could have been done. But it wasn't an easy call to make, not knowing how long Molly would be with us. Weeks, months, even years was a possibility, albeit remote. I knew somewhere down the line I'd need compassionate leave in quantity. So it made sense, to me anyway, to keep going until we had some idea how things might pan out.

We both hoped a visit from Dr Jarvis might help. Ali wanted to know if there was something she could take to knock her right out for a day or two, give her body a chance to mend and get back to a place where milder things: herbal remedies, massage, might help. But when Dr Jarvis called in later that day she explained that no such panacea exists, and instead we discussed anti-depressants, anti-anxiety medications, sleeping pills, all of which ran counter to Ali's gas-and-air approach to life. For a few minutes after the doctor left, she was as shaky as I'd ever seen her: angry with her body and mind for conspiring against her and, more than that, tired beyond reason. She'd been building herself up for a turning point and it hadn't come.

'I'm frightened of breaking down,' she said, as the two of us stood there just inside the front door. And I told her, 'Ali, you won't. And even if you did in some way, we'd just keep things rolling until you felt better.'

Then looking down at the doctor's prescription in her hand and back up at the strain on her face, knowing her reluctance to take that path, I asked, 'Why don't you give this a chance?'

And without missing a beat she came right back at me –

'Because I don't want to be that kind of person.'

That kind of person.

Four words that brought me up sharp, made me understand her completely; and not just understand but see the parallel in me: the reason I couldn't or wouldn't let go of work. Just as Ali wanted to get through without surrendering entirely her dream of motherhood, I wanted to without folding in my working life – I didn't want to be *that kind of person* either. Which was nonsense, of course. We both came to see that virtually everyone is *that kind of person* if they're pushed hard enough, but we hadn't come that far yet. Within minutes I was back working on my laptop, Ali had tucked the prescription behind the clock on the mantle (where it stayed) and the cracks widened again.

*

Thinking it might be a diversion for her, I talked Ali into meeting friends of hers for coffee that afternoon while I took Molly out with me. I pushed the pram into the North Laine, past the salon (where Jonathan came out to say hello), then on to Jessops to pick up more photos, Rymans for a new photo album. And ticking off my chores I realised suddenly that Molly and I had never been out before, just the two of us, and she was four and a half months old. So I slowed my pace to be aware. I felt confident with her now after our nightshifts together. We even marked our milestone with a pint at The Greys while she took her afternoon nap.

Then later, with Ali not back yet, I gave Molly her bath (also for the first time on my own; we'd always done it together or Ali alone) and enjoyed it so much I found myself willing Ali not to come home until I'd seen it through; though as it turned out I had time enough to get Molly dried and ready for bed, to play her a Ladysmith Black Mambazo CD while I warmed her milk and got her fed and settled for the night. I knew I'd done no more than complete once a routine Ali had managed alone many times. But still it left me on a high: proud of Molly and me and our little show of father-daughterly independence. I almost felt guilty we'd had such a nice time, and was pleased to see Ali's spirits had been lifted too when she got in an hour or so later.

*

We had an appointment for Molly the following morning over in West Sussex. So again I arranged to work at home, uncomfortable with the idea of Ali driving any distance when she was so overtired. Our destination this time: a children's care facility called Chestnut Tree House, sheltered behind a thick bank of trees off the A27 between Worthing and Arundel. In the weeks

160

and months ahead it would become a place of profound significance for us, but that first time all it meant was a chance to take Molly swimming, and the moment I saw the pool I knew what a waste it would have been to have gone to London instead. When she heard first, then saw, the expanse of blue water, a lifetime of bathtimes all in one, she was so excited she almost wriggled out of my arms (as weak as she was). And carrying her down the staircase into the pool, I was just as thrilled. To me it felt like a biblical scene, an old-style baptism, to be wading into the water like that with my child in my arms.

With a nurse on hand to supervise according to the rules, I supported Molly with just one hand cupped beneath her neck, moving her gently this way and that while her confidence grew; until at length I was whisking her all around the pool at a pace, getting her face covered in droplets of water and drawing looks of mock-disapproval from Ali and the nurse. I took my lead from Molly though, who was clearly loving every second of it. As close as she ever came to true independence, the joy on her face was unmistakable.

Then Ali came in too and we played around as a family for a while, splashing and being silly (just as Damon and Bridget had that day with their boys at Saltdean), before switching over to a smaller Jacuzzi-type pool filled with multi-coloured LED lights – on the spectrum of Molly's life experience, wild indeed. But with our reassurance she was soon enjoying that too, making a nonsense of any lingering doubts I had about going awol from work. *I'm meant to be here.*

When we were dry and changed, the nurse offered us a tour: happy to take the time to make us feel welcome. In fact it was evident from our very first experiences of it that Chestnut Tree House was more than simply a medical facility and that making people with troubles feel supported and welcome was actually its reason to be. On the ground floor, along with the pool, we were shown rooms for music, for internet and film, for quiet reflection, for sensory stimulation with all manner of

161

sights and sounds and textures for the children to experience. There were two wings to the house for overnight stays: one exclusively for babies, the other for older children: all the way up to teenage. Upstairs, more bedrooms and a lounge where parents and siblings could enjoy a measure of peace and quiet but still be close by. And finally down again, via another set of stairs, to a communal dining and play area: the hub of day-to-day life.

For me, those next few minutes were my first ever in close proximity to children with extreme disabilities: physical, mental, sometimes both: an experience that in my ignorance might have unnerved me once upon a time. Now, however, from the very first seconds it felt like a privilege to be in their company, and in spite of the noise (and air of organised chaos) curiously peaceful to be surrounded by life stripped of all its pretentious trappings. I sat there wishing I knew how to communicate better, how to make my presence as positive for each of them as theirs was for me.

We were invited to stay for lunch then, another unexpected gesture of welcome; and over the simple comfort of jacket potatoes with beans and cheese, we got talking to another of the parents there that day: a woman whose eldest son, with severe cerebral palsy, was in need of round-the-clock care. She told us how her life had changed beyond all recognition; how each day had to be planned in advance and organised around the needs of the child; how the pressure had tipped her husband over into a nervous breakdown from which he was only just beginning to emerge. (I met him briefly later that day and, though he tried to smile as he shook my hand, he looked shot through.)

With Molly there beside us, her mind so sharp and alert, her body so apparently uncompromised to any but the expert eye, I almost felt phony. Yet the likelihood was that she was almost certainly closer to the end of her life than that boy or possibly any of the children there that day. Which didn't make our situation any better or worse. It was different, yes, in that Ali and I

162

would be able to start again, God willing. But in the sense that our expectations for parenthood had been taken from us and completely redefined, every parent there was one and the same.

*

Ali went to Hove later that afternoon to see a hypnotherapist to discuss her insomnia, while I, with Molly laid across my lap, wrote advertising copy selling Nokia phones on the Vodafone network: a surreal leap to make within the compass of a day.

Then Molly and I set about the bath-milk-bed routine again, though with less milk drunk and more tears. Perhaps she could sense that this time I *was* hoping Ali would come home to give me an hour in the pub with Damon and James. But having left for a half-hour appointment beginning at five, she still hadn't returned by six. Or six-thirty, or seven, or seven-thirty, and her phone was going straight to messages.

I began to feel afraid. Could she have had an accident? Fallen asleep at the wheel? It was there again: the mortal fear: *Don't speed.* And the more time passed the worse it got, until I'd sunk into imagining what it would be like to lose Ali, for it to be just Molly and me for a while, and finally me alone: a wreck, a shell, finished. The horror of it became so intense I thought I might actually be physically sick –

Then bang in the middle of that miserable extreme, Ali suddenly came bouncing through the door, as cheerful and upbeat as I'd seen her in weeks, the change in her so striking my fears evaporated at once; and I sat back relieved while she explained how kind the therapist had been once she'd heard Ali's plight, how determined to help her that when the allotted time for the end of the session had arrived they'd pushed on regardless. Ali was buzzing with it. She even insisted I go to the pub as planned, saying it'd be good for me to have a break. I had no idea how good until the first couple of pints were inside me and I realised what a state I'd got myself into. As the alcohol took its sweet, necessary hold, all up and down the length of my spine and around my neck I could feel the stress popping out of me like broken bedsprings.

*

It wasn't until Saturday afternoon, with rain beating against the windows outside and wind screaming down the chimney, that I remembered Ali's Dave would be somewhere up Ben Nevis by now. So I sent him a text to see how he was.

'Bitterly cold,' came the immediate reply. 'Feel like my face has been slapped by a thousand wet fish.'

I was sat on the floor by a roaring log fire, arranging photos into the albums, with my Dave on the sofa nearby with Molly on his lap (and Jeff Stelling anchoring Soccer Saturday on TV), the three of us peaceful and content.

Though part of me did wish I was climbing with the boys, a thousand wet fish and all, it was lovely to see Dave and Molly so entranced with one another. With no need for words it was understood that the chance for them to bond like that would be one of a kind most likely. And again it felt like Molly appreciated that, as if she sensed the rarefied love encapsulated in those hours by the fire with her dad and one of her two Uncle Daves. She played her part perfectly, waiting until I placed the very last photo in the album before calling for food.

*

We all knew that things were about to get harder. For one the coming week would bring confirmation of the date for Molly's surgery: an awareness that contributed to making the next day, Sunday, the salvation of our week once again.

In the morning, Ali, Dave and I divided up the household chores. While she pottered inside, he and I got the garden looking healthier, clearing away the dead leaves, pruning the roses

164

in readiness for winter, breaking up an old TV aerial that had been rusting in a corner for ages. Just stuff: things that needed doing before the colder months.

Then early afternoon, Gordon and Sally arrived and she and I worked in relay to concoct a splendid Sunday dinner with elements garnered from her kitchen and ours: a joint of lamb, two packs of sausages, potatoes, parsnips, whatever we had: an elastic dinner, as my mum would call it, with her years of feeding many mouths.

Molly followed proceedings avidly, delighting in all the comings and goings, the boisterous banter of the men, the softer intimations of the women, as well as all the attention she got from whoever happened to be near. It felt every bit the perfect happy-family day. If you'd wandered in off the street and witnessed the laughter, the fake confrontations, the easy affections flowing back and forth, you'd have thought ours was just the place to be on a Sunday afternoon. With Dave there, Gordon and Sally too, it felt like Ali and I could charge ourselves up for the week with the strength we'd need. And for those precious hours between Monday and us, the fortifications held: a buffer of steaming gravy, of treacle tart, and the illusion that it would take no more than let's-pretend to make the magic of it last.

Respite

Chestnut Tree House

All the time Molly was with us, Ali kept a record of everything relating to her in a bright red, lever-arch binder. It began life as a fun thing, a place to note milestones, but over time had taken on darker colours. The latest entry made was for 23rd October: the now confirmed date for Molly's surgery, three weeks away.

In preparation I decided to call a family gathering (my side) – something I set in motion that Monday afternoon with an e-mail to my brothers and sister, doing my best to infer, without actually saying it, that this could be their last chance to be with Molly. And again, only less unexpectedly this time, I fell into the trap of wording it over and over until it said what it needed to say, by which time I felt awful. Even to have written about Molly like that felt like a betrayal.

Needing to be on my own for a while then, I ran a hot deep bath and sank low into the water, trying to submerge as much of myself as I could, a wet flannel draped over my face. But it was hopeless. My demons swirled in the steam all around me, forcing me to confront a future without Molly; and beyond, as I tormented myself now, perhaps even a time when Ali might retreat to the haven of her family, now the prospect of making a new one with me seemed so fraught. For the first time to me our bond felt under threat: prone and defenceless like an open wound. Finally I was seeing what might have been obvious to others, that Ali and I were just two people, no more than two years into a marriage. We *could* be broken. It *was* possible. Lying there, with the last of the warmth leaving the water, the endurance I saw it would take to build us up again seemed unimaginable: a mountain summit far above the clouds.

*

Worse still, after the early encouraging signs in the wake of her session with the hypnotherapist, Ali was back to getting next to no sleep, and literally no sleep now more often than not. Her own demons, distracted temporarily, had returned more intent than ever on doing her harm.

That Tuesday morning I got up for work as normal. I showered, dressed, made coffee for the train: a sequence that always ended with a kiss for Ali, an exchange of good luck for the day before we parted. Yet this time, when I leant over her, the entreaty on her face not to be left was so plain, so unequivocal, no husband worthy of the role could have gone to work that day – even with Sally there to lend a hand.

When Dr Jarvis phoned shortly after to see how we were, with Ali's agreement I asked her to come as soon as she could; and later that morning we sat down together: her, Ali, Sally and me, determined this time to pool our resources (of professional skill, love, common sense) and make good on Ali's realisation that the time to accept help had come. Meaningful sleep was a must: she'd made her peace with that. And in the end it hadn't been a surrender at all, but an act of honesty and courage.

*

I was more self-aware about work after that day. I began to re-cognise the value in it for me: the repeated patterns, the reass-uring predictability of each project: the brief, the thinking time, the solution. Oddly I found that good ideas were coming easily to me, probably because I had no concern that they wouldn't. Work had become simple. Not intellectually, not physically, but emotionally. I felt relaxed there. When I saw others around me losing their cool now or digging their heels in over the smallest things (as I'd done myself many times), it made me stare, laugh at them as if they were mad.

And yet I was fragile in my security.

That afternoon, I put in a holiday request for two days: the one before Molly's surgery and the day itself. I tried to keep the specific reason low-key, not wanting to attract more attention than I could handle. But one way or another word got out, and when it did they wouldn't let me take the time as holiday and insisted I take it as compassionate leave instead.

It was a simple gesture of, as the name suggests, compass-ion, and one that with no warning at all broke me, smashed its way through the dam I'd built to keep me from crying at work. When Eleanor, our traffic manager at the time, conveyed the message, I mumbled a thank you, got up and walked out with-out another word. I headed for the stairs to avoid bumping in-to anyone in the lift. I got outside and across the road, aiming for the path by the Thames again, for that same bench as bef-ore, where I dropped my head into my hands and fell to pieces, like someone had taken all the bones out of me. I was sobbing and shaking, my ribcage jerking in and out in spasms (the way a child cries) with snot running from my nose –

Until, just as before, I saw myself: the Samaritan case beside the river revisited; and from the depths came that same compulsion to laugh, only this time all my body gave up was a sickly rasping sound like something from a dying animal.

Lifting my head for a moment then, through the blur I saw two workmates (one was Eleanor) out walking the agency dog. They could see me too, I assumed, with my eyes all bloodshot, a thick wad of toilet roll gripped in my hand, and I was grateful they chose to pass on and let me be. Briefly I considered sending in a text to tell them I just couldn't handle it today and was going home. It was tempting. But I pulled myself together finally and went back in. In the end it felt easier to stay on my feet than to fall and trust myself to get back up.

*

Thinking back now to the mess I was in that day and the look of desperation on Ali's face the day before, I can't quite believe that at first I questioned the need for what came our way next. A few weeks before, the staff at Chestnut Tree House had suggested we come for a weekend of respite care: a chance for Ali and I to stay at the house, to sleep, read, go out if we wanted to – all with nurses on hand to take care of Molly day and night, from Friday through to Sunday lunchtime. It seems so glaringly obvious from here what a good idea that was. But when a specific arrangement was arrived at for that Friday I was sceptical. My inclination whenever I had free time was to spend it with Molly, so to find myself unpacking an overnight bag in a guest room, with her downstairs in the care of strangers, was a struggle for me. Realising though that Ali spent all week caring for Molly and so probably needed the break, physical and mental, more than me, I resolved to make the best of it. We both did.

We began with lunch down in the dining area, where we got talking to another of the parents: this time a father of two girls, the eldest of which he'd recently lost at the age of five to a degenerative muscular condition that sounded particularly harsh. And as if that wasn't cruel enough he was now in the throes of losing the younger girl too to the same condition. Their genetic probabilities were identical to ours: autosomal recessive – three to one in their favour, and they'd lost twice in a row. No wonder he looked the way he did: so beaten up. Or spoke the way he did: all twitches and stutters and doubt.

'The one good thing to come out of this is that I found my Catholic faith,' he told Ali. His *Catholic* faith. I remember being struck at the time by the oddity of that construction, and suspicious of what sounded like another death-bed epiphany as Father John's words echoed inside my head: 'If there isn't a God, then life just isn't worth living.'

But then (again as if God himself had chosen to answer me) from the corner of my eye I watched as his daughter, disabled in body though not in mind, was winched electronically into a position that would allow her a few minutes of relative comfort while she was fed. And I recognised with a sinking feeling how desperately he must love her, and how it had to be killing him to see her suffering that way; and worse still, squaring up to an outcome she was old enough to understand.

Ali and I had read and heard a lot already from people who had forged their philosophies in the face of profound tragedy; who had been through hell and come out the other side with a method for living. Yet there was rarely much of consolation in what they said, because it always came across as wisdom only the passage of time could have given them, never the guttural cry of the here and now. This man was different. He was screaming out from the flames even as he burned; and seeing that, I saw how little I knew. What on earth did his faith, Catholic or otherwise, have to do with me?

*

It wasn't until after we'd spent the afternoon sleeping back in our room that either of us really began to relax. We went down early evening to help settle Molly (the darling of the nurses already) then returned to the dining room, where another family: mum, dad and three daughters, the eldest significantly disabled, were just starting their meal. I assumed the loud shrieks the girl gave out every couple of minutes were commonplace for them, and they were certainly no trouble to us. But still the mum felt the need to turn to us, embarrassed.

'Sorry about the noise,' she said with a resigned smile, rolling her eyes towards the ceiling. 'It's normal for us.'

To which Ali replied with bright spontaneity:

'Oh don't worry, it adds to the atmosphere.'

Which I thought was such a kind, disarming and, above all, funny thing to say. It gave me a glimpse of the goodness in her heart and still makes me laugh to myself whenever I recall it.

*

That night she and I walked a narrow, dark and dangerous path just a few feet from the fast-moving A27 to get to the nearest pub ten minutes away. And there it felt good to get a couple of drinks inside us, to enjoy a conversation in convivial surroundings, even if it was more than either of us could manage to relax entirely so soon. The anguish ran too deep for that, the alcohol serving only as a mild and temporary anaesthetic.

It did loosen our tongues, however, constructively for once. Very calmly, Ali helped me to appreciate that she needed me to be gentler with her, more tender; that my determination to be unrelentingly strong for both of us was making me distant and cold. And in turn, I found delicate words to convey to her that the only time I got to unwind now, even for an hour, was alone or with my brother, and that I needed her to help make the atmosphere in our home less strained if she could, so it could be a refuge for us both. A candid exchange: the stuff of argument defused before an open fire with our fingers intertwined and a

171

pair of pints on the table there in front of us. Without either of us being conscious of it, respite care had begun to take effect. It was one part what was happening with Molly up the road at Chestnut Tree House and one part what was starting to happen between us that night in the pub.

*

We pushed ourselves further the next day. Knowing Molly was in the safest hands and feeling we ought to be meeting the opportunity half way, we drove the few miles to nearby Arundel for a 'splore. It had always looked so pretty in passing from the road, its cathedral and castle vying for admiration, and up close it didn't disappoint with narrow cobbled streets and a legion of cake shops adding to the charm.

In our subconscious quest for peace we gravitated to the cathedral first where, by chance as we arrived, preparations were underway for what appeared to be a mass of some significance (all the bells and whistles were in evidence). So Ali and I took a pew about a third of the way down to watch and let the soothing beauty of the place take hold of us: the gothic architecture; the heady funk of incense and wood polish so evocative of my youth; the altar boys hurrying back and forth in white and red. It was a captivating scene and it got to both of us, but particularly to Ali, for whom, as I had to keep reminding myself, the majesty of such a place was something unfamiliar. In that high, echoing chamber she leant against me. And I held her, rocking her gently while she cried, almost silently, for what seemed like a long but much needed time. It felt like a good place to grieve: a healthier, more natural way for Ali to express herself than the wired, sleepless suffering of the weeks gone by.

We could have stayed longer, and would have, I'm sure, had I not observed over Ali's shoulder at least half a dozen priests, a dozen altar boys, and what I took to be the bishop of the diocese congregating in the vestibule now, making ready to begin their procession up the central aisle.

At a time like that, as any mum would say, 'you're either in or you're out.' So with a whisper I gave Ali the Devil's choice:

'Do you want to stay for mass or go for a cake?'

And I watched her catch her breath and collect herself.

'A cake,' she managed through her tears.

We sidled out then, past the disappointed-looking clerics, into the sunshine, where a ladybird fluttered down and alighted on Ali's jacket. God must be despairing of us, I smiled to myself, as I tried to coax it onto my finger. He sends us a bishop, no less, to say mass just as we happen to walk in off the street, and still we entrust our souls to a slice of Victoria sponge.

*

Feeling better for a cry and a cake, Ali took herself to bed back at the house while I took a book to the parents' lounge, but got caught up instead in an old Frank Sinatra film, Pal Joey, on TV.

It felt nice to be alone, pleasant to contemplate the prospect of a meal out at the pub with Ali that coming night. I was really starting to appreciate what the weekend away was doing for us. Ali was sleeping; I was unwinding; and Molly: it was funny, as I glanced out of the window I noticed a nurse pushing a pram through the gardens and was slow enough to think to myself, 'That's the same pram as ours,' before realising it *was* ours, that Molly was being taken for a turn in the fresh air. It caught me off guard, made my heart flutter to see her that way from afar, not knowing whether she was sleeping or awake looking up at the trees. It was a sweet moment, like happening upon my life from the outside and seeing only the beauty in it.

I was jarred from my reverie then as the lounge door swung open noisily and in came the woman I recognised as the mum of the family we'd sat near at dinner the night before: the one who'd apologised for the noise. She seemed pleased to run into company and the two of us fell into conversation. Or rather, I listened while she vented about the challenges of caring for a child with severe disabilities.

'It's a full-time job,' I remember her saying – 'even with all the benefits the state provides.' Then with a trace of bitterness: 'In return for being free to wash their hands of you.' She told me too about the network of helpers she employed and had to co-ordinate constantly, who surrounded her family every day as they tried to get on with their lives.

Briefly I gave her the basics of our story too, but I could see she was fixated on her own, relishing the forum for self expression that sometimes only a stranger can provide. I didn't mind though. She was personable enough. And more than that, real: real in her flashes of anger and bitterness, her moments of despair, all of which I could relate to more readily than the saintly stoicism of the dad we'd met the day before.

It was also valuable to me to get another woman's perspective on things, not least of which the strain such circumstances can place on a marriage.

'Oh yes,' she said with a sigh. 'We've been through all that.' *All that.* 'I think I must have driven my husband mad.'

He looked to have survived the experience though when he joined us later on, and seeing them together it was evident that they'd kept the love between them growing. It showed in the way they were together, in the way their arms cuddled naturally around each other when they stepped out onto the terrace to take some air, as well as on the faces of their two younger girls, who came in shortly after, full of life, giving me hope Ali and I too might have greater fortunes to come. They were off home soon with Dad to watch X-Factor while Mum was set to stay overnight to be close by for her eldest should she be needed. I wondered whether she ever gave herself a break. When I mentioned we were planning to dine at the pub, she said that sounded like fun but she didn't feel ready yet to leave her daughter long enough for something like that.

'Eventually,' she said, without conviction.

Her daughter was twelve years old.

*

For the second time then, Ali and I made the disconcertingly hazardous journey to the pub on foot, with traffic flashing past us in the fading light. Again a pair of pints, and food this time: enormous T-bone steaks, a bottle of red; and things were good between us. Ali was lovely company, and not just because she'd had a rest but because she too was appreciating now that our escapes had to be manufactured sometimes, helped along with a conscious effort. Otherwise, it was easy to feel we might never enjoy ourselves again.

Afterwards in our room we watched light-hearted late-night TV, melting into the absence of milk and quotas and tears, just for once. We knew that Molly was with people who knew what they were doing and we slept through, unthinkably, until nearly noon the next day.

When we did finally make it downstairs, a little embarrassed (nobody minded: I think they regarded our lie-in as evidence of a job well done), our stay was rounded off with a Sunday roast, cooked and served with a smile by their big-hearted chef. After which we said our goodbyes and drove back along the coast to Brighton, three in number but all of one mind: what a wonderful place and what very special people. They'd helped us find the courage to go on. And to think I'd arrived only forty-eight hours earlier, doubting we needed respite care at all.

Surgery

Rickmansworth

First thing Tuesday back at work, Eleanor, irrepressible, lovably manic, told me she'd looked up Chestnut Tree House on the web the minute I'd gone and started up a collection. Which did make me feel self-conscious this time, having more money raised on my behalf after the Ben Nevis climb. But then I suppose that's what charity's about, putting good causes under people's noses, and I was pleased to hear several hundred pounds had been raised: enough to pay for the weekend: for us or another mum and dad, it didn't matter which.

The afterglow of the weekend was short-lived, however. Later over lunch I wrote a long email to Damon who'd asked me to explain the issues and our concerns about Molly's surgery. It was the first time I'd seen everything down in black and white like that, pros and cons, like a list to mull over a house move or a change of job; and it depressed me, set my stomach churning with the fear we might be getting it terribly wrong.

Then that night, satisfied that Ali had Sally for company, I stayed at Dave's again (taking a last gasp of irresponsible air), where he asked me for a copy of what I'd written to Damon so he too could understand and feel able to ally with us in our decision. Damon and Dave: my rocks beside Ali. It felt like the further we went the fewer people I could handle being around.

*

At home too, with the date for Molly's surgery almost upon us, tensions began to build again. Ali slipped back into the cul-de-sac of asking the same unanswerable questions over and over. I fell into frustrated silence and withdrawal in response. Our relationship was seizing, an engine running out of oil, and I think we both recognised the tragedy in that finally at the same time, and decided to deal with it once and for all.

Sat in the car, moving glacially around the M25 on route to Rickmansworth for the family gathering, something just seemed to give between us. In our confinement there was just no getting away from the need for us to talk; and more, to actively listen to each other to try to understand what was happening to us. Broadly we had the same conversation we'd had that first night at the pub near Chestnut Tree House. Again Ali spoke of how distant and severe I'd become, how I'd 'raised the drawbridge'. And again I conveyed that if we couldn't devote just a portion of our lives to avoiding the toughest issues and being at peace, then I honestly felt I could crack. Like I said, nothing new: the exchange was very similar, yet it felt as though in the intervening days we'd been pondering as much on what made us wrong as right, and had come back with demands adjusted, with a real determination to align ourselves at last. And really, without trying to be overly simplistic, that was all it took. Not

177

to make everything immaculate overnight, but to put us back on convergent paths with renewed respect, understanding, and simply enough when it came to it, love.

∗

Still it was hard to contemplate the next day. The underlying, unspoken reason for bringing the family together was so stark. *Molly might die on Friday.* There was no getting around that, and the feeling of sadness weighed heavily on us both.

I wanted to put a brave face on for Ali. This once it seemed like the right thing to do. So to prepare, before anyone arrived, I drove to Tesco to buy some beer and wine to go with lunch and to be alone for a while, and there discovered that my capacity for crying in supermarkets wasn't exclusive to Sainsbury's. While the teenage girl at the checkout bleeped my bottles and snacks, I stood there staring into space with tears dripping off my cheeks. There was nothing I could do to manage anything better and I didn't care enough to try.

'Are you all right?' she asked me, pausing momentarily with a bag of Wotsits in her hand. More of a security question than a tender enquiry.

'No,' I said. 'Not really.'

Then cheering me up more than she could ever know, with a stroke of innocent genius, she asked:

'Do you have a Clubcard?'

Which made me laugh so instantly and violently a great gob of snot came flying out of my nose onto my top lip. Then God knows why, I put on an American accent and answered, 'No, I'm a Nectar man.' After which I was laughing so hard she had to call me back to give me my change.

Outside I sat in the car for a minute trying to collect myself, before remembering suddenly how close I was to the cemetery at Woodcock Hill where my dad's buried. Though I loved him dearly I'd never associated him much with his resting place so I

178

Five months to eighty-nine years

rarely went there (there was more of him in the house and garden at home), but the urge to go there that day was strong and in the end I was glad I did. I spent a while clearing dead leaves away from the grave to make it nice for Mum. Then I spoke to Dad out loud softly, asking him how he coped when he lost *his* first child. I stayed ten minutes maybe, just enough to give me what I needed, then went back to the house to face the day.

*

I could see from the cars parked outside (there was Dave's battered and long-serving VW Golf) that the family had started to arrive: from the youngest: my great-nephew, Daniel, all the way up to my then nearly nonagenarian Auntie Agnes (Aggie). And as soon as I got inside I saw that the gathering was going to be fun, that the day would pass as I'd probably always known it would, with endless cups of tea and cakes, chicken drumsticks and quiche, Mum and Maria in charge in the kitchen.

While the weather held I assembled everyone in the garden for a photo, acutely aware of the significance (Can a photo like

Thomas and Molly

that ever be less than significant?). I used the timer and ducked awkwardly into the frame at the last second. Then the boys got up a game of cricket while the girls chatted in the lounge, with Molly in among them looking more than content with events. The photo above with her cousin Thomas, Maria's son, is one of my favourites. That expression on her face, all caught up in the conversation and laughter around her. I'm so thank-ful we managed to catch it.

I made time too to catch up with Auntie Aggie, just the two of us: partly because I like her so much and partly to feel the benefit of her life experience. She'd been an air-raid warden in London during the Blitz. She'd delivered my brother Colin. So while never a mother herself she'd seen her fair share of life, its beginnings and ends, rough and smooth. When it came to Mol-ly, she had something very particular to say. Holding my hand as she spoke, she said: 'The ones you lose you keep forever.'

Which I asked her to explain, and she said: 'The thing is, if I was asked to describe any of you as young children, I'd have to go back to the albums because you've all changed so much and I've known you so long. But Stephen, I'll always remember in every detail just the way he was. And it'll be just the same with your Molly – you'll see.'

Then she squeezed my hand tightly and told me again:

'The ones you lose you keep forever.'

*

Elsewhere, it was always going to be a difficult day at times for Ali. Given the circumstances and timing, there was no escaping that. But we kept close throughout with little touches and gestures and the intimacy of eye contact. It made all the difference in the world to sense that we were past our lowest point now.

I came down the stairs at one point, saw her in the kitchen surrounded by my family and felt such a rush: the kind you feel when love is new, when you catch sight of the one you believe in, and all you want to do is fight through the crowd to get to them, to tell them how it is. *We can do this. I know we can.*

*

Those last few days in the run-up to the surgery were a curious patchwork. Tuesday, we were back at Chestnut Tree House to take Molly swimming (the last time?). Then on Wednesday Ali went to see a psychiatrist over in Hove: an appointment she no longer needed, if she ever had, but had wanted to keep as a courtesy and because we were both interested to hear what he might have to say. I went to meet her at the front door when I heard her getting back and listened to her describe how he'd quizzed her about her childhood, her upbringing, her past relationships, the circumstances surrounding Molly, all of it, before

Minnie (to me)

making his pronouncement. In Ali's own words:

'He reckons I'm suffering from 'adjustment disorder'.'

At which, roughly three seconds passed during which I tried my damnedest not to laugh, until Ali caught my eye and absolutely in sync we cracked up together, and spent the next while stood there in the hall discussing her 'disorder' in loud, Freud-inspired, mock-Viennese accents. 'So you're saying zat I'm feeling shit because my life is shit?'

'Ezzentially, yar.'

'Oh Doctor, zank you – you're a genius.'

But then maybe he *was* a genius. If his endeavours could get the two of us laughing like that, hugging and kissing, just forty-eight hours shy of the most intimidating day of our lives, who were we to question the encounter?

Then as if the prevailing mood of hilarity hadn't quite peaked, the phone rang. It was work, asking me if I wouldn't mind travelling into London to supervise the recording of two radio ads for Vodafone, in Hindi. What anyone thought I could contribute, I had no idea. But in the context of that week, it didn't even seem strange.

*

The last day before Molly's surgery was uniquely special for us. The weather was unseasonably warm for October: enough for the three of us to eat lunch al fresco at a restaurant called Due South on the seafront. Ali had spotted the solitary table from a distance; and though I thought the place might be too snooty for a couple with a baby, it turned out to be perfect. The food was delicious and the staff attentive but easy-going – as though they knew our circumstances and the way we needed things to be. In place of main courses we ordered three starters to share, which smelled so appetising on arrival Molly woke up at once demanding her own lunch. So out came the hot water, the Infatrini, the bottle, and we carried on regardless in a little triangle: Ali feeding Molly while I arranged forkfuls of each dish for the two of us, nibbling on Molly's fingers in between mouthfuls to keep her amused. It seemed so unlikely that we should be enjoying ourselves but we were, epitomised by the moment a sliver of onion marmalade slipped off a fork in transit and landed precisely on Molly's upper lip like a Poirot moustache. Another indelible memory made. *The ones you lose you keep forever.*

After, we went to another local favourite: Food For Friends (for coffee, cake and dessert wine), where Molly, to my delight, hummed and chattered away to her heart's content.

Sing up, little darling – let the world know you're here.

By the time we pushed her pram through the door at home an hour later, we were as ready as we were ever going to be.

*

According to our instructions from the hospital, Molly wasn't to be given any food after 2am. So we coaxed as much as we could into her around midnight – then tried to sleep, neither of us caring much whether we did or didn't this time, until Sally drove us all to the Alex shortly after 7am.

Strangely (or not, I don't know), I hardly felt nervous at all. Perhaps the scenario was too outlandish to register properly or my mind had shut down in some way to help me through. But most likely I was calm because it seemed impossible, too cruel, that we should lose Molly to the surgery and have more misery piled upon us. There was no more logic to it than that. We had to trust the surgeon now, the anaesthetist, the odds.

Inside we took a lift to the eighth floor, the High Dependency Unit, where Molly was checked in and assigned a room. Then for an hour or more we played with her, singing all her favourite songs, blowing raspberries on her tummy, giving her the love and affection her unknown bravery deserved. And in true Molly fashion she loved it: she looked delighted to be out on an adventure somewhere new, early in the morning with her mum and dad in tow.

Briefly we spoke with the surgeon again and Colin Farrell to clarify procedure and likely timescale. Then just before 9am we were given the nod. Ali carried Molly to the operating theatre, with me beside her and the nursing team around us: more like a scene from a hospital drama than anything real. Earlier they'd explained that only one parent would be allowed into theatre – but then later, though we'd made no fuss, probably *because* we'd made no fuss, they said the rule would be waived for us.

'You'll carry Molly in,' the senior nurse confirmed, 'give her a kiss for luck, then straight out. Okay?'

'Okay.'

Then suddenly we were there, inside the room just long enough for a fleeting impression – six or seven people around the operating table, green masks, bright lamps. Ali set Molly down, and we did what we'd been told to do: we kissed her for luck, turned and left immediately. The last image I had was of Molly craning her neck left and right to take in the scene: a look of excitement on her face: more adventures, more playmates.

Outside in the corridor Ali buckled at once. In a heart-breakingly child-like gesture she stamped her foot on the floor then went to sink down, dropping the façade she'd been holding together so desperately for Molly.

'You did so well,' the nurse said to her. 'You kept smiling so Molly wouldn't be anxious.' And again, with me supporting her on the other side: 'You did so well.'

We walked away then, my arm tight around Ali's waist, with no idea where we were going. We didn't know what to do, how to pass the time, so in the absence of any other ideas we went back to the room, where the indentation made by Molly's head was still visible on the pillow. And for the next twenty minutes I paced up and down while Ali sat in silence, until the claustrophobia became too much for either of us and we went downstairs to get outside for some air.

They'd told us to expect a wait of between an hour and an hour and a half to allow for complications. We thought we had a long wait ahead of us. Yet we'd been outside only five minutes, and away from Molly no more than half an hour in total, when my phone began to vibrate in my hand. I recognised the senior nurse's voice:

'The surgeon's been in to see you,' she said.

And I said, 'We're on our way.' That was all.

And we set off back through the building, with Ali staring at me: 'What did they say?'

'Nothing yet,' I told her, 'let's just go up and find out.' Then 'Don't worry, if anything had gone wrong they wouldn't be out so soon.' As if I knew.

I'd say maybe one in twenty wouldn't come through.

I kept telling myself the odds were heavily in our favour this time. But still, were we about to be taken aside? Would there be sombre expressions? Eye contact wavering? An invitation to step into the quiet room? I played out the whole scene in my mind while we waited for the surgeon to return. But no – when he did he was smiling: a smile that told us Molly was through safely, even before he explained that the operation had gone as well as it could have. (There was no punching the air, no 'Yes' moment – just a slow release of air through the mouth and a silent prayer of thanks). Then by way of illustration he went to his pocket and took out what has to be the strangest souvenir of my life to date: a small photo of the gastrostomy fixture taken from inside Molly's stomach. He seemed quite taken with it, like he was showing me a snap of his Lexus. I had no idea how to react. Should I have said 'Good job' or something? As it was I stared at it for a moment, then passed it to Ali, who likewise eyed it obliquely before slipping it quietly into her handbag.

*

That night, when all seemed stable with Molly, who was groggy but essentially okay, Sally kept watch while Ali and I crept out for a bite to eat at the nearest pub. It was a Friday, gone 8pm: the weekend back on Earth was up and running: girls and boys in sparkly going-out-gear, hair full of product, downing Bacardi Breezers and beers, with the two of us sat in among them like freshly-landed Martians. *Greetings. We come in pieces.*

Within the hour we were back at the hospital getting Ali and Molly settled for the night. Then Sally and I returned home to a silent house, where for the first moments inside the door we kept our voices to a whisper out of habit before realising what we were doing and laughing at ourselves.

*

Molly was given the all clear to come home the following day. We'd been anticipating three to five nights in the hospital, so it felt like a dream; and from the vantage point of knowing that all had ended well, so much easier to get through than we'd envisaged. Molly was grumpy but otherwise fine.

Gordon arrived Saturday afternoon, giving another dad and daughter a chance for a long and much-needed hug. (It felt like it was over. We were through, for the time being anyway.) We even took Molly for lunch the next day at The Hartington, another of our locals: the pub Damon and I had come to, to wet the baby's head, the night she was born. I'd been expecting to be sat beside Molly's cot in hospital, hoping, praying, trying to reassure Ali, and instead I was sat in the pub drinking pints of Harveys with Gordon, with sunlight flooding through the windows and Molly dozing beside us. All around us other families were doing the same: lots of them: a chaos of prams and clutter, of roast dinners being passed along, bottles being warmed, faces wiped, and grown up chatter interspersed with Ruby-put-that-down-please and Oscar-that's-not-nice-leave-your-brother -alone. It was life: ordinary, unremarkable, everyday life, and it shone. Molly was home and for now nothing else mattered.

Part Three

Space

Extra time

None of us thought much of the post-surgery advice given by the hospital which was patchy at best, worryingly contradictory at worst. Molly had thrown the system probably – by declaring herself good to go several days before the admin was in place. But still, despite Ali, Sally and I all taking and comparing notes, that Sunday night we flushed the surgery site through with saline solution instead of sterilised water because the information was so unclear. Not that a few millilitres of salt water would do any great harm, but it was annoying nevertheless that despite our best intentions we didn't know what we were doing.

Then against this backdrop of renewed tension, along with the emotional fall-out from both the run-up to the surgery and the surgery itself, unwisely I allowed the number of people in the house to creep up, so that by Monday afternoon, alongside Gordon and Sally, we had Mum, Maria, Maria's daughter Hannah, Hannah's boyfriend at the time (and two or three community nurses coming in and out with equipment and information that really needed to be given our full attention). It soon reached a point where as much as I loved all those assembled (with the exception of the boyfriend who I felt like beating up just to let off some steam), all I wanted was for us to be left in peace. And with Ali and I communicating effortlessly again, I knew she felt the same. We were in shock the two of us. We'd braced for the end and it hadn't come. So while everyone took that as a signal to be upbeat and celebratory, there was nothing she or I needed less than more tea and cake and goodwill. As the day stretched, my mood sank steadily until, over dinner that night, Ali mercifully spotted it was about to get the better of me and had me in my coat and out through the door before I knew it.

Minutes later we were sat in The Reservoir, yet another local pub, unwinding over a beer (ironically only possible because of the support we had at home). And it wasn't long before we were laughing at ourselves, softening with the change of scene, feeling guilty about how much we wanted to be alone. Yet the truth was we needed family and friends or to be just the two of us in about the same ratio as always, so it was hard sometimes to be the focus of attention, especially knowing we couldn't easily do without it. We could try though: take the success of the surgery as our cue to tackle more ourselves, be less dependent. There in the candlelight we even made a pact along those lines. I pledged to curb my aggressive tone and Ali promised to approach gently when she needed extra help and not launch at me without warning when she was already upset. We shook hands on it too, aware of how silly it all seemed in light of what we'd just been through. Then last, before home, we raised our glasses to Molly still being with us, and again to the fact that we, Ali and me, were still in one piece.

*

When I got in from work the following night I found just Ali, Molly and a pleasing air of calm. Though we *were* worried that we'd caused offence, we were also more confident we'd be able to manage now with less support, and the chance to show it arrived as early as the next morning.

Out of the blue, after significant improvement, Ali had been unable to sleep at all. When the time came for me to leave, she looked strung out, wobbly on her feet. So I emailed the office, told them I wasn't coming in. And for the first time, that came easily to me. She needed me more than they did. There was no more to it than that.

I took Molly with me downstairs to leave Ali to try to sleep. Then later when she came down I had her take me through all the chores she'd been doing either alone or with help from her mum while I was out: the constant cycle of washing and drying the feeding things; the right amount of sterilising fluid to use; which of Molly's things went in the Molly-only sterilised box in the fridge and which did not. Straightforward, practical knowledge, but with, as I saw now, an emotional aspect: the one that went with Ali knowing she wasn't solely responsible for keeping the wheels turning. When I thought I had everything down pat I sent her back to bed, then practised a while longer on my own, making sure we had another way now to turn to each other before turning to anyone else.

*

Molly meanwhile was doing okay, though my initial impression of her rapid recovery from the surgery did falter in the ten days or so that followed as I began to see how much the procedure had taken out of her. She was struggling more than before to clear her throat; her breathing was more choppy and laboured; though as always it was hard to be certain of the cause. Was it the condition? Just tiredness after the surgery? All we could do was follow the advice to flush the site with sterilised water each day to keep it clean while it healed, and take care not to knock against it or catch the tubing in Molly's clothes. Which was unsettling at first: the idea that we might inadvertently hurt her. But we got used to it. We learnt to trust our skill and sensitivity to do what was needed.

Otherwise we treasured our last opportunities to feed Molly by bottle: encounters I sought out now more than ever, aware that they could be my last, not just with Molly, but as a dad at all (there was no guarantee of more children in future after all). It should have been heart-breaking; it *was* heart-breaking yet indescribably beautiful too. Just to watch my first-born drinking for those last few times, with the knowledge we had, was to see the veil lifted, see the miracle of life in ways a luckier lot might never have shown me. If we had more sense the world would always look that way.

Losing Our Bottle

Watching me watching Spurs

Saturday next, the last day of October, Molly and I were downstairs soon after first light, playing music and dancing together in the lounge. I moved more gently than before the surgery. I knew I had to be careful. But not *too* careful: this was Molly after all. We danced to Pick Up The Pieces by the Average White Band. I blew the brass section on her fingertips. Then I tickled her face and neck for a while with an oversized feather plucked from a chest of toys and sensory stimulations leant to us by The Jennifer Trust: things that were lighter to the touch or especially tactile for Molly to explore: by any measure an uplifting

195

start to the weekend.

Then just after nine, one of our community nurses called in. Jill this time, with the unenviable job of showing us how to use a suction machine, like dentists use, to assist Molly if ever she became too weak to swallow at all. A precautionary measure, in other words, to combat the danger of her choking. She'd been home from the hospital less than a week. We'd barely had time to exhale. Now this.

Leave us alone.

While Jill demonstrated, ably and kindly, the basic technique (no more than point and suck, taking care not to push into the throat) I stared blankly, unable or unwilling to engage this time.

Irrational anger boiled up inside me. *This is a placebo. What good could it do? Really? If things got that bad.* Yet I knew it was as much indignation, horror even, at what I was being forced to contemplate, along with a deep-seated fear that Ali or I might fall short in some way when the time came, and not be calm or fast or skilful enough to come to Molly's aid. That was the worst of it by now: the worry she might suffer at our hands and leave one or other of us dealing with that all our days.

Of course none of that showed: the anger, the fear; at least I don't think it did. Ali and I soaked up the information the way we usually did: calmly, almost impassively, with all the damage being done on the inside. We were adding another string to our bow, that was all: a tutorial in mortality tucked in between her yoga class and Arsenal v Tottenham on TV. Jill left us with two machines: one to keep at home, the other to carry around with us in the bottom of the pram.

Down by the seafront meanwhile, another group of visitors had assembled (Sam and her family, plus Ali's cousin and husband down from Hull) with an open invite to join them if we felt up to it. Through the grapevine, word would have trickled out that we were jaded with company so they were offering us space. But as it was, after our depressing morning, and with the particular tension of the surgery dissipated now, we were glad of the diversion. In the lounge of the Royal Albion Hotel (the scene of our wedding reception) and later at home, it felt comforting to have some bustle around us, the children at play, and to be frivolous for a while over beers and pizza, suction machines temporarily forgotten.

*

I assumed I'd be on more secure emotional territory the next day when, in an effort to do something useful, I tried to install our new washing machine. But never having owned a new model before, I didn't realise I had to remove the long metal bolts they include to keep the drum in place during transit. So when it came to its debut spin cycle, the vibrations shook the house to its foundations: a development made more memorable because Ali and I were in bed having sex at the time. With all God gave me bobbling about I sprinted downstairs, where I found the machine six feet from its original moorings and shaking so violently I feared the kitchen windows would shatter. The stop button was a blue blur. I just jabbed a finger at the middle of it and at last got the thing to come to a halt.

By the time I'd worked out I was to blame (I noticed one of the broken bolts on the floor), Ali was already on the phone to Zanussi, giving someone in customer services there a piece of her mind, railing on about 'standards' and all the research she'd done to find what she'd 'understood to be a quality product'. I had to signal vigorously through the serving hatch, pointing in turn at myself, the washing machine and the broken bolt in my hand until she understood.

'It seems to be working again now,' she told them then, not for one second dropping the outraged tone. 'So you can cancel the engineer. I'll call on Monday if there's any further trouble.' None of which qualifies this apparently irrelevant interlude to feature here, save for the fact that I found it funny at the time, and in its life-goes-on absurdity curiously reassuring, like a man stepping on a dog turd on his way to the gallows.

*

The search for comfort took Ali and I up to the promontory at Devil's Dyke again the next day, where we took a walk heading east this time as far as the terrain would allow with the pram. The sky was clear, the expanse of Sussex spread out below us all the more verdant and alluring for a heavy soaking of rain overnight. We took pictures as always, several of which would number among our favourites later on. Then we dropped in at the pub on top of the hill. I had a Harveys, Ali a hot chocolate, Molly her usual. We felt blessed with our bonus time together as a family, even knowing we couldn't hide in the hills forever. The community nurses were coming again in the morning, this time to teach us how to feed Molly via the gastrostomy: something Ali and I tried to be relaxed about for each other's sake, though I've no doubt we were equally daunted.

*

When the morning came, I arranged to work from home again so we could learn whatever we needed to learn together. Bolus feeding, as it's known, was undoubtedly the biggest step out of our comfort zone so far. We felt we were being called upon to exhibit genuine medical know-how now and neither one of us felt even remotely competent.

Yvonne, our community nurse this time, began by reminding us of the need to use brand new, straight-from-the-packet equipment for every feed (babies being particularly susceptible to infection, and post-surgery babies doubly so). Which set the tone – I tried to concentrate even harder, if that was possible. Then she took us through the theory once before carrying out the practical demonstration with Molly eyeing her suspiciously throughout (how strange it must have been for her to feel her

Snuggled up for winter

hunger abating slowly with no breast or bottle in sight). Ali and I watched intently as we were shown how and when to open and close each of the tiny clips and caps on the equipment and gastrostomy fixture – essentially how to use gravity to regulate the flow of milk into Molly's stomach. The only thing I'd done that was comparable in any way was a task I remembered fondly from childhood – helping my dad to siphon homemade beer from a brewing bucket into bottles via a length of rubber hose. Not a comparison I should have shared, probably: there were sideways glances from both Ali and the nurse; but I didn't care: if that was my way of understanding the principle, so be it.

The process did look complicated though. It *was* complicated, appearing at several points to require more hands than we had between us let alone when one of us had to manage alone; and yet not so unfathomable as to make me think we wouldn't cope in time with some practice. There was a feeling of relative empowerment too, knowing that from now on we could make sure Molly got the nutrition she'd need for a healthy life. Within her own terms, of course.

After Yvonne had gone, I went to get on with some work. I checked my emails and found a note from one of the account handlers asking me to speak to a copywriter who'd just thrown a tantrum in the office. And for a moment, no more, I thought about ripping into him, telling him exactly what I'd been doing for the last half hour and what I thought of his antics in light of that. But my heart wasn't in it, not really. I'd come to accept that the day-to-day held the same sway as always for the people around us. A lonely feeling on one hand, distancing and cold. But on the other that sense of isolation probably toughened us up, helped us find the courage to come out of our corner for a fight that could only be lost.

Becoming The Experts

Team lunch

We earmarked Thursday night of that week, two days after our visit from Yvonne, to attempt our first bolus feed unsupervised. And though I didn't make the link at the time, it must have been the prospect of it that sent my spirits plummeting during the intervening days at work. All the constructs of the mind I'd built to keep me functioning began to fail. I felt old suddenly, unhealthy, a failure: the way many a forty-something probably feels sometimes but cranked up a hundredfold, like white noise running under everything.

Reading remained the one thing I could trust to take me out of myself for an hour here and there – I carried books with me everywhere. When I reached the end of John Reader's *Africa* that week, I picked up *A Burnt Out Case* by Graham Greene without a pause, literally one book down, the next one up, as if I was scared of what might creep in if I left any kind of gap.

*

But Thursday arrived, of course, like it or not, and by then I'd steadied myself again. Ali and I were afraid, but knowing there was no alternative, dutifully, after dinner, we took Molly up to the nursery, spread the equipment out on the table in front of us and stood there together staring at it.

Bolus kit (multiple parts)
Sterilised syringe
Sterilised water
Infatrini
Bottle warmer

We were so tense, so frightened of messing it up, as we read through the instructions again we kept snapping at each other, apologising, then snapping again, over and over. We read them out loud, then again to ourselves in silence, with Molly looking up at us. And what it came down to, what it was going to take to feed our daughter from now on (not the way it was written but the way it's imprinted in my mind even now) was this:

1. Draw 5ml of sterilised water into the sterilised syringe. Close the clip on the tube leading from the gastrostomy. Then open the cap at the end of that tube. (Forget to close the clip before opening the cap and gastric fluid would leak out.)

2. Remove the plunger from the syringe. Screw the syringe to the gastrostomy tube. Open the clip on the gastrostomy tube. Then raise the syringe to allow gravity to push the water along the tube to flush it through. (If it doesn't go

easily, re-attach the plunger and apply minimal pressure.)

3. Close the clip on the gastrostomy tube. Unscrew the syringe. Replace the end cap.

4. Take a new bolus feeding kit from its packaging. Pour pre-warmed Infatrini into the bolus container. Remove the cap at the end of the bolus tube underneath. Open the clip on the bolus tube and allow the weight of the milk to push any air through and out. Then close the clip at the last moment to prevent milk dripping onto the floor.

5. Open the cap on the gastrostomy tube and attach the tube leading from the bolus container. Open the clip on the bolus container tube and the clip on the gastrostomy tube. (Milk would now flow down into Molly's stomach.)

6. Raise and lower the bolus container to adjust the speed of flow using the pressure of gravity. Higher equals faster, lower is slower. (The pace should mimic that of a bottle- or breast-feed.)

7. Top up the milk to the required amount until it's all gone. Then close the clip on the gastrostomy tube, unscrew the bolus set and discard.

8. Draw another 5ml of sterilised water into the syringe. Attach the syringe to the gastrostomy tube, open the clip and flush through as before.

9. Close the clip. Detach the syringe to be sterilised and re-used. Close the end cap. Then finally leave the clip open to minimise wear and tear on the tubing.

10. Wind as normal. Settle to sleep. Then go downstairs, pour

two huge glasses of wine, slump down and exhale, wondering how the hell you're going to do this several times every day and night.

And yet less than twenty minutes after we'd taken Molly upstairs she was fed, content and asleep. It felt like a triumph: the sense of relief so palpable we were both close to tears.

What a time then for Ali to be asked out for drinks with the NCT mums that night. I even talked her into going (thinking she deserved a drink), though I worried after she'd gone whether I'd done the right thing. Six other women, all with healthy new babies: it can't have been the most straightforward company. But I worried needlessly again: she came back on a high. Between them they'd struck the right balance, neither talking about their babies all evening nor pretending they didn't exist. Pinot Grigio was drunk, oh-go-on-then cigarettes smoked, and keels evened out just a little before they returned to their babies and men.

*

While I was at work the next day, Ali fed Molly by bottle so we could tackle one more bolus feed together before either of us (meaning her initially) had to go it alone. And tackle it we did that night in a completely different frame of mind, with an air of celebration about us, a hint of swagger even, realising as we went that we *were* going to be able to cope; we *weren't* going to hurt Molly; feeding her could still be a time for bonding, even with all the equipment surrounding us; and that realisation as it dawned was so sweet, so unexpected, it made us playful, giggly and giddy all at once.

'One top-up for Old Toppenhausen – complete,' I declared, giving Molly yet another nonsense moniker as Ali and I got her buttoned up again, her face a picture of contentment, a smile across it that seemed to say, 'I love it when you're both here.'

Somehow we were still getting a kick out of being parents. And from that day on, together or separately, we took bolus feeding in our stride. Another summit had been scaled and conquered, but crucially this time by Ali and I together. Which did *us,* the *us* every couple knows about, the power of good.

*

Within days I could see Molly was gaining weight and strength, her newly invigorated young body temporarily outstripping the condition. But while satisfying to see, it also served as a reminder that the anguish surrounding the surgery had been only a taste of the real trauma to come. We'd been taking a bow after a dress rehearsal. It was meaningless.

Then came a reminder of a different kind, of the kind celebrations are meant to be made of: news that my friend, Emma, had given birth to a baby boy, which cast my mind back to our Indian meal all those months before when I'd coached her on what to expect of parenthood; when our becoming a dad and mum contemporaneously had been a source of joy for us both.

As I sensed my spirits beginning to spiral again, temporary salve appeared in the shape of another visit from our friend Tess, whose sunny and infectious disposition helped to keep us at a reasonable pitch. Then on Monday Ali and I tried to recapture the tone of the previous week with another trip to Devil's Dyke (I knew she needed diversion after being cooped up all week). But try as I did I couldn't muster any enthusiasm at all, and by the time we reached that high exposed promontory it was bitterly cold too: the onset of winter, with all the heartache it would bring, painfully apparent. Even the option of lifting ourselves with a temporary fix, a holiday perhaps or a weekend away, felt beyond us: the unknown had our lives held in check.

That week was one of the hardest times. With every passing day I sank further into a depression that reached its nadir that Wednesday night over something entirely inconsequential. All afternoon I'd been trying to decide whether to go for a curry and a beer with some friends (with Ali's blessing: she told me I should give myself a break). But as pathetic as it sounds, I just couldn't make up my mind: first at my desk; then as I walked to the bus stop; then sat on the bus. I kept wavering back and forth until finally I caved in on myself: the connection between fortune and self-confidence became absolute. I sank down into my seat on the number 49 bus going through Battersea, turned the collar up on my coat to hide my face, and cried; and in doing so realised the only place I wanted to be was home, where my malaise was understood and accepted, and where, as often as not, Ali and Molly would be able to patch me up.

I was pleased to find Gordon and Sally there too when I got in that night. I bathed Molly and settled her for the night. Then the rest of us ate dinner and played ten-pin bowling on the Wii. It felt homely, secure, far from the stress and strain outside.

I had the option to go out the next night too. But there was no indecision second time around. I went straight home, confident in my choice, aware that I'd acclimatised again, absorbed the surgery and the bolus feeding. We even had fish fingers for dinner and nobody cried.

*

Then, as if to close the chapter finally, two community nurses (not ones I'd met before) came to the house the following day to make sure we were carrying out the bolus feeding correctly. Ali had been given the thumbs-up already. Now it was my turn to be verified as competent.

And so, feeling nervous but equal to it, I led them up to the nursery when Molly's feed was due and carried out the process in front of them, speaking the theory out loud as I went, showing off like a schoolboy reciting a poem learnt by heart. I wanted to demonstrate definitively that this dad was on board, that I could be as tender and efficient as anyone. And with the help of my leading lady, I made the performance look so slick they didn't even stay until the end.

'I can see you're doing fine,' the senior one said, ticking the relevant box on her documentation. And I watched as they set off back down the stairs, smiling to myself, thinking, 'Yeh, you didn't see me blubbing on the bus.'

All Her Birthdays and Christmases

The look of love

When the weather turned mild again that month, we defcided to make the most of it and get out of Brighton. I took a week off and we set out to stay with Gordon and Sally again in Devon. Far and fun enough to feel like a real holiday, but with practical support too to help us feel secure.

My sense of our vulnerability was more acute now, post surgery. Giving Molly a bolus feed in the car park of a Little Chef on the way took some getting used to. But we managed –

and the fact that we had gave us both a confidence boost. Only the last hour of the journey was stressful. The strain of sitting upright so long began to take its toll on Molly, making it difficult for her to breathe, and Ali and I grew anxious.

'What should I do?' she asked me. 'Shall I take her out?'

I looked at the road ahead: wet with rain; the traffic fast and compact around us; and it was dark already (I'd hoped to complete the journey in daylight). I hated the idea of Molly travelling unrestrained at motorway speed. But with no choice seemingly (she was running out of strength), for the last fifty miles or so the law and ordinary dictates of safety were ignored. Ali laid Molly on her lap, while I gripped the wheel white-knuckle tight and crept along in the inside lane with impatient traffic roaring past us through the dark. *God help me to get you there safely.*

*

Though Gordon and Sally's home had always been a refuge for us, this time we struggled to settle: the opportunity for leisure was a double-edged sword: little to do meant longer to dwell. It occurred to me too that we might simply be too far gone now, beyond the point where anything: parental care, mother nature, help with our workload, could penetrate the gloom. Even the steady ally of alcohol felt more and more like a dull and maudlin palliative. And while books still helped a little (in a chair by the Aga I read Ryszard Kapuscinski's Another Day of Life at one sitting), it would take an outing altogether more eccentric to draw us out of ourselves.

In an effort to shake off our lethargy, on our third or fourth day, Ali and I set out with Molly into a chill, blustery afternoon in the direction of the local pub. Max came too, running ahead and behind, digging out oversized sticks to tempt us into play; until at length we arrived, hoping to spend some easy time together, beside a log fire perhaps. I had it all pictured in my mind. Yet the scene we walked into would have been more than at home in an Alan Bennett play.

Initially, at least, Molly was the star attraction. The barmaid made a beeline for her the moment we came through the door, launching into that now familiar line of baby questions: something that always made my stomach tighten, wishing Ali didn't have to be interrogated like that on top of everything. I knew that like me she'd be hoping the woman wouldn't push too far and force her to escalate evasions into lies, or give up a truth too personal to share with a stranger when all we wanted was a quiet drink.

I felt relieved when at length she seemed satisfied and went back behind the bar. Ali and I tried to bed in. The hiatus, however, was brief, the focus merely shifting from cootchy-cooing to dog-loving with the appearance of an amiable old gent who paused, as he was leaving, to fuss over Max. An unremarkable enough event until he took his wallet out to show us a photo of *his* dog, in pride of place behind a plastic panel.

'We lost her last October,' he told us. Then with a degree of detail I wasn't quite prepared for, 'to the nasal cancer.'

'Ohh,' Ali sighed, doing her best to be sympathetic.

'Ahh,' I gurgled into my pint, trying not to laugh.

Not that I didn't sympathise too. I've shed tears at the loss of a pet more recently than I'll admit. It was more shock, in my weakened state, at having nasal cancer introduced as an opening conversational gambit in the pub. And not just nasal cancer – but *the* nasal cancer. It was that *the* that tickled the darker side of me. There we were in our greatest hour of need and destiny had served up a man proffering a photo of his dearly beloved dead dog. How was this omen meant to be read?

Then with me fighting to compose myself and Ali still making sensitive noises, the man's wife appeared out of nowhere, pausing, as her husband had, to make a fuss of Max. I thought I'd managed to pull myself together, until –

'We lost ours in October, did he tell you?'

I ducked my head down. Ali whacked her knee against mine

under the table.

'Yes,' she said, with a plaintive sigh, 'to the nasal cancer.'

Which was the end of me, I'm ashamed to say. I buried my face in my scarf, trying to disguise my hysteria as a coughing fit and pointing vaguely in the direction of the toilets, practically ran across the pub to the safety of the Gents. That had to be the strangest morale-turning point in our whole story.

*

Back at the house meanwhile, Sally had kitted out the smallest bedroom, the one across from ours, with various things to help us with Molly: a table for feeding and changing her on; an electric heater; a kettle; even a mirror alongside her pillow so she could see her reflection, and mine too when I nuzzled my face beside hers cheek to cheek.

As for the bolus feeding, Ali and I had indeed become the experts in a remarkably short time. In fact it became routine so quickly I probably forgot too soon what a shock it could be to witness for the first time. Later that day I invited Gordon up to see the process for himself and sensed that he was surprised by the crudity of it, not much more than gravity and time. That, and a little unsettled maybe. I think it made him feel for Molly desperately, the way it had us at first, and intensified his love for her all over again.

*

Ali and I were just happy to see Molly gaining weight so visibly and looking content. Her quality of life was always our measure and on that basis we had reason to believe we were succeeding. I got it into my head we ought to celebrate the success of the surgery and our own efforts in coming as far as we had. So the next morning I asked Sally which restaurant was thought to be the best in that part of the world. Then I called and booked a

Dinner is served

table for two for that evening. A decadent feeling, even making the reservation: it seemed like an age since we'd done anything so extravagant, though I kept an open mind over whether we'd actually go. It would depend on Molly, of course, but as much on how Ali and I felt when the time came. And for a while that afternoon it didn't look good.

Again fighting our inclinations, we set out to go walking: an attempt to take some fresh air when I'd have taken the warmth of the fireside a dozen times over. The clouds were oppressive and low; the trees shrouded in mist; and the woodland around us smelt overbearingly of damp and decay as it prepared itself for winter; so that what began as a bid to lift ourselves, soon degenerated into a solemn trudge through a landscape that was making us both feel ill.

'I've got this awful feeling in the pit of my stomach,' I recall Ali saying as we walked. 'Like you get when you're coming to the end of a relationship and you know there's nothing you can do about it.' And for a moment only (I was so tired, so weak emotionally) I thought she meant us: her and me, and my stomach lurched. But of course she was talking about Molly, and automatically I searched for something comforting to say. My mouth even opened, I remember, only to close up again when I realised I had nothing left. I'd used all my scraps. All I could do was hold Ali's hand as we walked back to the house, where she ran a bath for herself and I closed the curtains in the bedroom and lay down in the dark feeling beaten again. Problems had always had resolutions in the past, no matter how hard to come to. But this. There *was* no resolution.

And yet I lay there for no more than a minute.

Bored suddenly of being depressed, I leapt up – determined not to sink again. Ali and I had each other. That had to count for something. I turned on the light and went quickly across to the bathroom, where by now she was sunk deep in the tub covered in bubbles.

'I want us to go out tonight,' I stated firmly. 'And I think we should.' (In my head it was Pompeii and Berlin '45 rolled into one: time to crack open the booze and dance while the volcano glowered and the bombs crashed against the walls.)

'Then we will,' Ali said softly, amused by my vehemence.

And we did. We smartened up, made an effort to look nice for each other. Ali put on a dress and made up her hair. I ironed a shirt and polished my shoes. And after Gordon had dropped us off in Plymouth, we had a ridiculously expensive, fairly good meal, with great wine, in a slightly stilted atmosphere that gave us the giggles and made us enjoy the occasion even more. We could still sit across from each other over a romantic meal and feel romantic, despite this being, as we both knew, only the briefest break in the clouds. Ali looked pretty, never mind how exhausted she was. And over puddings I had her laughing like a loon, loud enough to disturb the people at the other tables, which alone was worth double the price of the meal.

*

I was downstairs with Molly not much after six the next morning. Tired, of course: almost fundamentally so: the underlying sadness and stress was so sapping. But I'd learnt by now to appreciate the rewards of rising early, the joy of those first hours alone with Molly. There was something about the silence, the pre-dawn darkness, the knowledge that much of the world was still tucked up in bed, that made it unique. It was always easier to feel happy at that secret time of day.

I took the photo that opens this chapter that morning while Molly and I were playing 'hats' with things we found in her toy box and around the kitchen. It's the photo I look at most often to remind myself of the fun we had early in the mornings and how wonderful it was to be looked at that way, to be loved so unconditionally. I'll never forget that look in her eyes. I'll carry it with me to the end of my days.

*

I realise now that love was the driving force behind the rest of that day too, though I wasn't really in tune with it at the time. Between them, Ali, Sally and Sam had decided to do a birthday tea to celebrate Molly reaching six months: a silent and, for me, painful acknowledgement that in all likelihood she would never have a proper birthday. Sally baked and decorated a cake in the style of a country cottage, with walls and windows of icing and chocolate buttons for a roof; Molly's cousins came after school to play pass-the-parcel; and I got to climb up on a step ladder and Blu-tack a Happy Birthday banner across the kitchen wall.

As I've said, I knew intentions were good: how thoughtful it was all meant to be. But it hurt being a father that day, sticking that banner up, reading what it said, knowing it wasn't true and never would be. And by the time it all got going, Molly was too tired to enjoy it anyway and the noise all around her made me protective, anxious on her behalf, and even more miserable for myself. *Who is this for?*

I was relieved when bathtime came and I could retreat with her to the relative peace of the bathroom upstairs (she could

The 'birthday' tea

have baths again now as long as we were careful and kept the surgery site covered with cling-film). And it wasn't long before the familiar activity: the warm water, a couple of toys, soothed us, had the party-poopers smiling again. Sally came in with a bottle of bubble mixture. Then Ali arrived to wash Molly's hair (with me on bubble duty). Soon more visitors stopped by: first Juliette, then Gordon, and finally the boys. It was one of those parties suddenly where an unlikely room becomes the focus of the merry-making, and my mood lifted with it, floating up and around with the bubbles before coming back down with a pop.

Alone with Molly again for a minute while Ali went to get her a towel, my eyes welled abruptly, tears threatening to overwhelm me as they had so many times before. But instinctively this time I held myself together. Maybe it was as simple as not wanting to be seen for once. Or perhaps I was starting to see that regardless of what people say about grief: it's good to let it out and all that, sometimes it *was* better to keep it to myself, to recycle the pain and turn it into something I could use.

*

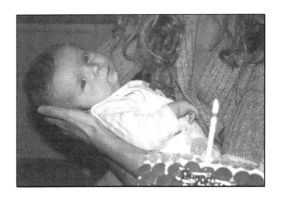

Best intentions

I enjoyed the next day more. Gordon, who'd been working at home all week to make the most of being near Molly, finished up for the weekend. We took a drive to Totnes for a meander, and from there on to Turtley Corn Mill near South Brent for a late afternoon early dinner.

He and Sally went ahead to find us a table while Ali and I fed Molly in the car, balancing a pint of hot water on the dashboard and spreading our paraphernalia of syringes, bottles and tubes among the armrests and coffee cup holders. We were so adept by now the venue didn't faze us at all. When Sally passed in some menus to peruse, they were absorbed effortlessly into the scene: bolus container at the correct height; Molly content; Ali and I with an eye each on the starters. I felt a mixture of pride at our endeavour and heartache at seeing my fledgling family so up against it, huddled together in a rainy car park doing the best we could do.

Inside, the meal itself was a treat – the food, the ambiance – but most of all the company and prevailing mood between us. In the lull between lunch and evening we had the place pretty much to ourselves, so Ali lay Molly along the bench in between

Pretend Christmas

us, where she could feel involved and make eyes at her grandad across the table.

Then finally, on the way home, we stopped in at the garden centre at Ivybridge: Sally's idea, to let Molly see the Christmas lights and decorations. Which could easily have been upsetting, and yet wasn't at all. Ali and I held her up to look at snowmen, nativity scenes, reindeers draped in LEDs, and it was fun.

*

We watched Children In Need that night on TV. Again something that might have been difficult but wasn't (I felt a kinship now with the lives I saw, just as I had at Chestnut Tree House). Gordon too remarked that he'd found it too tough to watch in the past. There was no need for anyone to say that things were different now. Upstairs, our own child in need, the object of so much of our love, was asleep. Through the speaker on the monitor, now and then as we watched, we could just make out the sound of her breathing.

The Signs

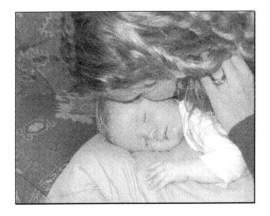

Sleepy girl

That visit coming to an end was especially difficult for us. Ali and I knew it could well be our last time there as a family. And we both felt hollow, and more than a little afraid, as we braced ourselves to stand alone again.

Downstairs early on the final day, in sombre mood I shared with Sally how I wished I could see for a moment what Molly would have come to look like as an adult (or a more grown-up child even, with her hair longer, her features more clearly defined): a needless, self-destructive notion that Sally did her best to entertain by hunting out family photos through the years to compare and contrast. But I'd sunk too low to be retrieved so easily. For those last few hours before we left I felt desolate.

Certainly I thought a lot about Molly's life-not-to-be as I guided us cautiously home through the densest traffic, and rain that didn't let up once during the six and a half hours it took to get back to Brighton. Plenty of time, while Ali slept and the windscreen wipers laboured hypnotically, to reflect on how far the three of us had come and how far we still had to go.

Ali, though sleeping again at night for the most part, was excruciatingly thin now from the stress, and my likewise stress-related eczema was worsening all the time. I now had uncomfortable patches over most of my body and hydrocortisone on my face constantly to keep outbreaks at bay. So yes, we were coping. People often remarked on how well. But probably not as well as it looked.

And what of Molly, the other girl asleep behind me? Was it possible that our fragile world with her was about to collapse completely and on some level Ali and I already knew it? Three times in Devon, Molly's milk had come back up after a feed: all of it, like a waterfall, and we'd tried not to dwell on it too long. We'd assumed, or rather hoped, we'd given her more than she could hold when her stomach hadn't adjusted yet to the larger intake. But the fact that she'd never been sick before, not once, set alarm bells ringing. As much as we wanted to believe otherwise, we had to acknowledge, at least to ourselves, that the final progression of her condition might have begun. It had only been a month since the surgery, two weeks of which had been recuperation: hardly any time at all to see Molly gaining weight or for Ali and I to draw strength. It seemed the surgery might not buy us extra time after all.

*

The nutrition lost when Molly's milk came up was a concern, of course, but as a principle source of worry it was a sideshow.

The real fear, and one of the main dangers associated with the muscular weakness caused by SMA, was that Molly might take fluid into her lungs. So from that time onward our nervousness struck a new pitch. For up to twenty minutes after a feed, we took to keeping her in our direct line of sight. Even a moment away to use the loo or answer the phone felt like it could be a moment too long.

My first day back at work I tried to prepare by searching online for what to do when a baby is choking. I'd assumed, rightly as it turned out, that something like the Heimlich manoeuvre would be too extreme, too violent for such a small body. And eventually I found an instructional video on YouTube showing a digitised baby being held aloft by its feet and struck repeatedly between its shoulder blades. I watched the footage half a dozen times to familiarise myself with the technique, angling my body to block the screen from view. Not that I cared about being seen not working; just because what I was doing seemed so far beyond the realm of conversation. What could I have said to anyone who had shown an interest? And more to the point, what could they possibly have said to me? Discreetly I printed off a written copy of the instructions and put it in my bag to show Ali that night after dinner. It was probably pointless. The advice related to solid obstructions when ours would be liquid after all, but at least it felt like I was doing something.

*

For the next week or so, Ali and I took on the fight. We agreed it was all very well the nutritionist giving us quotas to aim at to preserve Molly's strength, but it was *us* who had to bear the responsibility and trauma should the worst happen, and *our* child who was at risk of suffering along the way; so we chose to trust our judgement as Molly's parents and just try to be sensible.

We began to experiment with the amount we gave Molly at

each feed, and if she showed any sign she was going to be sick we stopped, never mind the quota. Which may not have been ideal but it did allow us to feel we were giving Molly herself the first word, then Ali and me, and last and definitely least all the charts and deciles and whatnot telling us what we ought to be doing. What we *ought* to be doing, we felt sure, was giving Molly all our love and making the rest of her life as happy as we could. And her smiles, her experiments with new sounds every day, her never-ending wonder at the world, made it possible to believe in ourselves. Yet the signs were ominous: we were neither in denial nor being naïve. Despite our most careful ministrations, Molly's body was now expelling, in its entirety, every second or third feed.

*

Then *I* started to get ill: something we'd both been trying desperately to avoid with all the concern that year about swine flu, as well as the added risk of infection following Molly's surgery. I'd been washing my hands obsessively a dozen or more times a day with anti-bacterial soap and de-sanitiser in a double effort to ward off germs. But working in London in a crowded office, riding trains and buses every day, it was only a matter of time. And sure enough, on the last Thursday morning of November, with the cold weather really starting to bite, I woke up feeling awful, and acutely aware that close contact with Molly would have to be avoided for as long as it took me to shake it off.

It felt ridiculous to be taking time off sick on top of everything else, but I couldn't risk getting any worse. So after calling the office I went back to bed to sweat it out, rising just briefly in the afternoon when Jill called in to show us how to rotate Molly's gastrostomy fixture (the way you would a new piercing) to stop the tissue growing over. The sharp stab of discomfort made her yelp, which in turn made Ali and I feel miserable, the moment lingering long after Molly had forgotten all about it.

Other than that the encounter sticks in my mind only because I held my breath through it, stepping out onto the landing when I needed to inhale so I wouldn't be breathing over Molly.

If anything the next day I felt worse. But I managed to get some work done at home, which cheered me a little. Enough anyway, with Ali and Molly out for the afternoon and early evening, to accept an invite to join Damon and James at the pub. Probably not the wisest course in my state of health, but with opportunities to get out so rare I dosed up on medications and went for it. And consequently three hours later I was back at home, knelt on the toilet floor, throwing up the six pints of ale I'd poured into a sick, recently medicated, didn't-bother-with-food stomach. I felt like an idiot: a middle-aged man puking his guts up like a teenager and feeling every day of his forty years.

Making my way downstairs afterwards, abruptly sober now and shivery, I half-expected Ali to be cross with me or dismissive at least, but she was neither. Very kindly she made me a fish finger sandwich: perhaps the finest, most appreciated sandwich ever made. I think she understood simply and doubtless shared my desperation to let off steam. And from my freshly mayonnaise-slathered vantage point I soon felt better, realising that I'd enjoyed my escapade in spite of its lowly outcome. Two friends with a familiar way of helping me to feel human for a couple of hours had seen me through.

*

By the weekend my health was much improved. When Brian, my eldest brother, phoned early on Saturday morning to see if he could bring Mum for an impromptu visit, I said yes at once. And the couple of hours they passed with us were a tonic: the two of them making for gentle, easy company; so by the time they left it felt like some peaceful karma had settled over us.

But then later that afternoon, roughly fifteen minutes after a feed that had appeared to pass without incident, Molly brought everything up more unexpectedly than anything we'd witnessed so far. And this time she found the experience so debilitating, so upsetting, it was a full half hour before the crying stopped and her jagged breathing pattern levelled out into a smoother rhythm, by which time we were half out of our minds, with no idea what we should have done for the best. Used the suction machine? Phoned for an ambulance? What?

The crisis had come and gone. We had to accept that such episodes would become more common now, more life-threatening, and just pray we would cope. But acceptance aside, the minute-by-minute pressure on us was appalling now. It was impossible not to dwell on how the end might come. Just because Molly was a child didn't mean her passing had to be peaceful – she might not simply slip away. And we had to live knowing the difference might come down to us, possibly just one of us. I was afraid of being on my own with Molly at the last, but I feared Ali being alone with her more. After everything she had faced already I thought that might be too much for her to bear.

*

I drove to Sainsbury's the next morning to do our weekly shop, something I usually found comforting. I like supermarkets. Yet for some reason that day the store seemed to be full of fathers with daughters doing just what I longed to be doing with mine, and it got to me. As I pushed my trolley up and down the aisles I tried to fight the sadness with make believe. I pictured Molly a few years older, sat in the seat in front of me while I chatted to her about the things we were buying (and not buying).

'Look Molly, a fish!'

'Which is prettier, Mollington, broccoli or cauliflower?'

'Rioja or shiraz tonight, Molls?

I dreamt of picking out things for her to smell: strawberries, basil, freshly baked bread; of rattling cereal boxes for her, pretending they were broken; of wheeling her through checkout,

223

soaking up the isn't-she-lovelies; when instead I must have looked like a ghost, one-to-avoid, to those lucky dads around me. I wanted to grab each one of them by the collars, make them swear to love every second of what they had.

I knew Ali too must have had countless private paroxysms of pain. Cycling home later that day after collecting more photos from town, I saw her wheeling the pram across The Level. And when I came up alongside her I could see she was fighting back tears, adrift somewhere in a moment of her own. So I got off my bike, and without words (just a brief eye-to-eye that said it all) we continued on together. It was tough to see her so low. I wanted so much to be able to protect her, shield her and Molly. But all I could do was walk up the hill beside them with all the truth of our predicament descending around us like a cloak.

*

The first day of December, the start of the party season, began for us with a meeting with Molly's surgeon to hear his post-operative assessment. After a very brief examination, he declared he was satisfied with the way the site was healing. Then with no warning at all, he reached out and rotated the gastrostomy fixture through three hundred and sixty degrees, just as Jill had, which earned him a shout of indignation from Molly and very nearly an irrational punch in the stomach from me.

He did seem concerned, however, when we told him about the sickness problem. There was no reason, he said, why a baby who'd not been prone to vomiting prior to surgery should become so afterwards: a statement we recognised immediately as bad news. It confirmed our fear that it was indeed the SMA causing the trouble and not the aftermath of the surgery. From a surgical point of view everything was as it should be, he took pains to reassert, beginning to sound like a man who wanted to tick his box and get away. Any further concerns would need to be directed to our paediatrician.

Though there was bad news on that front too. We were told that Dr Trounce was on indefinite sick leave – which made Ali and I feel even more dejected. Aside from our concern that he might be seriously ill, for us he was linked intimately to Molly and her well-being: we'd grown accustomed to the idea of him being there somewhere in the background if we needed him. It wasn't until later, when we heard one of the community nurses tutting 'He just won't look after himself properly', that we realised it was probably just overwork and a rest would be enough to see him right.

Regardless, immediately after our meeting with the surgeon, we were introduced to his temporary replacement: Dr Davidson, who, fortunately, we also took to quickly. Her accent reminded me fondly of my relatives in Northern Ireland and helped put me at ease as we brought her up to speed with Molly's history and voiced our more recent concerns. Her impression was that Molly still looked and sounded surprisingly strong, certainly in comparison to other children she'd seen with SMA; though she was candid with us too, warning us as sensitively as she could that we should be clarifying in our minds what our end-of-life wishes for Molly were going to be.

I don't want to have any.

I had to leave before the end of that appointment to move the car (the money was about to run out on the parking meter). I drove it around to the rear of the hospital, normally closed to traffic, and waited there, watching the motorcycle couriers coming and going with their life-and-death packages. And as I sat I wondered how Ali would be getting on inside without me; what she and Dr Davidson had found to talk about for another half an hour. Was Ali explaining that Molly was being sick now after feeds more often than not, losing vital calories, compromising her ability to fight infection, worrying us to distraction? Or telling her it was getting harder every day to allow ourselves to sleep, or leave Molly alone even for a moment?

And so our lives continued to contract: to close in on us to the point where we measured our limited pleasures in the plainest of units: a bellyful of good food, a cuddle on the sofa in front of the TV, a sip of wine held in the mouth to savour. We were drinking a bottle between us most nights now; never enough to be drunk in charge; just a consistent low level to dull the ache.

Even now the *illusion of bliss* was there. Apart from the hour after feeds, which was terribly angst-ridden now, Molly remained a source of profound joy to us. She was quick to be amused, playful, inquisitive, as responsive as ever to music and motion: miles in almost every respect from the picture conjured by the words *terminally ill*. Which is what made her condition so hard to predict: the end could come today, tomorrow, next week or next month. There was even an outside chance she could stabilise and be with us a relatively long time. I reminded Ali of that often, perhaps half convincing myself. But of course I knew no more than she did, and probably intuited a lot less. With the sensitivity she'd built up over months of caring for Molly, I've no doubt Ali was more instinctively aware than me that things were different now and infinitely more serious.

By one of those odd quirks, on Friday of that week, for the first time since the diagnosis, I stayed late at work to help them prepare for a pitch. That was 4th December, 2009. It turned out to be the last day I worked that year.

High Dependency

My little girl

Ali and I were up early the next day doing chores, working feverishly again, the way we had that day after church, craving the motion, the notion of control perhaps, even over something as domestic and ordinary.

By the time we'd finished, Molly was ready for a feed: a process that since the day before had taken on a new component. She'd been prescribed a drug called Domperidone. Administered before each feed it was intended to speed up her digestion, the theory being that milk would spend less time sitting in her stomach and consequently be less likely to cause her to vomit. We were hopeful. If we could beat the sickness problem, Molly had no other significant symptoms beyond the obvious muscular weakness (which at her age didn't preclude a good quality of life). The only downside, as far as I could see, was the further complication of an already time-intensive task: the drug needed to be given via the gastrostomy at least ten minutes before the Infatrini which, with all the fiddling around, would add another quarter of an hour to the feeding regimen. It feels selfish now to comment on our physical and mental shape, but the two of us were shattered. There were precious few breaks for me, next to none for Ali and just briefly that morning I stamped my feet psychologically. I grumbled aloud for the first time, baulking at the endless toil. *Daddy was just tired, Molly. I'm sorry.*

Then early afternoon, Damon and Bridget called in for an impromptu visit with their younger son, Jake, who did his best to entertain Molly – who was unusually out of sorts and plainly uncomfortable. Ali put it down to the flu jabs she'd had the previous day, which was perfectly plausible. Maybe the Domperidone didn't suit her, or the effort of keeping milk down was simply becoming too much. Whatever the proximate cause, she struggled throughout their visit: it was obvious to all of us. Her breathing was snappy and shallow, her spirits impossible to lift for more than a few seconds at a time.

Ali looked so unhappy when we were alone again, my heart ached for her. So I tried to do what little I could to cheer her up. I walked round to Sainsbury's to get us something nice for dinner. I bought mussels, prawns and squid to make a seafood pasta, a bottle of Gurwurtstraminer. I wanted to give us a Saturday night treat, even within our limitations. And for a while it almost worked: we ate our pasta, drank our wine, watched the easy nonsense of X-Factor. With Molly safely in bed, it looked like our evening would pass inconsequentially, until –

Until we heard Molly, on the monitor, clearly in distress.

As we often did, Ali and I both went to her that night and

took turns trying to re-settle her with our different techniques. Ali cradled her, whispering reassurances. I hummed a few bars of Sing Sing Sing quietly and took a few tentative dance steps. But as hard as we tried there was nothing either of us could do to console her. Every time she came close to dropping off she fought it tenaciously, hauling herself back up to consciousness, dare I say it, like a drunk, afraid of falling asleep when she felt she might be sick.

'She'll keep herself awake if she can see me,' Ali said. So she stepped out onto the landing and waited behind the door while I kept on trying. And very soon after, that's when it happened. Over three hours since Molly's last feed, well beyond the point where we thought there was any risk, abruptly everything came up and out of her at once (or so it appeared to me).

Immediately I set her down on her front with her head angled off to one side and called Ali in to help. Molly looked pale, and desperately tired now, as she had all day, only worse. And for the briefest moment Ali and I just stood there looking at her, totally at a loss for what to do. Which is when (something I'll never be able to forget) Molly snapped bolt awake suddenly – her eyes wide, shocked, staring right at me like she expected me to have the answer.

Things are meant to be safe when you're here.

With hindsight, knowing what we found out later once we'd seen the X-rays, that must have been the moment she aspirated – inhaled fluid deep into her right lung as she lay on her side. The colour in her cheeks, what little there was left, drained away to nothing. Her breathing became shallower still. For a few seconds I was paralysed by the dread that she was about to die in front of our eyes.

Stupidly then, I know now, an unnecessary delay, I told Ali to run next door to find our neighbour, Graham: a paramedic. I thought, by the look of Molly, he might be her only chance: she seemed so close to the precipice. I lay beside her, stroking her hair, trying to reassure her while I listened out for sounds from downstairs, praying Graham would be home, that Molly wouldn't die with me on my own. Then presently he arrived in the room, took one look at Molly and told us to call an ambulance. 'If you're in doubt, you should always call,' he said. There was no magic remedy. All he could do was pat her back gently to ease her airways. I felt foolish, annoyed with myself for having wasted those extra minutes.

Ali made the call. I stayed with Molly, faintly aware of Graham's wife, Saskia, sat behind me, squeezing my shoulder for encouragement. Then time evaporated. After what seemed like an incredibly short wait, the ambulance arrived. Even allowing for my judgement of time under stress it can't have been more than two or three minutes. I was stunned when the first member of the crew walked into the room.

Downstairs I grabbed the bare essentials: house key, mobile and wallet. Ali carried Molly out to the ambulance. We climbed in and at once I heard the bleeping sound as the driver put the vehicle into reverse and began backing down our narrow cul de sac. It's an acquired skill, and momentarily I worried he might struggle. But of course, his daily bread and butter, he handled it with ease. Then, as he turned at the bottom of the road and set off, I took in my surroundings: my first thought being that at the age of forty I had never been inside an ambulance before. Was that unusual? It was white-bright, fluorescent. I looked up and saw a No Smoking sign, wondering whether it would really occur to anyone to light up in the back of an ambulance. Then right away: this is England, of course it would. Other than that all I recall was feeling self-conscious that my breath smelled of garlic and wine, which felt inappropriate, disrespectful to the situation, so I tried not to breathe much. I couldn't see Molly's face directly but I kept an eye on Ali's, which told me all I needed to know.

By now it was close to 11.30pm, Saturday night in Brighton, and my mind shifted to worrying we'd struggle to get through town. I pictured the roads clogged with the drinkers and fighters of your average weekend night; and for a moment my fears looked justified. Ahead, through the window, I saw the reflection of flashing blue lights and heard a siren screaming. Whatever's happening, I prayed, please don't let it hold us up. *Please.* But the roads ahead were almost preternaturally clear and I realised with a jolt, the flashing blue lights, the screaming siren, were us. We *were* the emergency, the Saturday night crisis, rushing through to A&E.

When we pulled up at the hospital, there were staff waiting for us outside. Ali and Molly were ushered straight through to an assessment room with me following close behind. They put an oxygen mask over Molly's face, a canula into her foot. She was mortally pale now. Ali kept looking at me for reassurance but I was fixed in concentration, knowing that the fastest way for the staff to understand and be aware of Molly's condition was for me to explain it to them. So I set about it, in a voice that sounded, to me at least, so much more authoritative than I felt inside. Yet the truth was I knew what I was talking about by now. As Dr Trounce had said to us back at the start, 'You'll end up being the experts yourselves'. And sure enough I heard words like 'compromised' and 'intercostal' flowing out of my mouth as I told them what they needed to know, recognising that we might only have minutes, even seconds, at our disposal. And finally, the hardest thing of all to say, I made it clear we didn't want any life-extending procedures beyond what would make Molly comfortable. They probably took no notice. They would have had protocols to follow, I'm sure, regardless of me, but I thought it was important to speak up.

With their standard entry assessments made then, they gave Ali and I heavy black gowns to put on, lined with lead to shield us from the X-ray machine while Molly was exposed to its full glare. Then immediately we were moving again, walking fast, a sizable group of us now: Ali on the trolley holding Molly; me alongside in among the doctors and nurses as they swiped us through doors marked STAFF ONLY – the insiders' shortcut to the Alex on the other side of the complex; where suddenly, through an unfamiliar door, we were on familiar territory. The eighth floor, High Dependency, just six weeks after we'd been there for the surgery.

Though still struggling to breathe, Molly sensed the change in atmosphere at once: much more peaceful, and calmed a little as the nurses settled her in. They taped an oxygen feed to her face leading up through her nose, hooked up a saline drip to the canula and clipped an oxygen monitor cable to her big toe (her *big* toe, as if anything about Molly was big), after which all they could do was monitor her, wait and see.

An hour passed then which Ali spent sat with Molly, trying to comfort her, while I paced the room, until a doctor came in at last with the X-rays. 'We're not sure at this stage,' I remember her saying, 'But the most likely scenario is pneumonia.' *Pneumonia?* Molly had aspirated, surely. Did the one cause the other, I wondered? (At the time I didn't challenge it.) But for the rest of the night that was all we had. The duty nurse came in every half an hour to check on Molly, who appeared to be stabilising slowly. And around 3am I felt reassured enough to lie down on the parent's bed in the adjoining room. Ali stayed ever-present meanwhile, telling Molly how much she loved her, making sure she could feel her mum's presence right through until dawn.

It Was Definitely A Tuesday

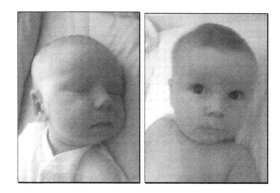

Early memories on my phone

There was a natural balance, I discovered, to the way particular tasks fell to one or other of us. For just as Ali was the one to remain steadfast at Molly's side all night, when the duty doctor requested a meeting in the morning to confirm our end-of-life wishes for Molly, it was plain at once that the task would go to me. In mirror opposite to the travails of the night, it was something I felt I could do and Ali felt she could not.

I was shown across the corridor to an office where, with the duty doctor and a senior nurse, I discussed every possible scenario in detail. They wanted to know exactly what they had our permission to do, what amount and type of intervention would be acceptable to us, given that losing Molly was inevitable sooner or later. Ali and I knew that in America, for example, the

233

treatment favoured in the later stages of SMA was often highly invasive: the use of ventilators and such to help the patient live as long as possible. But with due respect to other parents to do what they think is right, we didn't want that for Molly. We took her quality of life as the guiding light for our decisions, so the answers I gave were along those lines. As each agreement was reached the doctor wrote it down, had me check over the wording, then we moved on to the next.

'We do this so when a new doctor comes on duty, they will know your wishes without having to trouble you at what might be a very emotional time,' the nurse explained.

'I understand,' I said.

And I did. I'd been thinking about little else for weeks.

When we'd finished I gave the document one last look over and added my signature as directed at the foot of the page: our end-of-life wishes for our daughter: a piercing echo of the birth plan Ali had written just seven months before. Then I crossed the corridor again to our room and sat down quietly beside her. Without a word she took my hand, the two of us more grateful than ever to have each other to share the load.

*

It must have been because it was the weekend that none of the staff we knew were on duty. We had to start again, getting used to unfamiliar people coming in and out offering their opinions. And the more I listened, the more I grew concerned at what I perceived to be a lack of understanding of the seriousness of Molly's condition. Later that morning there was even mention she might be moved to a general ward, which I found astonishing. It would mean strict enforcement of visiting times for one. And more crucially, as far as I was concerned, a significant misreading of the situation. I was more than prepared to fight any attempt to have her moved.

Fortunately, if fortunately could ever be the right word, the

X-rays, once they were reviewed properly in context, made the extent of Molly's plight plainly apparent. The images revealed a white mass obscuring the entire length of Molly's right lung. As I'd thought, she had indeed aspirated: defined in the dictionary as 'the sucking of fluid or foreign matter into the air passages of the body.' Which would explain the suggestion of pneumonia, almost identically defined as 'inflammation of one or both lungs in which the air sacs become filled with liquid.' *Aspiration.*

How I've stared at that word and wondered how it could have such opposite meanings: something we hope for one day and what befell Molly that first Saturday night of December 2009.

Medical definitions aside though, just looking at Molly, watching her breathe for a while, was all it took to see how poorly she was. One whole side of her chest appeared flat, misshapen. Yet remarkably she was stabilising still and being fed again now – the smallest amount, very slowly via a pump: just enough to keep her ticking over while they worked out what to do.

By lunchtime I felt confident enough to walk home, twenty minutes or so on foot, to collect a few things to keep us going. I made bacon and egg rolls and wrapped them in foil to keep warm (just as Sally had when we'd been there for the surgery). Then later in the day she and Gordon arrived from Devon to lend a hand. We didn't want many people with us but this familiar and capable cavalry was a welcome sight. Our ranks were strengthened, our spirits raised.

*

As Ali had stayed up all night with Molly, it was agreed I'd stay on alone the second night while she went home to try to sleep. I was slightly surprised to be given the responsibility but happy too at the prospect of one-on-one time with Molly when I assumed I'd had my last. And by now she'd rallied considerably so I felt confident we'd be okay.

Throughout the evening and night I moved back and forth between her cot and the parent's bed a few feet away as there was very little I could do. Like her mum, Molly had spent most of the previous night awake so she slept deeply and peacefully, the air of serenity around her completely belying her situation. I could see for myself though that her breathing had improved and some colour had returned to her cheeks. She was fractious and awake for an hour at most, throughout which I lay curled in a protective arc around her on the cot, singing to her quietly and holding her hand. Which is how and where I was found by the new duty nurse when she came in to check on Molly at the change of shift. As policy they're trained to ask a security question of anyone on the ward they don't recognise. So she asked, 'Can you tell me Molly's date of birth please?' And for a few seconds I stared at her, totally befuddled, adrift between states of consciousness and so tired I couldn't begin to think straight.

'It was definitely a Tuesday,' I said, drawing a blank.

At which she laughed softly and smiled. It must have been the kind of answer shattered, stressed-out dads sometimes gave and it seemed to put her mind at rest.

She sat with us then for a while at the end of the cot (probably double-checking I wasn't a nutter), saying how pretty Molly was, things like that. She had a kind, motherly/grandmotherly way about her, a warming Caribbean accent, and I was glad of her company. I felt lucky to be where I was. The alternative would have meant being at home, helpless and worried; about Molly of course, but as much about Ali not having me with her should anything happen. It was strange to picture her alone in our bed at home. I wondered if she was asleep at that moment, gathering her strength for whatever lay ahead. I hoped so.

*

Throughout that weekend, all the doctors who assessed Molly expressed the same opinion: that in all likelihood she would be capable of recovering, returning home, though I suspected they weren't as familiar with her condition as they might have been; doubts which were confirmed late Monday morning when Dr Davidson, our now familiar paediatrician, called in and sounded a more sceptical note. Sensitively but frankly she made it clear that recovery from such a serious physical trauma, even for an otherwise healthy person, would be a long and complicated process. And looking at Molly that day, a washed-out likeness of the bright-eyed girl she'd first examined just a week before, I had to acknowledge what she was saying, even if I wasn't quite ready to accept it. I tried to remain stoic on the surface, for my own sake as much as for Ali's. But even so, that discussion felt like a defining point. It left Ali and I expecting the worst at any time: a bleak juncture to have arrived at.

As the doctor was leaving, my mobile buzzed in my pocket: my sister, Maria, and I could hardly speak to her as I fought to keep my composure. I said I'd call her back. Then Ali and I lay down on Molly's cot, one either side of her, quite literally surrounding her with our love and protection, as if we expected to lose her there and then. I nuzzled into her hair to breathe her in for what I thought could be the last time, and we stayed like that in silence for a while, until our fragile peace was shattered by a support worker crashing into the room to change the bins with no regard at all for where he was. I was shocked. I wanted to yell at him to be quiet, to show some respect. But to be fair, as soon as he absorbed the scene on the bed, he seemed to understand and completed his tasks as quietly as he could.

Is this the end? It felt like the end, but it wasn't of course. A doctor had expressed caution, that's all. Molly wasn't going to die on cue. A few minutes went by, the intensity eased and the mundanities of life began to reassert themselves. I needed a pee, then a sandwich or something. Life didn't stop.

*

237

In fact life, with all its dark comedy, continued as it always had. Minutes later, in the parents' kitchen, trying to perk myself up with a coffee, I found myself sat opposite another dad (I presumed) who I could tell was itching to strike up a conversation. He kept shifting around in his seat trying to catch my eye. And though I sharpened my body language to an extreme of leave-me-alone, he was like that cab driver the day we got the news, blind to even the most hyperbolic stay-away signals, and eventually he had to break the silence.

'Kids!' he declared, rolling his eyes. 'What's yours in for?'

I didn't answer. I didn't even look up.

'Mine's broken his leg,' he went on. 'Fell off a swing.'

So I nodded. Then lifted my head to look at him, giving him a good long opportunity to register my tear-reddened eyes, my sleep-deprived face, my it's-nothing-personal-mate-but-please-piss-off demeanour. And still he sat there looking at me like a Labrador waiting for a stick.

'And you?' he asked again.

Please go away.

'My daughter's not well.'

'Oh, I'm sorry to hear that,' he said, still full of good cheer. And hoping that might be that, I sank down in my chair, trying to make myself look even more depressed and unamenable to conversation than I was. But no –

'What's the trouble with her?' he piped up.

So, unable to see a way out and much too tired to find one, in two or three short sentences I gave him the bare facts: SMA; terminal; coming to the end now; and assumed by any ordinary standards of interaction that would be enough to restore some quiet to the room.

'That's very sad,' he said then, crestfallen for a moment, and he sat back in his chair looking down at his thumbs.

'Yes,' I said quietly, almost to myself. 'It is.'

And at that I softened just a little. I could see he meant well, even if he couldn't take a hint, and we settled into silence again

238

for fifteen, maybe twenty seconds, until –

'So do you *live* in Brighton?'

It was almost funny. I'd just told him that a few doors down the corridor my only child was fighting a losing battle for her life. Now he wanted what? To talk house prices? Parking? The way the seagulls rip up the refuse bags and make a mess in the streets? Without another word, I got up and walked out.

*

We spent a quiet afternoon after that at Molly's side, with little idea where fate might be taking us next. We'd heard of parents of children with Type 1 SMA who'd been in and out of hospital many times before reaching the end. *This could be our life now, for the foreseeable.* There was no way of knowing. The night shift passed to Ali (Sally came in with a Tupperware box of home-made cottage pie, veg and baked beans to sustain her) and this time I headed home, where Gordon and I split a bottle of wine and I climbed into my own bed for the first time in three days. The last thing I did was prop up a photo of Molly on the bed-side table so I could see her in the night if I woke up. It's still there: in a frame now, but in exactly the spot I put it that night.

*

Early the next morning, Tuesday now, Sally drove me back to the hospital, where Ali relayed that the night had passed peace-fully. Molly had been awake more than the previous night but not distressed. In fact, confidence was boosted sufficiently for the doctors to try her without the oxygen feed for the first time just after I arrived (Ali had wanted to wait for me). But it was-n't successful. Molly struggled badly. So they reconnected it set to a lower rate and we agreed to try again later if she seemed stronger. After which there was little for Ali or I to do except settle in for the day, a limboland experience now, past the peak of the initial crisis perhaps but a long way short of anything we could term recovery. (And how high could we pitch our hopes anyway?) We took turns at Molly's side; made coffee and tea; tried to read or rest intermittently; and washed our hands. I've never washed my hands so much in my life: the same antiseptic soap and alcohol gel again and again before each physical contact with Molly: a faint chemical smell like vodka on our fingers all the time.

Only once during that morning was the pattern broken, and then in the most unexpected way. A nurse came in to ask us if we'd like a visit from a gang of bikers who were riding along the south coast between children's hospitals giving out Christmas presents. What could we say? With the same weary, amused fatalism we exchanged looks and shrugged, 'Why not?'

And so it came to pass that a few minutes later our intimate family vigil was extended to incorporate one of the rarer sights of my forty years: a half dozen to a dozen hairy middle-aged men, dressed from head to toe in leather, standing around the foot of Molly's cot singing Christmas carols. Which in its own faintly ridiculous way was kind of glorious, as if all the good in the world had taken the reins again for those few minutes. And what a sight for Molly to behold too. I watched her give them all the once over with a look that stated, as plain as day: 'Tired I might be, but I like this. This is all right.'

Otherwise, that third morning was punctuated only by the comings and goings of staff, still trying to work out what to do: a process in which I tried to play an active part (or at least refused to be passive); and they were receptive to that: every turn in tactics and let's-see-how-she-goes was debated, agreed in advance. And I always double-checked the notes the doctors and nurses made on the paperwork in the corner of the room.

By then the list of drugs being used was growing steadily –

Mini-Morph: the cute name they give to morphine in a children's hospital (a weaker version presumably).

Amoxicillin: an antibiotic to combat any infection in Molly's lungs caused by the aspiration.

Claritidine: to inhibit the natural secretions in her throat and mouth so they wouldn't contribute to breathing difficulties.

Domperidone: to speed up the process of digestion to make Molly's milk less likely to come back up.

Ibuprofen (definitely) and Codeine (possibly) at intervals to deal with discomfort and to lower Molly's temperature.

And finally Calpol: to ease the pain caused by the early stages of teething, as if Molly needed that as well.

I did say that seemed like a lot to be coursing around inside a six-month old. But they told me they'd known far worse, that Molly's treatment, as multiform as it might seem, was still comparatively light.

*

In the background, meanwhile, Sally and Gordon were doing a commendable job treading a difficult line: staying close enough to be supportive but recognising the intimacy of our situation and keeping a respectful distance. They came in with lunch for us that afternoon; and later Ali's Dave turned up unannounced with a wonky bunch of flowers. We were pleased to see him. It helped Ali to have a change of company. But we decided to hold back on anyone else making the trip (I knew Sam wanted to bring the children; Maria wanted to bring Mum). Aware that these might be our last days with Molly, our last hours even, I made it clear that until we were sure Molly was coming home, vital and immediate support would be our limit. Whatever time we had left: Molly, Ali and me, needed to belong to us.

Still, by mid-afternoon, with Molly seeming much better again (full of chatter) and Dave keeping Ali company, it felt safe to get out with Gordon for two fast pints down the hill at The Barley Mow. It was his suggestion and I half wondered whether he was going to sound me out about allowing more visitors. I even began to explain my view in anticipation, but didn't get far. 'Hey,' he said, palm to me, 'Understood.' His brothers had been set to travel from Yorkshire with their wives that coming weekend but he'd already let them know to make other plans.

*

The shift came back to me that night: my turn to be eating the homemade food from the Tupperware box with everyone sat around me for company, until it was just Molly and me again.

She settled easily, as she had the first time. So I sat with her until she was sleeping deeply then stretched out on the parent's bed to reply to some well-wishing texts. It wasn't long though before I was slipping in and out of consciousness, the tiredness reeling me in; though I never quite surrendered my awareness of Molly's breathing. Nor, as I came to realise, my sense of the meaning of each of the various bleeps and alarms coming periodically from the hospital equipment: which ones I could safely ignore and which should have me leaping to my feet.

The one I knew to concentrate on, and always stay partially alert for, was the device used to monitor the oxygen circulation in Molly's blood. (Late that afternoon they had tried her again without the oxygen feed and this time she had held her ground. If she could continue to breathe without help, we'd know she was rallying significantly and really might have a chance of coming home.) I knew, because I'd asked one of the nurses to explain it to me, that the numerical read-out on that monitor had to stay above 91. For as long as it did it meant Molly was managing on her own, getting all the oxygen she needed. Anything under and an alarm would sound, as it did somewhere between once and six times an hour all night, causing me to spring off the bed each time to stare alternately at Molly and the monitor, trying to decide if it was time to call for help. But without fail, every time, the read-out stayed under 91 for just a few seconds, ten at most, before Molly found reserves from somewhere and the numbers climbed back over the threshold again. It was as if

242

she was playing with me, reassuring herself, even in her sleep, that her dad was close by.

The only other important alarm, needlessly loud beside Molly I thought, sounded each time the milk bottle attached to the pump ran dry (every three hours or so), at which point a nurse would come in to replace it.

*

As dawn broke and Molly stirred, I raised the blinds so she and I could look at the sky. Then I lay alongside her singing songs, scouring my memory for anything I knew right through, which from an overtired brain came down to I Will by The Beatles and I Thought About You by Frank Sinatra. When we tired of those, I pulled the cord on her man-in-the-moon toy and sang along to that too with the nonsense lyrics that had slowly come to be over the months:

This is the story of Molly-housy-house,
Cheeee – ky – like a churchy mouse.
And if she went to Scotland –
she'd shoot a grousy-grouse, cos
this is the story of Molly-housy-house.

Meaningless and loaded with meaning, I must have sung it a couple of dozen times, the two of us quite content looking into each other's eyes, until the sun had risen further in the sky and the first nurse of the day came in to ask me about Molly's milk. As she only needed to be connected to the pump for twenty of every twenty-four hours, I could decide when to give her a rest. So I elected to keep going, reasoning it would be better to save the gap for when Ali arrived so she could hold her more easily, maybe take her for a walk.

It proved to be the wrong decision.

I was alone with Molly when her milk came up, just as I had

been at the weekend. But this time there was no warning at all. No crying or grouchiness or apparent discomfort. One minute she was fine, then abruptly discontented and everything came up and out. With her being fed so slowly now, I hadn't realised there was even a risk of another aspiration.

I kept my head though this time. I knew there were doctors and nurses just a few feet away. I pressed the call button, eased Molly onto her front and patted her back gently (like Graham had the night we came in), and seconds later a nurse appeared at my side to turn off the pump and make sure Molly was in no immediate danger. Then, briskly and without fuss, she and I changed the bedding. And by the time we were finished, Molly was smiling and chattering away as if nothing had happened. She'd had an ordinary baby occurrence and shaken it off. I felt myself glow inside with relief, pride, even an odd kind of hope.

When it was just the two of us again, I looked around at the room and saw that for the first time since arriving at the hospital over three days before, Molly wasn't connected to anything. No oxygen. No drip. No milk. No monitors of any kind. She'd made it through the night on her own, and I was overwhelmed suddenly by the enormity of that and smothered her with kisses, a few tears and another spluttered song or two to celebrate. *It's so amazing to have you here.*

Then tentatively I gathered her up into my arms (I knew Ali was due any moment: she'd texted from the car), carried her to the door and out into the corridor, over a threshold she hadn't crossed since Saturday evening and it was Wednesday morning now. The nurse at the monitoring station looked up.

'Is it okay to take her out for a bit?' I whispered.

'Of course,' she smiled.

And so, very carefully, as carefully as I'd ever done anything with Molly, I carried her along the corridor towards the main door, through which, by a wonderful coincidence, I could see and hear Ali pressing the entry buzzer. She looked up, saw me and smiled; then after a moment's delay, registered that I had

Molly in my arms and the change in her expression was a picture to behold. I pressed the door release to let her in.

'Hello,' was all she could manage, as she wrapped her arms around the two of us.

'We decided to form a welcoming committee,' I told her.

'Wow,' she said, with welling eyes. 'Hello Molly.'

And for the first time in many months I saw my wife's face radiate happiness as we cuddled ourselves close around Molly (with doctors and nurses, patients and visitors, coming and going around us) like a solitary still at the centre of a time-lapse film. What a delicate paradise our parenthood was, but with the capacity to thrill still. Crushed between us, Molly was all smiles, all here-and-now. Yet again she was the one taking care of us, pointing out into the unknown, letting us know that all we had to do now was be strong and push on.

*

That was roughly 9am. By afternoon, Molly was holding court. When Dr Davidson called in after lunch she could scarcely believe she was looking at the same child. Our discussion just two days before had been all about medication, end-of-life wishes, the when and where and how. Now, for the first time, we talked about taking Molly home, agreeing that we'd make a definitive decision between us later that day.

In the meantime the admin was set in motion. Oxygen was ordered for delivery to the house; another consignment of Infatrini was sent for (this time in puncture bags to be used with the pump); the community nurses were warned that Ali and I would be needing instruction in the new feeding system (a session was booked for the next day) and more regular back-up at home from now on. There was an air of action about us again, some roll-our-sleeves-up. Breast feeding. Bottle feeding. Bolus feeding. Now pump feeding. Though Ali and I knew we'd arrived at the last remaining option we felt positive, confident we

245

could deal with it, the practical side at least. From a workload point of view, it might even be easier. And psychologically, the slow-release method of pump feeding would mean less danger of Molly aspirating again. At least these were the things we told ourselves. We even started to wonder what Christmas might be like. Unlike any other, that was for sure.

Then with all that going around in my head, and Ali out of the room for a moment, the cleaner reappeared: the one who'd annoyed me so much by being so noisy and insensitive on his previous visit. This time, however, he took every care to work as quietly as he could. And when he paused to look at Molly I could see the kindness in his eyes.

'How is your baby?' he asked, in what I took to be a strong Polish accent.

'Much better today, thank you.' I told him. 'We're hoping to take her home tomorrow.'

'Ahh, that is good,' he said. And for a few seconds more he stood there leaning on his mop, regarding Molly tenderly, before getting on. After which I always thought of him as a rough kind of angel sent down to keep watch over us.

Part Paddy, Part Viking

Difficult days

But do we ever really know what is coming?

And where there are angels, there are –

Black dogs.

Mid afternoon, with our outlook appearing so much brighter, Gordon drove me back to the house, where a huge delivery from the NHS was waiting: boxes stacked as high as me in the hall. And shortly after, I bumped into a neighbour who told me there were more nextdoor, including dozens of bolus kits we'd never need now.

For an hour I pottered around the house, then declined the

offer of a lift back to the hospital, thinking I'd walk instead, get some air. It felt like days since I'd breathed freely. So I strolled up through Hanover to Queen's Park from where, over to the south-west, I caught a spectacular view of the last of the day's sunlight colouring the clouds over the sea. It was so striking, a Turner painting come to life, I paused a few minutes there on a bench. It was cold now, almost dark, but still and peaceful.

I didn't see the dog at first.

At least not one in particular; there were several of them off their leads, running around together while their owners talked. But I noticed very clearly when, about thirty yards in front of me, a young and wild-looking Alsatian, came to a stop suddenly and stared right at me through the fading light. For four or five seconds it froze in that pose, trying to discern what I was, to distinguish my shape from the surrounding shadows. And whatever it decided I was, it didn't like. It began to bark, then to growl. Then with no further warning it launched itself into a full-pelt sprint straight for me. It must have covered the distance in three to four seconds – it was beyond surreal. I had no chance to do anything more than shout out as aggressively as I could and prepare an outstretched boot to try to connect with its head before its teeth connected with me.

Only at the very last second, when the dog got close enough to see me clearly and appreciate my size (I was sitting and must have looked smaller from a distance) did it veer off to stand its ground a few yards back, baring its teeth menacingly. The owner, having heard me, called it away then, and shouted over an apology, something about the dog being young and untrained, then wisely perhaps took his leave before I'd had time to collect myself.

It was nothing really, the incident. It happened so fast – too fast to seem real. But it shook me. And as soon as I was alone my blood began to boil. *How dare he let a dog like that run loose. What if it had run down a child instead of a grown man like me?* And from there, in a nonsensical chain of causation, *What if that child*

248

had been Molly? It was the warped reasoning of a downtrodden man picking a fight in a pub, *somebody's going to pay*, and marching on towards the hospital I couldn't calm down. In my mind I played out an absurd, hideous montage of violence: a fantasy of fighting first the dog, killing it to save my child, then turning my anger on the owner. It was horrible: my reaction to the incident more than the incident itself, as well as being the darkest of omens to contemplate as the familiar and distinctive Noah's Ark shape of the Alex came into view.

Minutes later I was inside: the eighth floor again: the High Dependency Unit, where I realised with ambivalence I felt safe. Within that ark, good people were taking care of my daughter, my wife and me. On the outer walls, window cleaners worked dressed as superheroes so the children could see Spiderman go past from their beds. As traumatic as our time at the Alex had been, it had still been a haven for us. Now the time had almost come to leave, I was afraid.

*

Towards teatime, Gordon and Sally drove over to join us. Not with food this time, as things seemed to be improving so much with Molly. This time they offered to babysit for an hour so Ali and I could pop out for a bite instead. After the relentless pressure of the hospital we were glad of the opportunity and made the short walk down to one of the pubs in Kemp Town, where we had two quick drinks but didn't eat as nothing on the menu appealed. Instead we stopped at a kebab shop on the way back, perched on flimsy plastic chairs beside an overflowing bin and ate messy food like kids coming home from a club.

Though we were gone less than an hour we were anxious to get back, but all was well. We found Gordon and Sally sat either side of a very talkative Molly, who plainly felt she had a lot to say for herself after all she'd been through. She'd been charming the socks off her grandad (I could see that) who was sat

249

there looking and sounding as exhausted as the rest of us, but enamoured beyond words.

And before long it was time to part again. With a fifth night beckoning, the shift passed back to Ali. There was every hope that the following day we'd bring Molly home. So the rest of us went back to prepare.

*

I had hoped to walk again to the hospital in the morning, just to stretch my legs (and avoiding dogs this time), but the early morning call from Ali wasn't positive. She was anxious, fretful again, far from the relative calm of the night before. So I called down to Sally that I would like a lift after all, dressed as quickly as I could, and she dropped me at the back of the Alex with a promise to return in an hour with some breakfast.

When I reached the room I could see right away that Molly was in trouble again. Slipping from the path of slow recovery she'd seemed set upon, she was pale again and thoroughly out of sorts. Ordinarily when I entered a room, even the most disconsolate, grumpy Molly would be diverted temporarily, but this time she hardly noticed me. Her chest looked constrained, immobile, her breathing unbelievably arduous now, all from low in the torso. It was impossible to imagine anyone, and certainly not a small child, sustaining that degree of labour for long.

Concerned, I went looking for familiar faces in the corridor, yet that morning there were none to be found. I was unnerved by the predominance of light blue nursing uniforms (and even then only two or three) which signified less experience and seniority than dark blue.

Where the hell is everybody?

I knew, and Ali obviously knew, this was exactly how Molly had been just prior to her trauma on the night we came in. And like that night, we took turns trying to soothe her; and also like that night the situation worsened abruptly. Suddenly Molly was fighting to breathe at all. It looked like her fragile frame might give up there and then.

I hit the call button for a nurse. Then recognising immediately that we might only have seconds, I ran to the corridor again to get help, and for the first and only time that week found it deserted. The only member of staff I could find anywhere was a junior, a light blue, sorting bedding in an adjacent room. So I pulled her in to look at Molly, who by now was plainly in life-threatening distress. The young nurse looked fearful –

'Shall we turn up her oxygen?'

She was asking *me*.

'Where is everyone?' I barked at her.

'They're in a meeting,' she spluttered.

'Then get them – go.'

And she set off at a pace up the corridor.

On the monitor, the 91 monitor, the numbers started to fall. The alarm sounded: the one I recognised so well from my second night there with Molly. On that occasion the numbers had wavered up and down constantly, but now they were tumbling: down through the eighties, seventies, sixties. Ali was staring up at me, imploring me silently to do something. But what?

Aegyptopithecus.

From my vantage point I could see along the corridor to the doorway of the room where the senior nurses must have been meeting, because from it suddenly a wave of dark blue emerged and came rushing our way, stopping only just short of running. And still the numbers kept falling: through the fifties, forties, down and down.

Kenyapithecus.

The room flooded with staff. Doctors and nurses surrounded Molly. I could no longer see her. I stepped to the bottom of the bed to give them room. Across to my right, I could still see Ali, still see the monitor: the thirties, twenties, and on towards the single digits now.

251

Australopithicus.

Above the piercing noise of the alarm and the sound of the staff exchanging instructions I heard Molly's bowel empty and something inside me died for the love of her, with the agony of being so powerless. In that moment I'd have gone with her, or for her, in the blink of an eye if I'd known it would see her safely on her way. I could only pray that her innocence and ignorance would be enough to keep her from being afraid.

Then the display hit zero. The alarm sound changed, just as it does in the dramas, to one continuous note –

Was it over? Had she gone? *Molly May.*

All I can remember thinking coherently was: *Not here. Not in this clinical place with all these screaming alarms being the last thing she hears. Not here.* And somewhere my desperate plea was heard.

Nicky, the senior nurse, placed a hand-operated pump over Molly's mouth and nose to assist her. I was aware of the sound of Ali sobbing, her eyes begging for the impossible. And that's when the continuous note from the monitor separated again to individual bleeps, the numbers began to climb back from nothing to something, and there on the bed below us Molly's chest started to rise and fall again. Irish blood on my side, Yorkshire heart on Ali's: part-Paddy-part-Viking. Against impossible odds she was making a last stand. She hadn't quite done with us yet.

Star Treatment

If I could only have one photo

Having survived – I can't say recovered this time – again Molly was given an oxygen feed running up into her nose. She fought it less this time. She was much weaker now. Other than that, all the equipment was switched off and disconnected. The nurses and doctors filtered out. Only the pump they'd used to bring Molly back to life remained on the table by the bed as a temporal reminder of what might otherwise have been a dream.

Coming to, it occurred to me then that Sally would be arriving at any moment with breakfast, so I sent a text: 'Things coming to an end here. Please hold back until you hear from me.'

Then rather than trying to settle Molly back into bed, which seemed pointless now, we lay her on a pillow across Ali's lap in the chair, and in an echo of the early hours of the Sunday just passed, I watched as Ali stroked her hair and sang softly to her. Every once in a while we swapped over and I did the same.

Without being told, I knew that what we'd done in our panic, call for invasive intervention, was beyond what we'd agreed. To come to Molly's aid in the thick of the crisis had been the only plausible decision, if you can call it a decision. But moving forward, Ali and I acknowledged that firmer lines were going to have to be drawn. Nicky and I talked it over soon after, sat side by side on the parent's bed –

'You know we can't really take that path again, don't you?'

'Yes,' I said to her. 'I know.'

Molly meanwhile, heavily sedated by now, was drifting restlessly in and out of consciousness, while still showing moments of remarkable lucidity. Every few minutes she opened her eyes wide (like she was waking from a dream) as if to confirm that we were still there, before drifting off again. With all the equipment turned off now, the only sounds in the room came from the high-pitched rush of the oxygen feed and the push and pull of Molly's lungs labouring for breath. Which made everything that much more visceral and human somehow: the end of life approaching with scant regard for all our kit and caboodle.

After a time a nurse came in to tell us that Gordon and Sally had arrived and been shown through to a quiet room. So I said it was fine to have them come through, which they did, staying a few minutes only before withdrawing again to let us be. And eventually it was time, under the hardest of circumstances now, for Ali and I to prepare for our sixth night there: the two of us again like the first night; though unlike the first night neither of us slept more than a fitful drop of the head here and there. We kept watch constantly, though our efforts could do little more now than provide company for Molly, who battled on, clammy to the touch, her stomach muscles overcompensating to drag air into her body. It looked far too taxing to maintain: I could only guess at how tired she must be, and hope the Mini-Morph would be easing any discomfort.

*

By morning we knew a decision had to be made urgently about where we wanted to be with Molly when she died. So I began by confirming with the hospital that we were welcome to stay put should we want to (we were, of course). And for the first hours of that Friday morning that's what I imagined we would do. I didn't want to take Molly home, though that was clearly an option. Though I knew we'd have all the support we'd need, I had all manner of worries about returning there. Short term: like whether the phone would ring constantly (or less rationally whether someone on our street might unknowingly be having a party). And long term too: like whether Ali would come to hate our home if we lost Molly there. But in the end it was Ali who had the presence of mind to decide what to do, and right away I knew she was right.

'I think a hospital is for making people better,' she said, 'and Molly isn't going to get better. So maybe we should take her to Chestnut Tree House.'

The idea hadn't even crossed my mind but the moment Ali suggested it I knew it was what I wanted to do. My only doubt was whether we could we get Molly there safely. So for a while more we procrastinated, until something happened to convince us the time was right to go: the one incident, in the otherwise exemplary care we received throughout Molly's life, that I still have trouble stomaching. One of the doctors (not a favourite of mine) came in and asked me, in hushed faux-sensitive tones, whether I'd mind answering a few questions to help him complete the coroner's report. *The coroner's report.*

There I was, with my wife next to me cradling our soon-to-be-lost first-born, and this man wanted me to help him round up his paperwork. It's a scene I've re-enacted in my mind many times, and often what I think I ought to have done was tell him quite plainly to fuck off out of the room and show some respect. But at the time the preservation of peace and dignity there struck me as more important (which, of course, it was). I gave him his answers quickly and quietly, and he left with Ali's eyes burning a hole through his back. 'Was that *really* necessary?' she asked, incredulous.

∗

By the time Dr Davidson looked in mid-morning to see how we were, the sun was blazing into the room. Jill was there too. So I tried to glean from them some idea of how long they thought Molly might have. Though I realised it wasn't an exact science, and they said as much, I got my answer indirectly when at one point Dr Davidson and I went to complete the same sentence.

I said: 'After all, this could go on for – '
And as I said: 'Two or three days,' –
she said: 'Twenty-four hours.'

And with that we had our focus. I went to the kitchen to get a coffee for some energy and by the time I got back, Ali's mind was made up.

'She keeps pointing to the window,' she said, looking down at Molly. 'She wants to get out of here, somewhere nicer.' And so, with Molly's finger pointing out into the sunlight, a celestial signpost for us, we decided to go for it.

∗

Chestnut Tree House is about forty-five minutes by car from the Alex: a journey that, initially at least, the hospital suggested we could make on our own. Not satisfied, however, that Molly would be able to cope in a car, and not wanting the responsibility of travelling without support when there was a real chance she could die on the way, I insisted on an ambulance and arrangements were made.

'I've spoken to Chestnut Tree House,' Jill told us. 'They said they'd be happy to have you.'

It was comforting to feel their welcome reaching out to us.

I packed up our things quickly: Molly's toys, our rucksacks, some leftover snacks and drinks. We didn't amount to much as we made to leave what had been our home for almost a week: in a couple of minutes the room was as bare and clinical as we had found it. Then I loaded up Gordon and Sally with as much as they could carry and asked them to go ahead to the car while I made one last check around.

Nicky came in to wish us well and give us both a hug.

'You've done brilliantly,' she said to us, 'I've never seen two parents more devoted to a child than you two this week.' And by then I knew she'd lost a child of her own, not so long ago, so she really understood.

Minutes later the ambulance crew arrived and helped Ali up onto the trolley with Molly in her arms. I told her I'd pop back to the house to grab us a change of clothes, collect the car and follow. Then I put my hand to her cheek, kissed her, and leaned across to touch my lips to Molly's forehead.

'I'll see you in less than an hour,' I said.

And I watched, surprisingly calm, as they were taken away, my only hope that nothing would happen on the way.

*

Downstairs, in dazzling sunshine, I climbed into the back seat of Gordon and Sally's car with the last of our things.

'Are you all right, Matt?' Sally turned to me.

'Yeh,' I said.

But none of us was all right, not really. We sat in silence until they dropped me off at the end of our road.

'Don't rush,' I said to Gordon as I got out.

Don't speed.

'Just get there safely.'

'We will,' he said. 'Don't worry.'

And I strode up to the house, running into Graham as I did, giving him a potted version of events since we'd last seen him almost a week before. Once inside I stuffed things into a holdall: clothes for Ali and me, toothbrushes, toiletries: enough for three days: as good a guess as any. Graham knocked to see if I needed a lift anywhere. And as I reversed down the road, Ruth, from next door the other side, waved me down to tell me more supplies had been delivered: pumps, syringes, milk in puncture bags. All I could say was the same as I'd texted to Sally the day before: 'Things are coming to an end now.' And I pushed on, taking the now familiar A27, driving neither fast nor slow, just moving as the traffic allowed. And though I did wonder, each time I slowed or quickened, whether *this* delay or *that* piece of luck might make the difference, it didn't honestly trouble me. I knew that whatever influence I'd been able to exert over our lives for the past six months had come to an end now, and I let myself be at peace with that.

*

When I got to Chestnut Tree House, I parked and checked in at reception where I was asked to wait for a member of staff to collect me. I rubbed some antiseptic gel on my hands from the dispenser and when the nurse came out, as soon as I saw her face, I knew Molly had gone. As we set off along the corridor together she tried to break the news to me.

'Now you do know,' she began, 'that Molly was very unwell when she set out to come here, don't you?'

'I know,' I said.

258

'And you knew there was a chance –'

I interrupted her as gently as I could:

'Has she passed away?'

'Yes,' she said.

'Did she die here?'

'She did. A few minutes after she arrived. I'm so sorry.'

'It's all right,' I said, reaching out instinctively to touch her wrist, to comfort her through comforting me. 'I'm just glad she got here.'

Ahead of us, as we turned from one corridor into the next, I saw Sally, her eyes full of compassion; then a few feet further on, Gordon, looking much as I imagine I looked myself: shell-shocked, worn out. He gestured towards one of the bedrooms.

'Alison's waiting for you through there.'

Inside the room (I was pleased they'd given Molly the same one she'd stayed in before: an ordinary, fun-looking kids' room full of toys and books and lively colours) Ali was sat serenely in an armchair holding Molly, who was still warm to the touch, still as beautiful as can be. I had seen death up close only once before: my dad. And among my feelings that night, I remember being surprised at how soon, with the animating life-force gone from his body, he no longer looked like himself. Molly though, her younger features taut, was still very much herself. Her hand curled around my finger, as it always had, like a gesture of con-solation. And for the last time I touched the tip of my nose ag-ainst her lips: our Daddy-and-Molly kiss. I could feel tears run-ning down off my cheeks, but there was no anguish or ringing of hands now. Ali and I cried quietly, solemnly. We were neith-er hysterical nor inconsolable; just humbled and overcome by the very frail beauty of life.

Coming to myself then, I asked her how things had passed. She said Molly had been at ease from the moment the ambul-ance left the hospital (perking up for the thrill of being jolted around one last time). At Chestnut Tree House they'd transfer-red her to the bedroom they'd prepared and got her tucked in, at which point she'd taken a good long look at her surroundings: people and place, before drifting off to sleep. Then sensing that Ali would be fit to drop, one of the nurses had asked for a bowl of soup and a buttered roll to be brought for her, which Ali ate at a table in the corner while Gordon and Sally sat with Molly, everyone chatting and unwinding after the tension of the hospital and the journey, lifted by the feeling of loving care permeating the air. And Molly, I'm sure, picked up on that and chose her moment. When the nurse went to check on her again, she said simply, 'Oh, I think she's gone.'

And so she had, in her sleep, at Chestnut Tree House, with her grandad holding her hand, her gran stroking her hair, and her mum a few feet away. Of all the endings I'd feared, all the dread scenarios that might have been, that sweet and gentle release, for us as much as for Molly, struck me as so wonderfully kind. In the end the difference between life and death had been infinitesimal, the crossing peaceful, barely anything of significance at all.

*

We stayed there like that for a while, then Ali got me to ask for the external doors of the room to be opened onto the grounds (they were alarmed so the staff had to help us). After which we set Molly down softly on the bed and stepped outside, the eponymous chestnut trees swaying in the breeze above us.

Hand in hand we walked across the gardens, gravitating towards a fountain they keep there bearing the names (on individual pebbles) of each of the children who've died at the house. I counted eighty-ish, whispering their names aloud to myself as I went, wondering where their parents might be now and what stories they'd have to tell. For now at least, Ali and I were at peace, satisfied that we'd done all we could do and things hadn't ended badly: it really was as straightforward as that. We remarked upon the beauty of our surroundings. We spoke about nature and the passage of the seasons. We shared thoughts and feelings about God, the afterlife, and what form such a thing might take. Above all we exchanged a wish that if there is such a thing as a spirit after we pass, that Molly's would be free now to roam unencumbered by the limitations of her body. Then abruptly we realised we were freezing cold, shivering, our teeth beginning to chatter. Completely run down, we'd come outside without our coats; and it was mid-December now after all, two weeks to the day until Christmas.

They let us back in through the fire doors to the main living area, where we saw Gordon, Sally and several members of staff stood in an odd-looking congregation by the fireplace, looking down at something in the grate: a tiny bird, I saw when I got closer, hopping from log to log, fluttering its wings: barely real, like something from Walt Disney. It must have come down the chimney: an unlikely accident of chance and timing. But for Ali and me to see something like that moments after talking about spirits being set free was quite something, more than poignant, regardless of how you choose to see such things.

I don't recall what happened next. I must have walked away, I was so tired. But later they told me the chef had caught the bird in a towel and released it into the air outside.

*

Could there be anything to laugh about on a day like that? You might think not. But then you weren't there a few minutes later when Gordon set off the alarm in the toilet by pulling the help cord instead of the light switch.

*

Chestnut Tree House worked its magic in other ways after that. Firstly, by the staff assuring us that Molly would be welcome to stay in their care until the funeral, which was a huge comfort to us. Instead of being somewhere meaningless and impersonal, she'd be with people who'd known her in life and taken pleasure in her company. (They explained that the temperature of the room would be brought down, and a silver star placed on the door as an indicator to staff.) And secondly, they invited us to stay the night if we wanted to, to be close to Molly. Not just Ali and me, but Gordon and Sally too. We were fortunate they happened to have rooms free, but at the time it felt like such a kindness, so sensitive to our feelings. And so, of course, we all decided to stay.

I went back outside then to text the news to my family and friends (most of whom were expecting word at any time) and was deeply moved by the spontaneous and heartfelt replies that began to arrive back right away. Then Ali and I went up to bed to rest. I think Gordon did the same, while Sally drove back to Brighton to collect their overnight things.

*

That night the four of us went out for dinner at the local pub: the one Ali and I had visited twice the last time we were there. And in our own kind of way, we enjoyed ourselves. There was an air of nervous exhaustion pervasive between us that made for easy laughter, for anecdotes and fond recollections of Molly: an atmosphere I recalled from the night we lost Dad. Then too, laughter had come as readily as tears.

Certainly it would have taken a perceptive eye to register the strain on our faces from across the room. Sally: normally composed, uncharacteristically scatty. Gordon: usually at the heart of conversation, quietened by the intimate role fate had given him at Molly's passing. And Ali and me? God knows what our faces told of the hurt we'd endured and would go on enduring further into the future than we knew that night.

Later, when everyone was in bed, she and I went out again for some air, and bumped, literally, into the house doctor as we bleeped ourselves back in through the night door.

'You must be Alison and Matthew,' he said. 'I'm so sorry to hear your news.'

And I felt ashamed momentarily, wondering what he must think of us tumbling in through the door like that, giggling and playful, still tipsy from the pub (though I'm sure he'd seen it all before).

'Thank you,' we both managed, pausing just long enough to be polite, forcing the gravitas a little. For us it was too soon for condolences. All we wanted was to unwind, to have liberty to stand down at the end of our long day and before a week that we knew would place fresh demands upon us.

In the morning, Ali and I returned to Molly's room to pass a few minutes with her. It was colder there now: the aircon had been left on through the night. She looked paler, a fraction less like herself. There were no tears this time. We both gave her a kiss on the forehead and left quietly.

Then finally we sat in the quiet room with the doctor we'd met briefly the night before, Dr Cairns, who talked us through the same paperwork I'd already signed in Brighton (we were in West Sussex now so it had to be completed again). After which there was nothing to stay for, nothing more to be done, except walk out to the cars and drive home.

Four Days

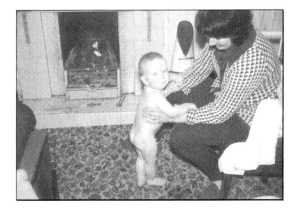

Me, about Molly's age

Back in our road in Brighton, Gordon and Sally waited in their car to give Ali and me a chance to come into the house alone: a thoughtful gesture, an awareness of a moment that might have been difficult for us, yet wasn't particularly. At that juncture I don't think we cared much whether we were alone or not. On balance I think we preferred the company, so it wasn't long before I was back on the doorstep gesturing for them to come in.

I built us a fire then, high and hot with both coal and logs, and we spent the rest of the afternoon and evening gazing at it, watching the flames dance, listening to the crackling wood: the oldest comforts of all: companionship and fire. We were warm, we had wine, we could rest, and that felt like plenty.

264

*

By Sunday, however, with Gordon and Sally on their way back to Devon, I could feel the strain taking hold again: the end of the short period of release: the beginning of the last round of responsibility. Ali and I had to make a conscious agreement to give ourselves one last day of peace, to not even think about Monday and plans for the funeral until we had to.

Instead I asked Dave to drive down to keep us company: a comfort for me, and good for Ali too, his easy affability catching just the right tone. I cooked a lazy meal of whatever I could find in the freezer. We watched the final of X-Factor. The only punctuation came when Dr Davidson phoned to offer her condolences and ask us if we had any unresolved questions about Molly's treatment. But I had none I could think of. I remember feeling faintly embarrassed that the X-Factor music was audible in the background. That, and the fact that I thanked her for all her help and support.

'You did a good job,' I told her.

A strange choice of words, probably, from a misfiring brain: she was slightly unsure how to take it I think. But I meant what I said sincerely. In my clumsy way I was trying to remind her of something she plainly already knew: that for the parents of a terminally ill child (or the family of any terminally ill person) it isn't just the *what* that matters but the *how*. Courtesy, respect, tenderness: those memories, the good and bad, run deep.

*

When the alarm went off in the morning, we'd both been lying awake so long already it seemed laughable. Yet despite the signal to rise, neither of us moved. What confronted us, arranging a funeral for our child a week before Christmas, was so far beyond our experience, so intimidating, the effort of will it took just to swing our legs around onto the floor felt monumental. I wanted to hide, curl up into a ball until it was over. As it was, we cuddled together for courage for another half hour before Ali had the presence finally to get to her feet.

Downstairs we ate breakfast because we knew we ought to. I made a pot of coffee. Then we took the only thing we had to work with and started there. The staff at Chestnut Tree House had suggested a Funeral Director in Worthing: people they'd worked with before and trusted, which was something at least: a personal recommendation. Ali phoned them and arranged a time for us to call in that afternoon. Then (it was all Ali at first) she found our two local crematoria on the internet: Woodvale and Downs, and made appointments for us to view their various chapels – religious and secular. If we came now, the man at Woodvale advised her, there was a gap between services. And so five minutes later we were in the car.

Neither of us was too sure how to go about viewing chapels (there hadn't been much call for it in our lives). So we each did the things that occurred to us. We guesstimated the number of friends and family who would want to come and counted seats to match. I went to stand at the front to gauge how it would be to speak from there, while Ali pressed the buttons that opened and closed the curtains, worried that they'd make an ugly noise. Was there a suitable place to project photos? Was one chapel any less sombre than the other? And how had the lives of two hitherto lucky people come to this anyway?

To have observed Ali and I that morning would have been to see next to nothing of what was going on inside. In our nervous state we joked constantly. There was even a hint of slapstick about us as we bluffed our way through those early hours. We'd arrived suddenly in a land of long faces, of solemnity for hire in units of half an hour to an hour, and it was a lot, as exhausted and uncertain of ourselves as we were, to take in. We were the same people we'd always been: not keen on stuffiness, inclined to laugh in stony faces –

Something we very narrowly avoided doing later that day at

the Funeral Director's office in Worthing. We'd been left alone for two minutes while they made us a cup of tea. Long enough to take in our surroundings, and to note that absolutely everything about the place was sombre: the wallpaper, the furniture, what the staff wore, their hairstyles, the way they talked, the oil painting of the founder. All of it downbeat and grave, the way it had to be, I suppose. And consequently so difficult for us to relate in any way to the package of fun that was Molly. Instead we found the place funny, and only just managed to compose ourselves, and look appropriately gloomy, when the lady came back with our tea (and sombre biscuits).

In a parallel-universe kind of way, what we were doing was reminiscent of organising a wedding: so many of the tasks were the same: choose a date, estimate guest numbers, compare venues, arrange catering, get the order of service printed, organise transport, someone to conduct the service. With uncanny similarity the list went on. But in place of a timescale of months, we had three to four days and Christmas very nearly upon us. So we had the Funeral Director make two provisional bookings with crematoria for that coming Friday and pushed on.

Our last stop was a visit to Saint Barnabas Hospice nearby, another Chestnut Tree House suggestion, to meet the chaplain there for advice on how a memorial service for a child might be structured: a chat that made us feel better for having some idea, and for realising we could do pretty much as we liked.

*

We were less disoriented by Tuesday morning, both of us engaging with the challenge more intently now that Friday seemed likely to be the day.

Jill came by early to wish us well and take away our surplus medical supplies: so another child could have use of them primarily, but also so the sight of them wouldn't be tough for us. She and I managed to fill her little car twice over: the boot, the passenger seat, the back seats, and all the floor areas front and back. It was striking to see it all stacked up like that.

Then with time pressing, Ali and I set out again, beginning by leaving a note at the priest's house beside the church to see if Father John would be free to conduct the service. And from there to Worthing again: an appointment at the town hall this time to register the death. (Needless to say, a bleak experience. But we coped. We held hands. It didn't take long.) Then back to the Funeral Director, the two of us more focused now, the hysteria gone, as the process was explained to us. They made no charge for their services for a child's funeral, they said, aside from the cost of booking the crematorium. Common practice, apparently. I didn't know.

Otherwise that meeting was memorable mainly for Ali and I being given a brochure of children's coffins and caskets to browse. From the bewildering array on offer, everything from Star Wars to Doctor Who, superheroes to fairy princesses, and all the major football teams, we settled quickly on a simple white casket. Then, knowing Christmas was fast approaching and a booking had to be made, we finalised our venue: Downs Crematorium. And our time: 1.30pm, Friday 18th December – though we still had no-one to conduct the service.

Thankfully that worry was removed soon after we got home when Father John called to confirm his availability. I was relieved and pleased: the man who'd baptised Molly would also be part of her life at the last. He walked up to the house that night to sit with us, to offer what comfort he could, and to reassure us, much as the chaplain at Saint Barnabas had, that the service would be ours to construct as we wished. His only stipulation: that there should be at least one bible reading and one hymn, which is how Ali and I would have had it anyway.

When he got up to leave he took our hands, as he had once before, and prayed aloud for Molly and for Ali and me. Again he'd proved to be a calming presence in our hour of need, as well as a likeable and sensitive man. And as I shut the door behind him I felt better. We both did. We now saw him as one of the small group of people who made the prospect of the funeral bearable. We had our venue, time, date and priest. We slept a little easier that night.

*

Those first two days were a blur. We moved from one appointment to the next, too busy to be distraught, aware that if the service was to be a fitting farewell, collapsing in on ourselves wasn't an option. But we were grateful all the same for a different kind of day on the Wednesday: our day between days, it was the one we'd set aside for constructing the service itself. A soothing task when it came to it: hunting out bible readings, finding hymns and other pieces of music and poetry; whatever came to mind really, for what we were determined would be a simple but beautiful gathering.

Ali set the tone, ordering a selection of yellow flowers, the colour of Molly's bedroom, to brighten up the chapel. Then we chose a piece of music to play while everyone arrived: Brahms' Lullaby, because it played on Molly's projector at night to help her to sleep. We anticipated words of welcome from Father John and a hymn to begin: How Great Thou Art: my favourite from childhood (and sung slowly and softly, as moving as any hymn I know). A reading then, because I didn't want to have to go first, which Ali intended for Tess:

You can shed tears that she is gone,
Or you can smile because she has lived.
You can close your eyes and pray that she will come back,
Or you can open your eyes and see all that she has left.
Your heart can be empty because you can't see her,
Or you can be full of the love that you shared.
You can turn your back on tomorrow and live yesterday,
Or you can be happy for tomorrow because of yesterday.

You can remember her and only that she is gone,
Or you can cherish her memory and let it live on.
You can cry and close your mind, be empty and turn your back,
Or you can do what she would want: smile, open your eyes, love and go on.

My dedication, still to be written, would come next followed by a Gospel reading: Mark 10:13:16:

People were bringing little children to Jesus to have him touch them, but the disciples rebuked them. When Jesus saw this, he was indignant. He said to them, 'Let the little children come to me, and do not hinder them, for the kingdom of God belongs to such as these. I tell you the truth, anyone who will not receive the kingdom of God like a little child will never enter it.' And he took the children in his arms, put his hands on them and blessed them.

After that, bidding prayers; reflections from Father John; another hymn: Abide With Me; and a poignant poem Ali found for her brother to read:

It is not growing like a tree
In bulk, doth make man better be,
Or standing long an oak, three hundred year,
To fall a log at last, dry, bald, and sere:
A lily of a day
Is fairer far in May
Although it fall and die that night;
It was the plant and flower of light.
In small proportions we just beauties see,
And in short measures life may perfect be.

Finally, a slideshow of our favourite photos of Molly; a closing prayer and a carol for Christmas: Silent Night, with the first verse repeated so we could end on *sleep in heavenly peace*.

We were satisfied. On paper, at least, it felt meaningful, per-

270

sonal to Molly and us. And with it done the day itself became that little bit more imaginable and fractionally less daunting. I typed it up and we emailed it, along with a photo of Molly, to a lady the Funeral Director had suggested to arrange the layout and printing. Within the hour she came back with a design we both liked, so we gave her the go-ahead. Another task complete, our confidence growing.

The slideshow, however, provided another level of difficulty altogether. It was heart-breaking, now that Molly was gone, to comprehend that there would be no more photos now, no new expressions or moments captured, and the first playback of the chosen photos against the song Ali wanted: Kirsty Macoll's recording of The Kinks' song, Days, floored us both completely. It was one of the very rare occasions Ali and I cried together; which was wonderful in its own way, grieving as one like that, though it did make me wonder how we'd manage on the day.

At the same time another consideration had begun to weigh on my mind: finding somewhere for our guests to congregate after the service. Hosting at ours would be stressful and cramped, so in glaring parody of Mary and Joseph, Ali and I trawled from inn to inn that afternoon trying to find a room. But with our request being for the last Friday before Christmas, one of the busiest days of their year, the answer was invariably no. We were down to considering the less salubrious local pubs, but even with the nicer ones I feared we'd be confronted with revellers: people doing nothing wrong, but who'd be so out of kilter with our mood.

'Cheer up mate, it might never happen.'

'Give us a smile, darlin'.

In the end I got so wound up thinking about it, became so fixated on everything being fitting and proper, when a resolution was found at last it felt like manna. Out of the blue, Ali recalled a small café up beside Queen's Park: somewhere she and Molly had been together many times. Sally spoke to them and they agreed to give us exclusive use for three hours, with food, mulled wine and winter punch served. In other words, a cosy, respectable, respectful place to be, and something soothing and boozy to drink. I couldn't have been more pleased.

In fact we were making such progress now, I had a wave of over-confidence and took the night off to watch Spurs against Man City on TV: a game I had to pause at half-time when Father John stopped by again to confirm we were happy with our plans for the service. He had us laughing a lot that night, telling us tales from his life as a priest that went a long way towards lifting morale. With one day left the only remaining challenge, so I thought, was to write the dedication; though what it would be like to deliver, I tried to push to the back of my mind.

*

Meanwhile, the last day before the funeral, Ali relayed that Sam had been trying to explain to her children what had happened, and what it meant in terms of not seeing Molly again. When Juliette had taken it in, she had said simply, 'But I didn't want Molly to die.' Such an honest, unadorned phrasing of what we were all feeling I thought. Even now you could roll up this entire book and it would fit neatly inside that little sentence.

Otherwise, from the sublime to the ridiculous, we discovered we had no way of connecting my Mac (containing the slideshow) to the projector we hoped to use. So thinking we had no choice we drove to Churchill Square Shopping Centre to look for a lead, on one of the last shopping days before Christmas; hardly the ideal preparation for the toughest day of our lives; and after an unsuccessful visit to the Apple store we baled out, realising we'd have to re-work the slideshow onto Ali's laptop, notwithstanding the fact that I'd stood on it getting out of bed the previous week, so it only had half a working screen.

In retrospect, these absurdities were probably our salvation. There just wasn't time to be afraid of the coming day. Into the evening now, and still with nothing written for the dedication, we arrived back at the house to find Gordon and Sally outside. I think they'd expected to find us in tatters and were surprised to be confronted by the two of us intensely focused and active. Too busy to cook we phoned out for Chinese, which Ali and I ate quickly and mechanically before going our separate ways.

Downstairs she set about constructing the slideshow again, while upstairs I began to write at last, so by the time she came up around midnight I had a rough draft ready to read out loud. Yet even in front of Ali, in the privacy of our bedroom, it was beyond me. I could barely speak or breathe for all the emotion it brought up. Father John had recommended I bring a copy to pass to him if I found it too difficult. 'Eighty percent of them can't do it, you know,' he'd counselled me. 'Not when it comes to it.' But determined to do that one thing, I carried on into the night, adding, deleting, but mostly just reading it over and over, trying to break its back through familiarity until, close to 3am, I knew I was as ready as I was likely to get.

I got up to pee then, to check downstairs that the house was secure for the night: the doors locked, the cooker switched off. Then I came back to the bedroom where, out of habit, I opened the curtains a fraction to check on the car. And what I saw outside was so unexpected, so preposterous and magical all at once I could only smile, half in awe, half in resignation. While I'd been writing, a thick covering of snow had fallen in silence and was falling still – enough to mock even the best laid plans.

It seemed certain now that some, if not many, of our guests would be unable to come (Ali's relatives all the way from Yorkshire, surely). And in another mood I might have despaired, or cast my eyes up to berate someone or something for this cruel twist of fate at the last. But as it was I stood there by the curtains thinking how pretty the snow looked with no footprints to disturb it yet, and how delighted Molly would be with all the excitement that goes with heavy snow. At least everyone will

273

have fair warning, I reasoned to myself as I got back into bed. There'd be time enough to set off early and trust to good luck. And with that I snuggled up spoonwise to Ali, closed my eyes, and took whatever rest I could get until morning.

Silent Night

Me and my girl

Already, by first light, I could hear the first of the thrill-seekers sledging down the hill in the park next door. A cheerful sound: one to melt even the hardiest Scrooge. I lay in bed enjoying the squeals and peals of laughter. *What a day of contrasts.*

'Matt, do you have a shovel?' Gordon called up the stairs.

The first words of the day. I laughed out loud.

'What do you think this is? The Archers?'

'Right. No problem,' I heard him reply, and a moment later

the front door pulling shut as he set out in search.

I sat in bed a while longer making a few last adjustments to the dedication; then got up and straight out, intending to print off a copy at the internet café down the road. I passed Gordon (shovel in hand now, clearing snow from under the tyres of his car) and paused to help. It didn't look good. Each time he tried to drive away from the kerb, even with me pushing, the wheels spun in vain and the car only skated from side to side, unable to climb the camber of the road.

Nor did things look too promising down at the café, where there was no sign of life at all (someone else stuck in the snow) – so I phoned Damon, arranged to email the dedication to him to print and bring along, then set off gingerly back up the hill. By now there were cars sliding around everywhere. It was impossible not to find it funny. And ironic too that, while Ali's relatives would be trying to travel safely all the way from Hull, we had a job on our hands to get out of our road; though passing Gordon for a second time he was clearly making progress, and confident noises about us getting away on time.

Indoors by now Ali was sat at the dining table with a man the Funeral Director had sent, showing him how to operate the slideshow from her laptop: the one with half a screen. Whether he was getting it or not I couldn't tell, but as Ali appeared to be in formidable let's-get-this-perfectly-clear mode, I stayed out of it: a wise course soon rewarded when Sally placed a full English breakfast down in front of me.

'Blimey,' I said, 'Thank you.'

'Well, we don't know how the day will pan out,' she replied.

Classic Sally, and quite right. With the slideshow man heading out the door with Ali's instructions ringing in his ears, her broken laptop under his arm, and the snow still falling outside, we really *didn't* know. The only thing to do was enjoy the bacon and eggs and leave the rest to what-will-be-will-be.

*

By the time we got on the road: Gordon driving Ali and me to Chestnut Tree House, the landscape en route was stunning: the snow barely disturbed anywhere, just draped over the contours of the land, with ice crystals forming along the branches of the trees. But as beautiful as it was it needed to be manageable too, so I was pleased the roads had been gritted and the traffic was mercifully light. I was happy too to have Gordon with us, to be responsible for the driving and to chat to Ali while I used the time to collect myself.

*

Chestnut Tree House and its environs, idyllic at ordinary times, was really something to behold that day: the covering of snow pristine, the pond frozen over, the chestnut trees glistening under the thinnest frosting of ice. It was stirring enough to give Ali and I a lift as we bade Gordon a temporary goodbye and went inside, where we were shown to the quiet room and given coffee and biscuits.

I felt almost comically sleepy. I was yawning constantly. Ali was the same. Nerves, I suppose: our bodies trying to shy away from what had to be done. Yet shattered as we were, neither of us was overawed or fretful or anything much. The demands of the day were so far beyond our imagining, our ignorance made us peaceful. My thoughts now were mostly of practical things: Would everyone make it through the snow? Would the slideshow work? Would I be able to speak when the time came? Ali too was quietly focused. We sat together, our fingers intertwined, but mostly in silence.

Did we want to see Molly? The offer was made, but we declined. Both of us felt we had said our goodbyes and, what was left unsaid but understood, that seeing Molly again now might undermine what composure we'd been able to muster. We sat on in reflective mood, until Ali saw the black limousine pulling into the grounds at the front of the house.

Did we want to be there while Molly was moved to the car? Again we said no. Instead Ali gave one of the nurses a few personal keepsakes to place in the casket with her, and we waited by the front entrance to be collected when they were ready.

*

The car was divided into three. The front, with the Funeral Director and the driver. The middle, where Molly's casket was secured. And the back, where Ali and I sat.

'Please say if you get too warm or too cold,' the driver said.

Then he pulled away, the icy gravel crunching beneath the tyres as we drove slowly out of the grounds, along the connecting lane, and out onto the A27 heading back towards Brighton. Again, forcefully, that strange parallel to our wedding: that feeling of being a focal point for attention in public: the two of us sat in the back, hand in hand, as we had been that day.

Only one occurrence from that journey stood out. We were held at a red light somewhere when I noticed two boys at the side of the road, throwing snowballs at the waiting cars. They were playing only – nothing malicious, but I felt my blood rise instantly out of all proportion. *Don't – you – dare.* I fired my line of sight at the boy closest to us, willing him not to violate the peace of our journey (as if a snowball thrown by a child could have done as much). But he didn't see me, and I watched powerless as he raised his arm, first up then back, snowball in hand, ready to let fly at us. And that's when I saw the expression on his face change suddenly. It must have been the exact moment he realised what he had in front of him. A funeral car. And not just a funeral car, but one bearing – plainly visible through the windows – a casket for a child. With his arm still held aloft he froze in that position. Even the remnants of his mischievous smile held fast on his face: a facsimile of bravado, but layered now with a complexity of fear, shame. And what? Knowledge? Was that a first moment of mortal awareness, I wondered: one

278

that would stay with him as a fragment of memory all his life? I felt sorry for him then, my anger dissipating as quickly as it had formed. Then the traffic light turned green and we pulled away, the flow of traffic smooth all the way to the crematorium.

As we'd left Chestnut Tree House early to allow for conditions on the roads, we arrived with fifteen minutes to spare. So the Funeral Director asked us whether we'd prefer to continue driving or to sit and wait. We opted to drive. Yet even that decision made me edgy as the driver took us up towards Brighton racecourse, where some of the deepest snow of all lay undisturbed (I feared we may have been unwise to tempt fate a second time). But like the ambulance driver reversing down our cul de sac, he knew what he was doing, and after a brief detour we were back at the crematorium. He brought the car to a halt about halfway down the steep drive.

Below us I could see familiar faces: Mum and Maria waiting outside by the door; Damon chatting to Father John; Gordon making his way over to us as soon as he saw the car. He leaned in to assure Ali that everyone had made it safely in spite of the snow, though one or two were running late. Then, certain that I didn't want to talk to anyone else before the service, I asked him to move everyone inside, and the Funeral Director to retrieve my dedication from Damon.

Did I want to carry the casket?

No. I was sure about that. I knew some fathers chose to but it wasn't my wish. The driver carried the casket into the chapel. We watched from the car as the last of our guests went inside, until finally there was just the Funeral Director, Ali and me.

*

I tried not to make any eye contact as she and I made our way down the central aisle. All I saw were the faces of some of the children, simply because children are smaller and my head was down. We found our seats at the front on the right-hand side:

279

me by the aisle, then Ali, then Mum, who had Brian next to her for company. (As absorbed as I was in my own emotions I was still aware of how hard it had to be for our loved ones to see us that way). Then I lifted my head at last, saw the casket in place, (plain white, with a wreath of sunflowers on top) and took one look around the chapel behind me to take in the scene. Not the detail but the whole. Even indoors I could sense the snow: the way it muted the sound all around us. We could have been miles from anywhere.

When everyone had settled, Father John began. And though I won't pretend to recall every word of what he said, the gist was that death is a natural part of life and that we shouldn't be afraid to think about it, talk about it, contemplate its meaning sometimes because eventually it will come to us all. I liked that. I liked that he was sensitive and gentle, but didn't wrap things up in cotton wool too much. It got us off on the right foot.

Then Sally went up for the first reading, which she preceded by explaining that she was filling in for Tess who was still stuck somewhere in the snow: a show of composure that rubbed off on me. When she was done I felt Ali squeeze my hand for luck. I took a deep breath, stepped up to the front and from the first words I knew I'd make it through if I took my time. If you've come this far you'll already know much of what I said. But on the day itself, with hours instead of months and years to think it through, it went like this:

Our darling daughter, Molly May Cunningham, came into the world on the 19th May – barely seven months ago. And she took her time about it, putting her mother through nearly thirteen hours of labour before finally popping her head through the door just after 3.20 on a beautiful, sunny, Tuesday afternoon.

In the womb we knew her as Dennis – after Dennis Cove: the little campsite near Padstow where we first learned of her existence. Though Dennis she wasn't destined to be. Mainly because – after some initial confusion concerning the umbilical cord, we realised she was a girl and decided to name her Molly. Which all three of us agreed was a much better name than Dennis.

And soon, over the next few days, as she peered out at us with only one eye open, she earned her first nickname: One Eyed Molly. It was to be only one of a great many nicknames she acquired during her short lifetime. At various times she was Molls, Mollington, Molsenhausen, Emperor Wong, Splashingtons, Poopenhausen, the list could go on. And sometimes we called her Molly May, or even just Molly.

By any name she turned Alison and me into a family, and we both feel so blessed and privileged to have been her mum and dad.

We've tried to make today a gentle tribute to her memory. As you arrived you'll have heard Brahms' Lullaby: chosen for Molly because it played on the musical projector that helped her off to sleep each night. Around you, sunflowers and other yellow flowers because Molly always responded to that colour so happily. And the snow? Well, we're assuming that's just Molly's idea of fun.

You can see how pretty she was – with beautiful, bright blue eyes that drew people to her wherever she went. It was as though she made up for her physical weakness with a depth of connection and communion with those around her. As one of the kind nurses who helped us towards the end of Molly's life said, "it was as if she could see right into your soul."

In spite of her condition, Molly was a very happy child for the vast majority of her life. Probably never more so than whenever she could be in water – splashing around in the bath at home or in the swimming pool. Water gave her so much more freedom to move around – to kick her legs out, to make little waves with her hands – and all the while chatter away in her own little language of gurgles, giggles and dribbly smiles. The only exception to her love of water was when Alison tried to dip her in the sea, which wasn't well received. But you can't have everything.

Where there wasn't water, there could at least be motion – which she got to enjoy plenty of during her regular disco dancing sessions with her dad (who was grateful to have an appreciative audience for his outdated moves). Up-tempo stuff it had to be too for Molly – no ballads. She liked Sister Sledge and Ian Dury and The Blockheads. If it was up to her, you'd all be sat here now listening to 'Hit Me With Your Rhythm Stick'. Molly *would complain only if she sensed that I'd stopped moving my feet and was just going through the motions.*

I'll also never forget the special kiss she reserved for me. Back in the early days I think she mistook my nose for a nipple – and from then on always gave it a little lick whenever she could to make sure it wasn't. And over time, that simply became the thing she did with her dad.

I know Ali has enjoyed watching Molly's hair change colour so many times – keeping us guessing; the way she liked to suck her middle two fingers as though she was about to wolf-whistle; the way she seemed to thrive in the company of children, her cousins particularly – always so responsive to their voices and touch.

Without doubt Molly also opened a door on a world we knew so little about: some of the families we met through our visits with Molly to the children's hospice – Chestnut Tree House – where she later passed away: people facing up to all sorts of life-limiting situations with courage, dignity and humour. We've had the privilege too to meet and work with all kinds of professionals, from support groups and throughout the NHS, who work so hard with children like Molly and those with a range of other conditions. Some of those people are here today: generous people who spend their lives being kind.

Everyone here today has done something to help Alison and I face up to these circumstances. You've been a tremendous support in so many ways at a time when we've been tested so hard. Ali has asked me to mention particularly her mum and her sister; and I'd like to acknowledge my mum too, who lost her own first born. To all our family and friends here today, thank you from both of us.

I'll end now by relaying to you a strange and beautiful occurrence last Friday at Chestnut Tree House – shortly after Molly had passed away. After Ali and I had sat with her for a time, we took a few moments together outside in the gardens – where we talked about God and the beauty of nature and tried to imagine Molly's spirit being set free. Then before long, because it was so cold, we came back inside, where we found a small gathering of people (including Gordon and Sally who were with us) watching something moving around down in the empty fireplace. There – behind the glass doors, fluttering happily to and fro was the tiniest bird I've ever

282

seen: a blue tit, no longer than my finger. Not distressed at all. Just a free spirit that had chosen that day to say hello to us – or maybe even goodbye – who knows? All I know is that little bird was gathered up gently into a towel, taken to the garden and set free to fly away.

That's how we'll choose to remember Molly: as a free spirit, who leaves us today with our eternal gratitude and our undying love.

I exhaled long and slow after that, then sat back down next to Ali. And from there the service proceeded as we had hoped. Ali's Dave read the second reading; Father John spoke tenderly when called upon (I was so happy he'd been available to help); and the slideshow, *especially* the slideshow, was sublime. Ali had worked wonders to arrange it. I could hear tears being shed all around the chapel. But I felt all right. I think she did too. We'd done what we'd set out to do: given Molly a send off worthy of her memory and full of love.

I was glad too that although we'd planned the service down to the smallest detail, things actually hadn't gone exactly as anticipated. Tess hadn't arrived in time to read; Father John forgot to bring the bidding prayers (I just smiled and asked him to ad lib); the organist clattered through How Great Thou Art like a missionary falling down a staircase; and at the very last, though we'd agreed that Father John would press the button to close the curtain around the casket during Silent Night, when it came to it, it didn't feel like the thing to do, and somehow he'd divined that for himself. There was no indecision or fumbling: the occasion itself impressed upon us what was fitting.

When we'd finished singing, Ali and I went up to the casket to be together as a family one last time. Then I took her by the hand and led her out through the side door of the chapel with Father John following behind.

*

Outside: the ten minutes or more that came next are the most dreamlike of all to recollect. As our guests filtered out gradually we stood in line to greet them: first me, then Ali, then Father John. Some came out very moved and showing it. Others were quiet and withdrawn as they passed. But there's no consistency to the way I remember it. Mum, my siblings, Gordon and Sally: of all the people I'd expect to have been aware of in those moments, I recall next to nothing. Instead it was one or two of the less obvious encounters that stood out and stuck in my mind. Gordon's brother, Stewart, for example, who spoke to me with real feeling, saying how sad he was to have come so close to meeting Molly, only for circumstances to overtake us. I remember too my sister's husband, Steve, gripping my hand, telling me I was 'unbelievable' for speaking like that. And one more: Nicky, our nurse from the Alex, who hugged Ali so long it caused a bottleneck in the line.

Beyond that handful of memories it's all gone, leaving only a sense that there's something uniquely comforting about being hugged by eighty people in a row.

*

The ice underfoot outside the café at Queen's Park was lethal. I stood in the doorway watching everyone arrive: first their car wheels spinning, then each of them taking pigeon steps across the road. In the circumstances it seemed miraculous that everyone had made it: no bumps or cancellations, no falls or sprains. As cold as it was that day, the mulled wine inside was warming and welcome, and the venue provided just what it had promised: a dignified atmosphere, intimacy, somewhere to be together and at ease. I was proud that Ali and I had made it through and those hours passed easily and pleasantly. I chatted to Mum for a while; I listened to Father John explain how no-one ever talks to him at funerals, and to the various trials everyone had undergone to reach us through the snow – until, finally, it was time to wish them all a safe journey home, to gather up the few who

284

didn't have to drive and walk back into Hanover to find a pub.

We ended up downstairs at The Reservoir: Ali and me; her brother Dave; Tess; two more friends: Caz and Rob; and later, for a drink or two before bed, Gordon and Sally. I got the impression any or all of them would have stayed for as long as they were needed. But somewhere near ten, Ali and I knew we were done. We said our goodnights, then set off slowly over the ice towards home, first to sleep, then to wake and begin working out how to live.

After

I never intended this book to be about bereavement, not in the sense of what life's been like for us since Molly died. Even if I wanted to I'm not sure I'd know how to tackle a book like that, where to start, and certainly not where to end. Grief, I'm learning, has no resolution. The colours and tones change, that's all, sharpening and softening in turn.

Together Ali and I have done very well, I believe, all things considered. We're still very much in love. We laugh and play in harmony more than many. And we have an enduring respect for each other that comes in part from knowing where we've been. In many ways we've been fortunate. We have supportive families, good friends to call upon. We've been able to take holidays, to Thailand, America, Corsica, Scotland, and Ireland to be with family. Though it's impossible to leave sadness behind, having new adventures together has been important for the way we see ourselves, our reason to be. It's a lot for a marriage to take, losing a child, but we feel stronger now than ever and for that I'm profoundly grateful.

We try to keep Molly a part of our everyday lives. There are photos, keepsakes of her, all around our home. Not so many as to make the place feel like a shrine; just enough to help us feel she's with us. Ali writes letters to her occasionally. And for as long as I've been writing this book, Molly's face has been the first thing to greet me each time I open my laptop. She's been our touchstone, our anchor through months of heartache without her, as well as a source of hope that one day we'd be blessed with parenthood again.

Ali has been courageous, I think. She has questioned herself over every aspect of our time with Molly, worrying whether we did the right things at the right times, and whether there was more we could have done. She has worn a brave face while several contemporaries have started out or continued on the path of motherhood; more than one has fallen pregnant and tried to keep it from her, or, at the other extreme, broadcast the news with no sensitivity at all. She's picked out gifts for new-borns, written well-meaning messages to parents in many a card, and every time it must have torn her apart wondering why it had to be her child that was taken away. There was even an occasion (I was with her) when she was holding another woman's baby, as natural as could be, and she looked up to find every pair of eyes in the room fixed on her. I hope it's obvious this book isn't meant to be definitive of her experience through all this. I know she'd have a different story to tell, some of which would resemble this one and some of which would not.

As for me, for a long time afterwards the pain I felt was dull and blunt, so while continuous it never quite cut through me. I busied myself trying to take care of Ali, never knowing when, or even if, my own grief would come to the surface. It wasn't until May, five months after Molly had gone, when we reached what would have been her first birthday, that I really began to hurt and feel crushed by the weight of sadness in me. I thought I'd be indifferent to the arbitrary symbolism of dates, but when it came to that anniversary I could not have been more wrong: I cried every day for two weeks as everything hit me all at once.

Other manifestations were more indirect, harder to fathom. My confidence was shot, I realised. For many more months I felt paranoid and nervous whenever I drove a car. I was constantly afraid of accidents, wary of road rage, and consequently I often drove badly, inviting the danger and anger I was so anxious to avoid. In public generally and pubs especially, I picked up on aggression or menace with acute over-sensitivity. I worried intensely, irrationally, that I would go on losing the people I loved (and not some day, but some day soon) and I dwelt on such imagined traumas unhealthily for hours at a time. I had to wait for enough days and weeks and months to stack up where no-one got hurt, no-one died, nothing bad happened, before I could believe that fate would be kind again.

I'm much better now. I have my routines, my philosophies, my ways of getting by. Writing this book has helped, I'm sure. Whenever people hear about it, they almost always say, 'I expect it's been cathartic for you' or something similar; and they're probably right, but only in the sense that it's helped me to pass the time, because if writing it has taught me anything, it's that losing Molly isn't something I either need or want to get over. My memory of her doesn't have to be rationalised into a box or a book or anything else. She's part of what I am now: flesh, blood and bone, and that's all there is to it.

At Christmas each year Chestnut Tree House arranges a gathering, a chance for parents and siblings who've been touched by its presence down the years to spend time together in reflection. We sing carols, have tea and biscuits, make festive decorations for the tree back at the house. And it's nice, comforting, tenderly set apart from the clamour of daily life. Ali and I attended our second one back in 2011, and at one point in the afternoon a woman I'd never met before (one of the counsellors from Chestnut Tree House, Ali told me later) walked up to me and, with a smile, asked simply: 'Are you Molly's dad?' Which sounds like nothing, I know: the most ordinary question in the world. But to me: *Are you Molly's dad?* Present tense. No-one had used that simple construction, not since Molly had passed, and it caught me off guard. Until then I knew that I *was* Molly's dad. I just didn't appreciate that I was still her dad and always would be. It was one of those moments when I realised how far I'd come.

'Yes, I am,' I said, returning her smile, stepping forward to shake her hand. And again, silently inside, just for me: *Yes I am.*

*

288

Dear Molly,

I wanted the last word to go to you. Not many who have lived such a short time can have had so many pages written in their honour. I hope the fact that you have tells you something of the way I feel about you and the impact you've had on my life.

We've written this book together you and I: I really believe that. I may have done the thinking, the writing and reworking. But you covered all the losses of confidence, each crisis of faith with your sweet presence looking over my shoulder. You were the reason I never let this go when it got too hard and I'm proud of what we've done, darling. Thank you for giving me the courage to make something whole, something beautiful — to me at least. We shall have to find other ways of being close to each other now.

Your mum and I miss you very much. It's been lonely here sometimes without you. There's a gap in our family. We wish you could have stayed. Nothing ever outweighs that longing, though we do take comfort in knowing that you're safe, and have a strong sense of you watching over us.

It's strange, Molly, when someone you love so much passes. You start to look for them in everything — in similarities with the living, in your dreams, in all the signposts of the everyday. And if you're very lucky, or open enough to such things, you can find them sometimes or believe you have. But is that because they're really there? Or because we want it so much to be true? Did you really lick the end of my nose that night to wake me and reassure me after you'd gone? (It couldn't have felt more real: I sat bolt upright in bed). And was it really you who interceded for us when I asked you to help Mum — your Mama — through her cancer last year? Or you again that night that your mum saw a shooting star from the nursery window when she was wanting so much to be pregnant again?

And then sometimes I think it doesn't even matter: the beauty of the way you were, of the life you lived, stands alone, regardless of faith or physics or time. I could feel the truth every time you curled your hand around my finger. I could hear it in that long single note you loved to hum, like the one at the start of Walk The Line by Johnny Cash. Even if there was nothing more to life than that, it's still a lot. It's still incredible, endlessly miraculous, that we get to be together at all.

I know I'm well on my way to becoming one of those sentimental old men who shed tears (of joy or sadness) at the least provocation: I have you to thank for that. But still, I've learnt not to shy away from crying or to think it makes me any less of a man. I even go looking for it sometimes. There's a song I listen to when I'm on my own in the car: September Song sung by Willie Nelson. And from the opening lines referencing May to December (the months you were with us), it destroys me. Yet I play it still. Maybe because I'm seeing slowly that a life close to tears is a life closer to you. And I'm fine with that. I really am.

Our time to dance together again will come, sweetheart, I know it will. Until then, know that I'll love you always, and never ever stop being your

Daddy x

PS. I suppose you know you have a little sister now. She seems to know you. She goes crazy when we show her photos of you, pressing her hands to your face and trying to speak to us. Keep watch over her if you can, Molly. Point your finger if ever she needs you to show her the way.

Printed in Great Britain
by Amazon